CARMANGAY AND DISTRICT
PUBLIC LIBRARY

PERFECT PARTNERS

DISCARD

*Beautiful Plant Combinations
for Prairie Gardens*

Liesbeth Leatherbarrow
and Lesley Reynolds

D0036519

**FIFTH
HOUSE**

Copyright © 2002 Liesbeth Leatherbarrow and Lesley Reynolds

Design by John Luckhurst / GDL
Cover photographs by Liesbeth Leatherbarrow

All rights reserved. No part of this publication may be reproduced, stored in a
retrieval system, or transmitted, in any form or by any means, electronic, mechanical,
recording, or otherwise, without the prior written permission of the publisher, except
in the case of a reviewer, who may quote brief passages in a review to print in a
magazine or newspaper, or broadcast on radio or television. In the case of
photocopying or other reprographic copying, users must obtain a licence from
the Canadian Copyright Licencing Agency.

The publisher gratefully acknowledges the support of The Canada Council for the
Arts and the Department of Canadian Heritage. We acknowledge the financial support
of the Government of Canada through the Book Publishing Industry Development
Program for our publishing activities.

Printed in Canada by Friesens.

02 03 04 05 06 / 5 4 3 2 1

First published in the United States in 2002.

National Library of Canada Cataloguing in Publication Data

Leatherbarrow, Liesbeth.
    Perfect partners

    Includes bibliographical references and index.
    ISBN 1-894004-78-7

    1. Plants, Ornamental—Prairie Provinces. 2. Companion planting.
I. Reynolds, Lesley. II. Title.
SB453.3.C2L427 2002   635.9'09712   C2001-911697-7

Fifth House Ltd.   In the United States:
A Fitzhenry & Whiteside Company   Fitzhenry & Whiteside
1511-1800 4 St. SW   121 Harvard Avenue, Suite 2
Calgary, Alberta, Canada   Allston, MA 02134
T2S 2S5

1-800-387-9776
www.fitzhenry.ca

Contents

CHAPTER FOUR: FALL — 169

Foreword

Gardening authors Liesbeth Leatherbarrow and Lesley Reynolds have once again delivered a recipe for success in choosing plants for prairie gardens. The layout of this book and its featured plant partnerships will be useful to both beginning and seasoned gardeners in designing garden beds. Liesbeth and Lesley have provided complementary ideas and suggestions for gardeners who are either starting from scratch or adding to a mature garden. From bulbs, annuals, and perennials, to shrubs and trees, these effective combinations will add impact to any landscape.

Gardeners often use trial and error to make decisions about which plants fit together. This book takes away the guesswork by describing compatible and beautiful plant pairs, and to top it all off, provides easy-to-read growing information for each plant. If the featured combinations do not meet your needs, the authors offer alternatives for almost every plant. They also back up their suggestions with prose descriptions of each plant's attributes that are so colorful they almost take away the need for a photo.

Liesbeth and Lesley have gathered inspiration for their books from gardens across the prairies, and their joy and awe in witnessing the creativity of prairie gardeners is apparent in their writing. Their appreciation of gardening and their familiarity with gardening in the challenging prairie climate invite confidence in the plants described in this book.

Perfect Partners: Beautiful Plant Combinations for Prairie Gardens is sure to be added to my botanical library.

Olivia Johns
CALGARY ZOO HORTICULTURIST

Rock gardens provide the ideal growing conditions for the bellflower, penstemon, hen and chicks, and fleabane pictured here, as well as many other perennial partners. LLYN STRELAU

Acknowledgements

As we wind down this book-writing project, it gives us pleasure to reminisce about the friends and strangers who welcomed us into their gardens and took the time to "give us the tour" and share favorite plant combinations. To all those whose gardens we visited, we give our heartfelt thanks. Their inspired landscaping, generous spirit, and words of encouragement made the task of seeking out and photographing plant partnerships an exceptionally rewarding one. Not surprisingly, our photo expeditions were very fruitful. Binders bulging with hundreds of slides of lovely plant combos are proof positive that prairie gardeners are remarkably successful at "getting it right."

As Calgary-based writers, we have benefited greatly from the botanical gardens at the Calgary Zoo, which boast an excellent labeled collection of prairie-hardy plants, trees, and shrubs, and an ever-helpful staff who went out of their way to answer our myriad questions. We are truly blessed to have such an invaluable horticultural resource right in our own backyard; weekly outings to "see what's happening at the zoo" were an integral and enjoyable part of our project.

We are grateful to Olivia Johns, the Calgary Zoo horticulturist, and Clancy Patton, a superb plantsman with prairie gardening in his blood, for kindly reading our manuscript and making thoughtful suggestions for its betterment. Our book is much improved thanks to their contributions. Winston Goretsky and Llyn Strelau generously shared several photographs with us to help illustrate the text.

As always, we are indebted to the staff at Fifth House for supporting yet another book project and seeing it through to its conclusion. Without the assurance, friendship, and backup of Fraser Seely, Charlene Dobmeier, Catherine Radimer, Kathy Bogusky, and Richard Janzen, writing a book would not be nearly as satisfying or as much fun. We also appreciate the efforts of Ann Sullivan, our editor, who worked her magic on our manuscript to our advantage.

Finally, we offer our love and sincerest appreciation to Kate, Camille, Bob, and Vic. They have stood by us through thick and thin, putting up with the rigors of our self-inflicted tight work schedules and deadlines, and taking the many resultant inconveniences in their stride. Although we always say that next time will be different, they know better, and still they give us their unqualified support. We are thankful for their understanding and, who knows? Maybe next time things will be different!

Perennials and bulbs are perfectly paired in this lush border that features statuesque delphiniums teamed with downward-facing lilies and ornamental onions. LESLEY REYNOLDS

CHAPTER ONE

Introduction

ABOUT *PERFECT PARTNERS*

In many ways, gardens are works of art in which the interplay between light, form, color, and texture defines the basis for creating beautiful landscapes. Gardeners face many challenges on the road to developing a garden masterpiece. These include everything from designing and installing the "bones" of the garden, to selecting plants and arranging them in freshly prepared flower beds. The art of combining plants is ultimately the most important part of the process—the equivalent of an artist applying paint to the canvas. No matter how strong the "bones" of the garden or how unique the plant collection, if the combinations don't work visually, then there is still work to be done. For most gardeners, this task of "getting it right" gives great pleasure and lasts a lifetime.

Perfect Partners describes beautiful plant combinations that are standouts in prairie gardens. It is written for gardeners who are looking for ideas about what plants to place side by side in containers, perennial and mixed borders, woodland gardens, and rock gardens. Whether or not they have plant knowledge, many people just can't imagine what plant pairs will look like at maturity, and they don't have the time or the interest to experiment—they just want to succeed the first time. This book will help them do that.

Low-growing perennials mingle at the front of a border in a delightful floral and foliage tapestry.
LIESBETH LEATHERBARROW

Each entry in the book is accompanied by a full-color photograph and a paragraph describing the combination and why it works well. It is hoped that these explanations will help interested gardeners draw on their own experience to think up other plant combinations that might create similar, pleasing effects. To complete the entry, there is a brief "plant at a glance" summary for each of the two plants in a combination, listing plant size, soil and light requirements, flowering time, growing tips, and suggested alternatives.

The plants we recommend are hardy across the prairies, where climate zones range from Zone 2 to Zone 4. However, gardeners should never regard zone ratings as absolutes. Much is dependent upon garden microclimates, that is, the specific growing conditions within a particular area. Elevation, buildings and other structures, and mature trees all serve to alter, and often moderate, the climate within a garden.

Our selection of perfect partners is based on such attributes as plant form and size; flower shape, color, and bloom times; and foliage texture and color. Both partners also enjoy the same or similar growing conditions, which means they thrive growing side by side. Suggested combinations include annuals, perennials, bulbs, shrubs, and trees.

GETTING STARTED

Developing successful plant partnerships can be a lot of fun, but it can also be a bit overwhelming at first. A good idea is to start small. Evaluate what is already growing in your garden by identifying the combinations that please you, and then plan to reorganize or replace the rest—eventually! Don't be in a rush—beautiful gardens evolve one plant combination at a time. And remember, if you love a particular plant duo, regardless of whether or not it falls within conventional design guidelines, it stays! From start to finish, you should be gardening for your own pleasure, not to satisfy the tastes of friends, neighbors, and passersby.

For gardeners uninitiated in the basics of design, the two most important things to keep in mind when mixing and matching plants are contrast and balance. When you think of contrasts, think opposites, and look for them in the color, form, and texture of both plant blossoms and foliage. Examples of some contrasts that work include tall vs. short, big vs. small, round vs. pointy, smooth vs. hairy, shiny vs. dull, bright vs. subdued, simple vs. complex, flat vs. cup-shaped; green vs. silver, feathery vs. rigid—the list is endless.

Ironically, despite the fact that contrast is good, too much contrast is not good, and that is where balance comes into play. Both plants in a partnership should retain their visual integrity, each being enhanced by the other, with neither predominating. In other words, the partnership should be an equal one. In a big leaf-small leaf combination, for example, if the big leaves are too big compared to the small ones, then the small-leaved plant tends to fade or drop out of sight, resulting in an unequal partnership. That's not to say that very large-leaved plants have no place in a perennial or mixed border. They can be lovely accent or architectural plants, usually performing solo as a dramatic focal point, and not as part of a combination.

MAKING IT HAPPEN

The following garden design tips are presented as guidelines only.

◆ Group plants with similar soil, water, and light requirements.

◆ Place an emphasis on choosing plants with interesting foliage shapes and textures because foliage is usually decorative much longer than flowers are.

◆ Incorporate a variety of foliage colors into borders, including traditional greens in all shades, silvers, blues, purples, chartreuse, and the occasional variegated form.

◆ Choose plants with varying bloom times, both concurrent and consecutive, to ensure that there is something happening in your garden from spring to fall.

◆ Include trees and shrubs that offer all-season interest. Evergreens are essential to the winter garden, but many other woody ornamentals offer fiery red or golden fall foliage and colorful berries or rose hips that persist through winter.

◆ Remember to plant a variety of spring-flowering bulbs for interest early in the growing season.

◆ Include fall-blooming bulbs and perennials that survive several degrees of frost to prolong the growing season in fall.

◆ Choose some perennials that also offer year-round interest with attractive blossoms in spring or summer, colorful fall foliage, and seed heads that are good-looking when rimmed with frost or laden with snow in the winter garden.

The contrasting colors of purple and yellow shine in this artful container composition of nemesia, petunias, African daisies, licorice plant, and bacopa. LIESBETH LEATHERBARROW

The autumn leaves of Amur maple provide a brilliant backdrop to the tall flower stems of 'Karl Foerster' feather reed grass.
LIESBETH LEATHERBARROW

- Plant in drifts of color rather than in straight rows; drifts can consist of several plants of uniform color within a species, or for the plant collectors among us, single plants of similar colors from several different species.
- Rich, strong colors such as reds, oranges, and yellows work best in a sunny site.
- Cool blues, purples, pinks, and whites work wonders in lightly shaded borders and woodland gardens.
- Hot colors (red, orange, yellow) advance, appearing closer than they are, although they tend to "disappear" in evening light. Cool colors recede, appearing more distant than they really are.
- Plants with light-colored flowers and/or silver-leaved foliage glow in the moonlight and are ideal in a night garden, floating magically in darkened borders.
- Plant partners with complementary blossom or foliage colors (green/red, yellow/violet, blue/orange) magnify the differences between them, creating a special intensity in the combination.
- For a sense of unity, repeat a few specific plant groupings or color schemes at intervals throughout the garden.
- Include some areas of "visual calm" in the garden where the eye can rest momentarily from stimulation. Green lawns, a small grouping of silver-leaved plants, or a simple green deciduous or evergreen shrub all create spots of visual calm.
- Choose plants that appeal to all the senses: plants in a variety of colors, shapes, and textures to see; fragrant blossoms and foliage to smell; herbs, vegies, or fruit to eat; soft, hairy foliage, smooth bark, and silky seed heads to touch; leaves that whisper and rustle in the wind to hear.

This lovely perennial border utilizes repetition of color and plant form to create a balanced and harmonious effect. Liesbeth Leatherbarrow

PLANT SUMMARIES

The characteristics of each plant in a partnership are summarized as follows:

◆ **TYPE:** indicates whether the plant is a bulb, annual, perennial, groundcover, vine, shrub, or tree. Where applicable, plants are noted as being either deciduous or evergreen.

◆ **PLANT HEIGHT AND WIDTH:** measurements represent the expected mature size, provided the plant's cultural requirements are met; these dimensions will vary from garden to garden, depending on light, soil, and microclimate.

◆ **SOIL PREFERENCES:** classified as poor, average, or fertile. Few prairie soils are naturally fertile or rich in organic matter; many locations have a high sand or clay content and may be on the alkaline side. We recommend incorporating compost, peat moss, or well-rotted manure to improve fertility and tilth for all soil types. This also helps moderate soil alkalinity. Moisture and drainage are listed when they are important to a plant's well-being. Some plants require consistently moist soil; in these cases, evaporation can be minimized by using a 5- to 10-cm (2- to 4-in.) layer of organic mulch. Shredded leaves, compost, or wood chips all work well. Most plants prefer well-drained soils; the addition of organic matter to clay soils helps improve drainage. In some cases it may be necessary to dig in a quantity of coarse sand.

◆ **LIGHT REQUIREMENTS:** indicated as full sun (more than eight hours of direct sun per day), part sun (four to eight hours of direct sun per day), light shade (less than four hours of direct sun per day or bright filtered light), and full shade (no direct or filtered sunlight).

◆ **FLOWERING TIME:** classified as early spring (late March to mid-April), mid-spring (mid-April to mid-May), late spring (mid-May to mid-June), early summer (mid-June to mid-July), mid-summer (mid-July to mid-August), late summer (mid-August to mid-September), and fall (mid-September to hard frost).

◆ **GROWING TIPS:** summarize a plant's care requirements with regard to planting, mulching, fertilizing (in addition to annual topdressing with compost), staking, deadheading, drought tolerance, pests and diseases, and pruning.

◆ **ALTERNATIVES:** are plants that can be substituted into a plant combination to create a similar effect.

◆ Plant fragrant species close to seating areas or under windows where they can be fully appreciated.

◆ Populate borders with plants of differing heights, with tall plants generally located towards the back of the border and short plants closer to the front. For contrast, plant one or two taller "see through" plants or narrow, spiky "see around" plants towards the front of the border.

SOURCES OF INSPIRATION

When it comes to arranging plants in the garden, there are opportunities for inspiration, change, and refinement around every corner. Of course, some lovely plant combinations just happen, the happy outcome of a spontaneous or hasty planting job. Other outstanding duos are deliberate creations, the result of extensive research and experience, patient trial-and-error, or the practised eye of an artist familiar with the elements of good design. Most perfect partners, however, have been borrowed or copied from fellow gardeners, our very best horticultural resource. Look for ideas in the pictures of gardening books, magazines, and catalogues; at public lectures and slide shows given by horticultural societies and gardening clubs; and most important, during visits to real gardens in your community, both private and public. There is no better way to ascertain whether or not you like a particular combination than by seeing it up close and personal, growing somewhere in your community. And when you get the hang of creating pleasing plant partnerships yourself, be sure to share your successes with others, thus carrying on the very best of gardening traditions!

BOTANICAL NAMES

In this book, plants are listed by botanical and common names. Although common names vary from country to country, or even from region to region within a country, botanical names are a universal means of plant identification. They consist of a genus (a grouping of closely related but distinct species) and a species (a particular member of a genus that will breed true with others of its kind). Species are sometimes subclassified into varieties—plants with naturally occurring distinctive features, such as color, that are not sufficiently distinct to be classified as a separate species. Cultivars refer to cultivated varieties bred from superior plants.

Genus names are italicized and capitalized; species and variety names are written in lowercase italics. Cultivar names are capitalized, but never italicized, and appear in single quotation marks. For example, the maiden pink cultivar 'Arctic Fire' is named *Dianthus deltoides* 'Arctic Fire'; *Athyrium niponicum* var. *pictum* is the painted variety of the Japanese fern.

Hybrids, indicated by an x (times) sign, as in *Geranium* x (times) *magnificum*, are crosses between two or more species or even between genera of plants. They seldom come true from seed and many are sterile. First generation (F_1) hybrids are consistent in size, color, and vigor; second generation (F_2) hybrids are extremely variable and seldom as vigorous as their parents.

With the endless blue sky as a canopy, colorful prairie gardens are as beautiful as any in the world.
LIESBETH LEATHERBARROW

Foliage color, texture, and form, the essential components of garden design, are masterfully combined in this elegant mixed border. LIESBETH LEATHERBARROW

CHAPTER TWO

Spring

Spring makes its tentative arrival on the prairies in March. As warming temperatures loosen winter's grip on the land, we listen for the sweet song of the first robin, perched high on a tall tree at dusk. Late March brings the first precocious flowers of the prairie growing season as hardy little bulbs like reticulata irises and crocuses begin to emerge, scorning the blustery winds and wet snow squalls of the early prairie spring. In short order, other bulbs join their ranks: snowdrops, Siberian and striped squill, glory-of-the-snow, and early tulips and daffodils make their appearance during April, as do the first perennials of the season.

The pleasing task of choosing perfect partners for the early spring garden is actually undertaken in fall, when gardeners buy spring-flowering bulbs to tuck in amidst the last few flowering perennials of the waning summer. Most spring-flowering bulbs require similar growing conditions, so this is not usually a deciding factor in bulb partner selection. Keep in mind that not all spring-flowering bulbs are early bloomers and that the loveliest gardens are planned for both concurrent and consecutive bloom. The gentle colors of early spring bulbs make it easy to create harmonious plant marriages.

Pink and white flowering ornamental crabapples and spirea combine with brilliant pink 'Barcelona' tulips in this romantic spring garden. LIESBETH LEATHERBARROW

Planted in generous drifts to achieve blocks of color, daffodils and tulips are the mainstays of this spectacular spring bulb garden. LESLEY REYNOLDS

Yellows, blues, purples, and whites predominate, with a few cool pinks offering a welcome diversion. For variety in texture, and flower and leaf form, seek out early-flowering perennial partners like pulmonaria, Iceland poppies, and rock cress.

In May, the well-planned prairie garden is a kaleidoscope of color as mid-spring bulbs reach their peak. Species and hybrid tulips, daffodils, grape hyacinth, and miniature irises are joined by burgeoning perennials to fill borders, rock gardens, and woodland gardens with every color imaginable. The proliferation of spectacular tulip and daffodil cultivars, not to mention other bulbs, makes the plant partnership opportunities inexhaustible.

When planning the mid-spring garden, it's important to consider planting perennials, including groundcovers, and shrubs in the immediate vicinity of bulbs. The large leaves of tulips and daffodils, in particular, can persist well into summer and should not be removed until they have died back completely. Bushy perennials, groundcovers, and shrubs, with their fresh new foliage and blooms, fill the gaps occupied with unsightly bulb foliage and make the transition into summer a seamless one. Early-flowering perennials or those with attractive foliage are also enchanting companions for bulbs in bloom. These combinations make the most of the contrast between the fleshy, spiky bulb foliage and the softer textures and varying forms of the leaves of newly emerging perennials such as prairie crocus, primrose, and leopard's bane. Cheerful pansies, one of the few annuals tough enough to be planted out in early May, also offer a wide range of colors to match with spring bulbs.

By late May, gardeners are creating magical combinations of annuals, filling con-

In spring, prairie rock gardens are at their peak, filled with a profusion of alpines that are small in stature but big in color. LLYN STRELAU

tainers and flower beds with the best of a new crop of exciting cultivars. Since containers are designed to be viewed from close range, they are perhaps the most artistically challenging exercise in plant partnership. It's easy to group non-blooming young annuals together to test foliage compatibility, but gardeners also need a good sense of the flower shape, color, and eventual size of the plants. However, when container plantings flourish in balance and harmony, there is no more satisfying aspect of gardening.

The sweet month of June is perfumed with lilacs, peonies, and rosybloom crabapple and apple trees. Late spring brings yet more bulbous plants to the forefront with an abundance of irises, late-blooming tulips, and intriguing fritillaries and alliums for the border. Many of these bulbs are superb rock garden plants that are happy to be paired with moss phlox, soapwort, purple rock cress, and thrift in a garden tapestry. There are shade-loving bulbs too; anemones, bloodroot, and dog's-tooth violets bloom beneath a canopy of fresh new leaves. Many moisture-loving woodland perennials, such as columbines, Jacob's ladder, blue-eyed Mary, Virginia bluebells, and bleeding hearts, are also at their finest now, blooming in June before the onset of summer's dry heat. Their subtle beauty makes them among the easiest of perennials to mix and match effectively. Shade-dwellers tend to have the most attractive leaves of any perennials, offering boundless possibilities for amazing plant duos that depend more on foliage texture, form, and color than on ephemeral flowers.

As spring draws to a close, the prairie gardener is full of optimism. Newly planted trees, shrubs, perennials, and annuals are settling in and getting to know their neighbors. Who knows what perfect partnerships summer might bring?

Classic prairie favorites, peonies and irises invite you down the garden path with their fragrance and myriad colors in late spring. LLYN STRELAU

Alchemilla AND *Narcissus*

One of the most dependable plants in the border, lady's mantle always brings out the best in its flashier neighbors. It is also a lovely perennial in its own right, particularly when the downy, scalloped-edged leaves capture the early morning dew in sparkling droplets. In spring, emerging mounds of pleated, gray-green lady's mantle foliage softly enhance the golden trumpets of 'Dutch Master' daffodils. By the time these classic King Alfred-type daffodils finish their spring dance, the lush lady's mantle foliage obscures the dying bulb leaves. Secondary to its fabulous foliage are the airy sprays of tiny, chartreuse flowers, which are wonderful fillers for bouquets of red roses. Other excellent yellow trumpet daffodil cultivars are 'Golden Harvest', 'Golden Trumpet', and 'Unsurpassable'.

LADY'S MANTLE

Alchemilla mollis (bottom)
(al-ke-*mil*-ah *maw*-lis)

TYPE: perennial
HEIGHT: 45 cm (18 in.)
WIDTH: 60 cm (24 in.)
SOIL: fertile, moist, well drained
LIGHT: full to part sun
FLOWERING TIME: late spring to mid-summer
GROWING TIPS: avoid planting in hot, dry areas; use organic mulch for moisture retention and winter protection; deadhead to prevent self-seeding; excellent for hiding dying bulb foliage
ALTERNATIVES: *Alchemilla alpina*, *A. erythropoda*, *A. glaucescens*

'DUTCH MASTER' DAFFODIL

Narcissus 'Dutch Master' (top)
(nar-*siss*-us)

TYPE: hardy true bulb
HEIGHT: 50 cm (20 in.)
WIDTH: 10 cm (4 in.)
SOIL: fertile, moist, well drained
LIGHT: full sun to light shade
FLOWERING TIME: early to mid spring
GROWING TIPS: plant bulbs in fall (before September 15); use organic mulch for winter protection; fertilize before and after flowering; deadhead; allow foliage to ripen
ALTERNATIVES: early to mid spring blooming daffodils, such as 'Carlton' or 'Yellow Cheerfulness'

Allium AND *Spiraea*

LIESBETH LEATHERBARROW

Few sights in the mixed border are more arresting than bold 'Purple Sensation' ornamental onion against a contrasting backdrop of bright 'Goldflame' spirea. Regal 'Purple Sensation' produces one of the largest flowers among the ornamental onions, forming huge, starburst globes of dozens of tiny, purple-violet flowers atop tall, ribbed flower stalks. The broad, strappy foliage is unobtrusive, allowing the flowers to shine solo against the glowing spirea leaves, and it dies back soon after blooming. 'Goldflame' has amazingly colorful foliage that is bronzy gold in spring, soft gold in the summer, and red in the fall. As if that weren't enough, clusters of light pink flowers bloom all summer. 'Goldmound' is a smaller *Spiraea* x *bumalda* cultivar with golden foliage all season long.

'PURPLE SENSATION'
ORNAMENTAL ONION
Allium aflatunense 'Purple Sensation' (bottom)
(*al*-ee-um a-flah-toon-*en*-see)

TYPE: hardy true bulb
HEIGHT: 60 cm (24 in.)
WIDTH: 45 cm (18 in.)
SOIL: fertile, moist, well drained
LIGHT: full sun
FLOWERING TIME: late spring to early summer
GROWING TIPS: plant bulbs in fall; mulch for winter protection; fertilize before and after flowering; allow foliage to ripen
ALTERNATIVES: *Allium atropurpureum*, *A. christophii* (star of Persia)

'GOLDFLAME'
DWARF PINK SPIREA
Spiraea x *bumalda* 'Goldflame' (top)
(spy-*ree*-ah x bu-*mall*-dah)

TYPE: deciduous shrub
HEIGHT: 90 cm (36 in.)
WIDTH: 90 cm (36 in.)
SOIL: fertile, moist, well drained
LIGHT: full sun to light shade
FLOWERING TIME: mid-summer
GROWING TIPS: prune in early spring as buds begin to swell; deadhead; water well in fall
ALTERNATIVES: *Spiraea japonica* 'Golden Princess'; *Sambucus racemosa* 'Goldenlocks' (European red elder)

Anemone AND *Euphorbia*

LIESBETH LEATHERBARROW

Pure white snowdrop anemones and brilliant yellow cushion spurge are perfect partners for illuminating a patch of dappled shade. Individually, the plants of this duo make a strong statement in the garden; together, they present even more boldly, announcing their return each spring in no uncertain terms. The solitary, cup-shaped flowers of the anemone are supported on erect stems above dark green, deeply divided foliage. 'Flore Pleno' is a double form. The anemone blooms nod slightly, in favorable contrast to the spurge's flat, up-facing arrangements of chartreuse bracts that enfold small, dense clusters of bright yellow flowers. Always reliable, cushion spurge usually forms a perfectly symmetrical mound of medium green, rounded to oval foliage that turns quite red in the fall.

SNOWDROP ANEMONE
Anemone sylvestris (top)
(a-*nem*-oh-nee sil-*vess*-triss)

TYPE: perennial
HEIGHT: 30 cm (12 in.)
WIDTH: 30 cm (12 in.)
SOIL: fertile, moist, well drained
LIGHT: light shade
FLOWERING TIME: mid to late spring
GROWING TIPS: deadhead; drought tolerant once established; may be invasive, but is easy to control; excellent for hiding dying bulb foliage
ALTERNATIVES: white-flowered Triumph ('Calgary', 'White Dream') or Darwin Hybrid ('Ivory Floradale', 'Maria's Dream') tulips

CUSHION SPURGE
Euphorbia polychroma (bottom)
(ew-*for*-bee-ah paw-lee-*krow*-mah)

TYPE: perennial
HEIGHT: 40 cm (16 in.)
WIDTH: 60 cm (24 in.)
SOIL: average to fertile, moist, well drained
LIGHT: full sun to light shade
FLOWERING TIME: mid to late spring
GROWING TIPS: in areas with hot, dry summers, provide shade from afternoon sun; drought tolerant once established; sap may irritate skin
ALTERNATIVES: *Aurinia saxatilis* (basket-of-gold); *Doronicum columnae*, *D. orientale* (leopard's bane)

Anemone AND *Fritillaria*

With an amazing variety in flower form and color, fritillaries have the potential to become a collector's dream, if only suppliers would make more species available to the average gardener! One little treasure that is increasingly making its appearance in prairie gardens is Michael's flower, a low-growing fritillary that sports deep brownish burgundy, squarish, bell-shaped flowers with flared yellow tips. Its unusual coloring and diminutive stature mean that this plant should be paired with something small, lovely, and unaffected—white Grecian windflower is a perfect choice. The windflower's daisylike blossoms, flushed with pink, form a perfect understory for the slightly taller, pendant fritillary, and its yellow stamens perfectly echo the color of the yellow-edged fritillary blossoms.

GRECIAN WINDFLOWER

Anemone blanda (bottom)
(a-*nem*-oh-nee *blan*-dah)

TYPE: borderline tuber
HEIGHT: 15 cm (6 in.)
WIDTH: 15 cm (6 in.)
SOIL: average to fertile
LIGHT: full to part sun
FLOWERING TIME: mid to late spring
GROWING TIPS: plant tubers in fall; soak tubers in lukewarm water for 24 hours before planting; use organic mulch for winter protection; fertilize before and after flowering; allow foliage to ripen
ALTERNATIVES: *Arabis caucasica* (rock cress); *Iberis sempervirens* (perennial candytuft)

MICHAEL'S FLOWER

Fritillaria michailovskyi (top)
(fri-ti-*lay*-ree-yah mee-kale-*ov*-skee-ee)

TYPE: hardy true bulb
HEIGHT: 20 cm (8 in.)
WIDTH: 5 cm (2 in.)
SOIL: fertile, well drained
LIGHT: full sun
FLOWERING TIME: mid to late spring
GROWING TIPS: plant bulbs in fall; use organic mulch for winter protection; fertilize before and after flowering; allow foliage to ripen; likes dry summer conditions; drought tolerant once established
ALTERNATIVES: *Fritillaria meleagris* (checkered lily), *F. pudica* (yellow fritillary)

Anemone AND *Narcissus*

LIESBETH LEATHERBARROW

Yellow miniature 'Tête à Tête' daffodils and bluish purple Grecian windflowers are a winning springtime combination in a sheltered rock garden or at the front of a perennial border. Although both 'Tête à Tête' and the windflower are little plants that paint a colorful picture at ground level, their strong, complementary colors also allow them to be distinguished and admired from a distance. 'Tête à Tête' is a fragrant daffodil that, once established, produces a multitude of yellow blooms with tiny, soft orange cups. The daffodil's yellow coloring is repeated in the stamens clustered prominently at the center of the windflower's soft, daisylike blossoms, creating a visual link between the two. Some windflower cultivars worth trying include 'Blue Star', 'Ingramii', and 'Violet Star'.

GRECIAN WINDFLOWER

Anemone blanda (bottom)
(a-*nem*-oh-nee *blan*-dah)

TYPE: borderline tuber
HEIGHT: 15 cm (6 in.)
WIDTH: 15 cm (6 in.)
SOIL: average to fertile
LIGHT: full to part sun
FLOWERING TIME: mid to late spring
GROWING TIPS: plant tubers in fall; soak tubers in lukewarm water for 24 hours before planting; use organic mulch for winter protection; fertilize before and after flowering; allow foliage to ripen
ALTERNATIVES: *Chionodoxa luciliae* (glory-of-the-snow); *Scilla sibirica* (Siberian squill)

'TÊTE À TÊTE' DAFFODIL

Narcissus 'Tête à Tête' (top)
(nar-*siss*-us)

TYPE: hardy true bulb
HEIGHT: 15 cm (6 in.)
WIDTH: 2.5 cm (1 in.)
SOIL: fertile, moist, well drained
LIGHT: full sun to light shade
FLOWERING TIME: early to mid spring
GROWING TIPS: plant bulbs in fall (before September 15); use organic mulch for winter protection; fertilize before and after flowering; deadhead; allow foliage to ripen
ALTERNATIVES: miniature daffodils such as 'Dove Wings', 'Jumblie', 'Minnow', and 'Peeping Tom'

Anemonella AND *Corydalis*

For a charming vignette in the dappled shade of a woodland garden, try planting delicate rue anemone and corydalis next to each other at the front of a border or in a rockery. Both form soft, rounded mounds of feathery, blue-green foliage, but they differ in blossom color and form, the source of visual appeal in this pairing. Whereas rue anemone produces relatively large but fragile-looking, white, cup-shaped flowers in loose clusters at the ends of slender stems, corydalis produces short spikes of up to twenty rosy red, spurred, tubular flowers. They are sometimes hard to come by, but several rue anemone cultivars are worth searching out: 'Cameo' (double pale rose), 'Double Green' (double light green), 'Green Dragon' (single green), and 'Shoaf's Double' (double light pink, most readily available).

RUE ANEMONE
Anemonella thalictroides (right)
(ah-nem-oh-*nell*-uh tha-lick-*troy*-dees)

TYPE: hardy tuber
HEIGHT: 15 cm (6 in.)
WIDTH: 30 cm (12 in.)
SOIL: fertile, moist, well drained
LIGHT: part sun to light shade
FLOWERING TIME: mid to late spring
GROWING TIPS: plant bare-root tubers in fall, container-grown tubers from spring to fall; soak tubers in lukewarm water for 24 hours before planting; use organic mulch for winter protection
ALTERNATIVES: *Anemone canadensis* (Canada anemone), *A. sylvestris* (snowdrop anemone)

CORYDALIS
Corydalis buschii (left)
(ko-*ry*-dah-lis *bush*-ee-ee)

TYPE: hardy rhizome
HEIGHT: 10 to 15 cm (4 to 6 in.)
WIDTH: 20 cm (8 in.)
SOIL: fertile, well drained
LIGHT: light shade
FLOWERING TIME: mid-spring
GROWING TIPS: avoid planting in hot, dry areas; use organic mulch for moisture retention and winter protection; may go dormant
ALTERNATIVES: *Corydalis cava, C. solida* 'George Baker'; *Aquilegia canadensis* (columbine)

Antennaria AND *Potentilla*

LIESBETH LEATHERBARROW

The cheerful yellow, buttercup-like flowers of shrubby potentillas are commonplace in prairie gardens; less familiar are their low-growing herbaceous cinquefoil relatives, which include *Potentilla nepalensis.* Suited to rock gardens or borders, *Potentilla nepalensis* is a clump-forming perennial with saucer-shaped, crimson flowers and branching stems clad with five-part, toothed, and hairy leaves. To showcase the cinquefoil's glowing red flowers, surround it with a carpet of silvery gray pussytoes, a delightful native groundcover that thrives in dry, sunny areas of the prairies and foothills. Unlike the brash cinquefoil, everything about pussytoes is subtle, from the woolly, mat-forming foliage to the small, white or pink flower clusters, resembling cat's paws, that perch atop downy stems.

PUSSYTOES

Antennaria (left)
(an-ten-*nair*-ee-ah)

TYPE: perennial groundcover
HEIGHT: 15 cm (6 in.)
WIDTH: 45 cm (18 in.)
SOIL: poor to average, well drained
LIGHT: full sun
FLOWERING TIME: early summer
GROWING TIPS: requires excellent drainage; deadhead; drought tolerant once established; very low maintenance
ALTERNATIVES: *Antennaria aprica* (low everlasting), *A. parvifolia* (small-leaved pussytoes), *A. pulcherrima* (showy everlasting); *Achillea tomentosa* (woolly yarrow); *Androsace sarmentosa* (rock jasmine); *Veronica pectinata* (comb speedwell)

CINQUEFOIL

Potentilla nepalensis (right)
(po-ten-*till*-ah nee-pall-*en*-siss)

TYPE: perennial
HEIGHT: 45 cm (18 in.)
WIDTH: 60 cm (24 in.)
SOIL: average, well drained
LIGHT: full to part sun
FLOWERING TIME: early to late summer
GROWING TIPS: shear after flowering to keep plant compact and encourage reblooming; drought tolerant once established
ALTERNATIVES: *Potentilla* 'Gibson's Scarlet', *P. tridentata* (three-toothed cinquefoil)

Aquilegia AND *Geranium*

LESLEY REYNOLDS

Golden columbine and Endres cranesbill both take their names from birds: columbine, meaning "dove," describes the flower's form, whereas cranesbill refers to the resemblance of that plant's pointy seed pod to a crane's bill. The golden columbine bears fanciful yellow blossoms composed of five cupped petals that narrow into spurs that protrude behind the bloom, and five petal-like sepals. The fernlike leaves are divided into lobed leaflets.

More vigorous and spreading than the dainty, upright columbine, the Endres cranesbill produces mounds of shiny, five-lobed leaves that support the columbine's slim flower stems, hiding its somewhat disheveled post-bloom appearance. Composed of five notched petals, the cranesbill's wide, trumpet-shaped flowers are pink with a silky, silvery sheen.

GOLDEN COLUMBINE
Aquilegia chrysantha (yellow)
(ack-will-*ee*-gee-ah kri-*san*-tha)

TYPE: perennial
HEIGHT: 76 cm (30 in.)
WIDTH: 60 cm (24 in.)
SOIL: average to fertile, moist, well drained
LIGHT: light shade to full sun
FLOWERING TIME: late spring to early summer
GROWING TIPS: avoid planting in hot, dry areas; use organic mulch for moisture retention and winter protection; deadhead to prevent self-seeding; prone to leaf miners, remove affected leaves
ALTERNATIVES: *Aquilegia* hybrids (Biedermeier, McKana, and Songbird)

ENDRES CRANESBILL
Geranium endressii (pink)
(jer-*ane*-ee-um en-*dress*-ee-ee)

TYPE: perennial
HEIGHT: 45 cm (18 in.)
WIDTH: 60 cm (24 in.)
SOIL: average, moist, well drained
LIGHT: part to full sun
FLOWERING TIME: late spring to early summer
GROWING TIPS: use organic mulch for moisture retention and winter protection; deadhead
ALTERNATIVES: *Geranium cinereum* 'Ballerina', *G.* x *oxonianum*, *G. sanguineum* var. *striatum* (bloody cranesbill), *G. sylvaticum* (wood cranesbill)

Aquilegia AND *Mertensia*

LESLEY REYNOLDS

As with many fine plant marriages, that of columbines and Virginia bluebells is a case of opposites attracting. Few flowers are as delightful or flamboyant as the columbine. The uniquely shaped blooms dance in the wind like colorful, fluttering birds above finely lobed, green to blue-green foliage. In contrast, the beauty of Virginia bluebells is understated, the soft gray-blue-green leaves composing a perfect backdrop for any color of sprightly columbine. Virginia bluebells bring woodland charm to the garden with pendant clusters of fragrant, sapphire flowers sporting small tubes that flare into scalloped, bell-shaped cups. Best used in informal gardens, columbines and Virginia bluebells are lovely in the dappled shade of deciduous trees or in a partly shaded cottage garden border.

COLUMBINE

Aquilegia (top)
(ack-will-*ee*-gee-ah)

TYPE: perennial
HEIGHT: 30 to 76 cm (12 to 30 in.)
WIDTH: 30 to 60 cm (12 to 24 in.)
SOIL: average to fertile, moist, well drained
LIGHT: light shade to full sun
FLOWERING TIME: late spring to early summer
GROWING TIPS: avoid planting in hot, dry areas; use organic mulch for moisture retention and winter protection; deadhead to prevent self-seeding; prone to leaf miners, remove affected leaves
ALTERNATIVES: *Aquilegia caerulea*, *A. chrysantha*, *A. flabellata*, hybrids (Biedermeier, McKana, Songbird)

VIRGINIA BLUEBELL

Mertensia pulmonarioides (bottom)
(murr-*ten*-see-ah pull-mon-air-ee-*oy*-dees)

TYPE: perennial
HEIGHT: 60 cm (24 in.)
WIDTH: 30 cm (12 in.)
SOIL: average to fertile, moist, well drained
LIGHT: light shade to part sun
FLOWERING TIME: late spring to early summer
GROWING TIPS: avoid planting in hot, dry areas; use organic mulch for moisture retention and winter protection
ALTERNATIVES: *Mertensia paniculata*, *M. sibirica* 'Blue Bells'

Arabis AND *Bergenia*

Although rock cress and 'Baby Doll' bergenia are both easy-to-please, long-lived, evergreen perennials, the sheer difference in scale between the two is what makes them an appealing pair in the mid-spring border. Whereas bergenia produces rosettes of large, round, shiny, green foliage, rock cress develops into mats of smallish, elliptical, hairy, gray-green leaves. Interestingly, the petite, flat, white or pink flowers that smother rock cress foliage in spring have rounded petals that echo the shape of bergenia leaves. In stark contrast, pink bergenia blossoms are funnel-shaped and arranged in clusters at the ends of sturdy red flower stems. Reliable rock cress cultivars are 'Compinkie', 'Snowball', and 'Variegata'. Excellent bergenia hybrids include 'Bressingham Ruby' and 'Sunningdale'.

ROCK CRESS

Arabis caucasica (bottom)
(*a*-ra-bis kaw-*ka*-si-kah)

TYPE: perennial
HEIGHT: 20 cm (8 in.)
WIDTH: 50 cm (20 in.)
SOIL: poor, average, or fertile, well drained
LIGHT: full sun
FLOWERING TIME: early to mid spring
GROWING TIPS: trim lightly after flowering; to prevent winter drying of evergreen foliage, cover with mulch or evergreen boughs
ALTERNATIVES: *Iberis sempervirens* (perennial candytuft), *I. saxatilis* (rock candytuft)

'BABY DOLL' BERGENIA

Bergenia 'Baby Doll' (top)
(ber-*geen*-ee-ah)

TYPE: perennial
HEIGHT: 30 cm (12 in.)
WIDTH: 45 to 60 cm (18 to 24 in.)
SOIL: fertile, moist, well drained
LIGHT: light shade to full sun
FLOWERING TIME: mid-spring
GROWING TIPS: to prevent winter drying of evergreen foliage, cover with mulch or evergreen boughs; drought tolerant once established
ALTERNATIVES: *Bergenia cordifolia* (heart-leaved bergenia), *B. crassifolia* (Siberian tea), *B. purpurascens*

Arabis AND *Scilla*

LIESBETH LEATHERBARROW

Is it pure coincidence or poetic justice that the colors of spring on the prairies are as cool and refreshing as the usually chilly prevailing daytime temperatures? Take the lovely combination of Siberian squill and rock cress, for example. At a time when few other plants have emerged, the enchanting, icy cobalt blue bells of squill make their appearance, followed closely by the dainty, snow-white blossoms of early-blooming rock cress. This duo, with its contrasting flowers of crisp white and blue, is in tune with its environment, evoking images of the frosty mornings and brisk afternoons that define a prairie spring. 'Spring Beauty' is a superb Siberian squill cultivar with large, violet blue flowers. Reliable rock cress cultivars include 'Compinkie', 'Snowball', and 'Variegata'.

ROCK CRESS

Arabis caucasica (bottom)
(*a*-ra-bis kaw-*ka*-si-kah)

TYPE: perennial
HEIGHT: 20 cm (8 in.)
WIDTH: 50 cm (20 in.)
SOIL: poor, average, or fertile, well drained
LIGHT: full sun
FLOWERING TIME: early to mid spring
GROWING TIPS: trim lightly after flowering; to prevent winter drying of evergreen foliage, cover with mulch or evergreen boughs
ALTERNATIVES: *Iberis sempervirens* (perennial candytuft), *I. saxatilis* (rock candytuft)

SIBERIAN SQUILL

Scilla sibirica (top)
(*skee*-lah sy-*bee*-ri-kah)

TYPE: hardy true bulb
HEIGHT: 15 cm (6 in.)
WIDTH: 2.5 cm (1 in.)
SOIL: average to fertile, well drained
LIGHT: full sun to light shade
FLOWERING TIME: early to mid spring
GROWING TIPS: plant bulbs in fall; use organic mulch for winter protection; fertilize before and after flowering; allow foliage to ripen; self-seeds; drought tolerant once established
ALTERNATIVES: *Scilla bifolia*, *S. mischtschenkoana* (milk squill); *Chionodoxa forbesii*, *C. luciliae* (glory-of-the-snow)

Artemisia AND *Aubrieta*

Anything goes when it comes to choosing partners for elegant, silver-leaved artemisias, but some combinations are just meant to be. One artemisia pairing that always lends a touch of class to rock gardens or the front of sunny borders is made up of the compact, low-growing artemisia 'Boughton Silver' (better known as 'Silver Brocade') and mat-forming purple rock cress. The aromatic, deeply incised, silvery foliage of 'Boughton Silver' is evergreen; with good winter protection it is already performing beautifully by mid-spring, when purple rock cress bathes itself in a profusion of small, single or double, four-petaled, cross-shaped blossoms. Purple rock cress hybrids come in a range of colors from magenta to purple; some species have variegated foliage.

'BOUGHTON SILVER'
ARTEMISIA
Artemisia stelleriana
'Boughton Silver' (left)
(ar-tay-*mis*-ee-ah stel-la-ree-*ah*-nah)

TYPE: perennial
HEIGHT: 15 cm (6 in.)
WIDTH: 30 to 45 cm (12 to 18 in.)
SOIL: poor to average, well drained
LIGHT: full sun
FLOWERING TIME: late summer to early fall
GROWING TIPS: requires excellent drainage; drought tolerant once established; excellent for hiding dying bulb foliage; very low maintenance
ALTERNATIVES: *Artemisia schmidtiana* 'Silver Mound'; *Cerastium tomentosum* (snow-in-summer)

PURPLE ROCK CRESS
Aubrieta deltoidea (right)
(o-bree-*ay*-tah del-*toi*-dee-ah)

TYPE: perennial
HEIGHT: 15 cm (6 in.)
WIDTH: 60 cm (24 in.)
SOIL: average to fertile, well drained
LIGHT: full sun
FLOWERING TIME: mid to late spring
GROWING TIPS: in areas with hot, dry summers, provide shade from afternoon sun; shear after flowering to keep plant compact; drought tolerant once established
ALTERNATIVES: *Arabis caucasica* (rock cress); *Phlox subulata* (moss phlox)

Asarum AND *Tiarella*

LIESBETH LEATHERBARROW

Woodland and lightly shaded gardens provide fertile ground for experimenting with the foliage form and texture of shade-tolerant groundcovers, which are often much leafier than they are floriferous. Two North American native plants that are star performers in dappled shade are the Allegheny foamflower and Canadian wild ginger. With their widely differing leaf shapes and sizes, this duo creates an interesting patchwork quilt effect on the woodland floor. Whereas foamflower leaves are small, deeply lobed, and prominently veined in a simple pattern, the wild ginger's leaves are large, heart shaped, and veined in a pattern as elaborate as any stitched onto an heirloom quilt. As a bonus, foamflower produces small, delicate spikes of white flowers in spring and fabulous reddish copper fall color.

CANADIAN WILD GINGER

Asarum canadense (right)
(ah-*sah*-rum ka-na-*dens*-ee)

TYPE: perennial groundcover
HEIGHT: 15 to 30 cm (6 to 12 in.)
WIDTH: 15 to 30 cm (6 to 12 in.)
SOIL: fertile, moist, well drained
LIGHT: light to full shade
FLOWERING TIME: mid to late spring
GROWING TIPS: avoid planting in hot, dry areas; requires excellent drainage; use organic mulch for moisture retention and winter protection
ALTERNATIVE: *Asarum europeum* (European wild ginger)

ALLEGHENY FOAMFLOWER

Tiarella cordifolia (left)
(tee-ah-*rell*-ah kor-dih-*foe*-lee-ah)

TYPE: perennial groundcover
HEIGHT: 10 to 30 cm (4 to 12 in.)
WIDTH: 30 cm (12 in.)
SOIL: fertile, moist, well drained
LIGHT: light to full shade
FLOWERING TIME: mid spring to mid-summer
GROWING TIPS: avoid planting in hot, dry areas; use organic mulch for moisture retention and winter protection; tolerates competition from shallow tree roots
ALTERNATIVES: *Tiarella wherryi* 'Inkblot', 'Oakleaf'; x *Heucherella alba* (foamy bells), x *H.* 'Bridget Bloom', 'Snow White'

Athyrium AND *Sanguinaria*

By combining the lacy foliage of lady fern with the boldly lobed foliage of bloodroot, prairie gardeners can recreate some of the subtle beauty of natural woodland plantings. Shady spots beside a house, fence, or shrubs, or under the canopy of deciduous trees, can provide ideal growing conditions for this duo. Bloodroot is slow to establish, but it gradually forms a unique ground-cover of distinctive gray-green. Its exquisite but short-lived, pure white blossoms come in single and double ('Flore Pleno' syn. 'Multiplex') forms and are a bonus in early spring. Contrasting light green lady fern fronds, each consisting of numerous pointed leaflets called pinnae, initially strike an erect pose in the garden. However, as they mature, the lady fern fronds arch protectively over neighboring plants.

LADY FERN
Athyrium filix-femina (top)
(a-*thi*-ree-um fih-liks-*fay*-mee-nah)

TYPE: perennial
HEIGHT: 90 cm (36 in.)
WIDTH: 60 cm (24 in.)
SOIL: fertile, moist, well drained
LIGHT: light shade
FLOWERING TIME: not applicable
GROWING TIPS: avoid planting in hot, dry areas; plant with crowns just below soil level; use organic mulch for moisture retention
ALTERNATIVES: *Matteuccia struthiopteris* (ostrich fern); *Osmunda cinnamomea* (cinnamon fern), *O. claytoniana* (interrupted fern), *O. regalis* (royal fern)

BLOODROOT
Sanguinaria canadensis (bottom)
(sang-gwin-*air*-ee-ah ka-na-*den*-siss)

TYPE: hardy rhizome
HEIGHT: 25 cm (10 in.)
WIDTH: 30 cm (12 in.)
SOIL: fertile, moist, well drained
LIGHT: full to part sun in active growth; light shade after blooming
FLOWERING TIME: mid to late spring
GROWING TIPS: place rhizomes in ground horizontally, with growth points just below soil level; use organic mulch for moisture retention and winter protection; may go dormant
ALTERNATIVE: *Trillium grandiflora* (trillium)

Aurinia AND *Thymus*

LIESBETH LEATHERBARROW

Whether tumbling over a stone wall or nestling companionably at the front of a border, basket-of-gold and creeping thyme bring a touch of summer warmth to the late-spring prairie garden. Basket-of-gold could just as easily be named basket-of-silver-and-gold: the abundant panicles of alyssumlike, yellow flowers arise from rosettes of cascading, silvery green foliage. Although similarly profuse, diminutive thyme flowers are pleasingly different in form; the two-lipped, tubular flowers grow in short spikes and dense clusters that smother the plants in blankets of mauve. Thyme blossoms outlast those of basket-of-gold, persisting for most of the summer above mats of tiny, aromatic, almost oval leaves that come to a point. There are also white, crimson, and pink forms of creeping thyme.

BASKET-OF-GOLD

Aurinia saxatilis (right)
(ore-*rin*-ee-yah sax-ah-*till*-us)

TYPE: perennial
HEIGHT: 20 cm (8 in.)
WIDTH: 30 cm (12 in.)
SOIL: average to fertile, well drained
LIGHT: full sun
FLOWERING TIME: late spring to early summer
GROWING TIPS: shear after flowering to keep plant compact; drought tolerant once established
ALTERNATIVES: *Alyssum montanum* (mountain alyssum); *Thermopsis lupinoides* (false lupin)

CREEPING THYME

Thymus serpyllum (left)
(*ty*-mus sir-*pil*-lum)

TYPE: perennial
HEIGHT: 10 cm (4 in.)
WIDTH: 30 cm (12 in.)
SOIL: poor to average, well drained
LIGHT: full to part sun
FLOWERING TIME: late spring to late summer
GROWING TIPS: requires excellent drainage; to prevent winter drying of semi-evergreen foliage, cover with mulch or evergreen boughs; trim lightly after flowering
ALTERNATIVES: *Arabis caucasica* (rock cress); *Phlox subulata* (moss phlox); *Saponaria ocymoides* (rock soapwort)

Caragana AND *Spiraea*

LIESBETH LEATHERBARROW

Although it is tempting to dot shrubs throughout a mixed or woody ornamental border, it pays to plan for a shrub pair every once in a while to capitalize on their "star performance" status when they bloom in spring. Two compatible drought-tolerant and low maintenance shrubs that bloom at the same time are spring-flowering spirea and fernleaf caragana. Both have arching branches that reach for the ground. Whereas the spring-blooming spireas have small but substantial leaves and tiny, white blossoms in showy clusters along the length of their branches, fernleaf caragana is a treelike shrub with branches clothed in lime green, linear, needlelike leaves and yellow, pealike blossoms. Caragana flowers also develop into brown seedpods that snap! crackle! and pop! when dispersing seeds.

FERNLEAF CARAGANA
Caragana arborescens 'Lorbergii' (right)
(ka-ra-*gah*-nah ar-bo-*res*-kens)

TYPE: deciduous shrub
HEIGHT: 4 m (13 ft.)
WIDTH: 3 m (10 ft.)
SOIL: poor to fertile
LIGHT: full sun
FLOWERING TIME: late spring
GROWING TIPS: plant with graft union aboveground; rarely needs pruning though branches may be trimmed in early spring; drought tolerant once established
ALTERNATIVES: *Caragana frutex* 'Globosa' (globe caragana), *C. pygmaea* (pygmy caragana)

SPRING-FLOWERING SPIREA
Spiraea (left)
(spy-*ree*-ah)

TYPE: deciduous shrub
HEIGHT: 1 to 2.5 m (3.3 to 8 ft.)
WIDTH: 1 to 2.5 m (3.3 to 8 ft.)
SOIL: fertile, moist, well drained
LIGHT: full sun
FLOWERING TIME: mid to late spring
GROWING TIPS: drought tolerant once established; prune after flowering and once leaves have fully emerged; water well in fall
ALTERNATIVES: *Spiraea* x *arguta* (garland spirea), *S. trilobata* (three-lobed spirea), *S.* x *vanhouttei* (bridalwreath spirea)

Cerastium AND *Saponaria*

LIESBETH LEATHERBARROW

The drought-tolerant duo of snow-in-summer and rock soapwort are two of the many low-growing, prairie-hardy perennials that provide a tapestry of pink, purple, and white blossoms from spring through mid-summer. An arresting sight tumbling over a wall or carpeting a hot, dry slope, the dazzling white flowers of snow-in-summer truly live up to the plant's common name. This tough, low-maintenance groundcover produces an abundance of small, star-shaped flowers above slender, silver-gray leaves. Snow-in-summer should be avoided in rock gardens, where it may overwhelm dainty alpines. Rock soapwort is less invasive than snow-in-summer, although the small, bright green leaves and tiny, rose-pink flowers trail prettily, a soothing complement to the stark white brightness of its companion.

SNOW-IN-SUMMER
Cerastium tomentosum (right)
(kay-*rass*-tee-yum toe-men-*toe*-sum)

TYPE: perennial groundcover
HEIGHT: 15 cm (6 in.)
WIDTH: indefinite
SOIL: poor to average, well drained
LIGHT: full sun
FLOWERING TIME: late spring to early summer
GROWING TIPS: trim lightly after flowering; drought tolerant once established; may be invasive, but is easy to control
ALTERNATIVES: *Arabis caucasica* 'Snowball' (rock cress); *Phlox subulata* 'Schneewittchen', 'White Delight' (moss phlox)

ROCK SOAPWORT
Saponaria ocymoides (left)
(sa-po-*nair*-ee-ah o-kim-*oi*-dees)

TYPE: perennial
HEIGHT: 8 cm (3 in.)
WIDTH: 45 cm (18 in.)
SOIL: average to fertile, well drained
LIGHT: full sun
FLOWERING TIME: late spring to early summer
GROWING TIPS: shear after flowering to keep plant compact; drought tolerant once established
ALTERNATIVES: *Saponaria* 'Bressingham', *S. caespitosa*; *Arabis caucasica* 'Compinkie' (rock cress); *Phlox subulata* 'Apple Blossom', 'Emerald Pink', 'McDaniel's Cushion' (moss phlox)

Chionodoxa AND *Puschkinia*

LIESBETH LEATHERBARROW

Like many other prairie-hardy bulbs, striped squill and glory-of-the-snow originate in the mountains of the Middle East. With a toughness that belies their delicate appearance, these darlings of the early spring garden gracefully withstand the frigid prairie spring weather. Each striped squill bulb pushes up a short flower spike that bears up to six outward-facing, star-shaped flowers of the palest frosty blue, each petal etched down the middle with a greenish blue stripe. Glory-of-the-snow has a more relaxed aspect than its partner, producing racemes of up to three pale lavender-blue flowers. The upfacing blooms are centered with white, complementing the icy hues of the striped squill flowers. The foliage of both bulbs is linear to strap-shaped and disappears quickly after blooming.

GLORY-OF-THE-SNOW
Chionodoxa luciliae (right)
(key-on-oh-*dox*-ah loo-*sill*-ee-eye)

TYPE: hardy true bulb
HEIGHT: 20 cm (8 in.)
WIDTH: 5 cm (2 in.)
SOIL: average to fertile, moist, well drained
LIGHT: full to part sun
FLOWERING TIME: early to mid spring
GROWING TIPS: plant bulbs in fall; use organic mulch for winter protection; fertilize before and after flowering; allow foliage to ripen; self-seeds
ALTERNATIVE: *Chionodoxa forbesii*

STRIPED SQUILL
Puschkinia scilloides (left)
(push-*kih*-nee-ah ski-*loy*-dees)

TYPE: hardy true bulb
HEIGHT: 15 to 20 cm (6 to 8 in.)
WIDTH: 5 cm (2 in.)
SOIL: average to fertile, moist, well drained
LIGHT: full to part sun
FLOWERING TIME: early to mid spring
GROWING TIPS: plant bulbs in drifts in fall; use organic mulch for winter protection; fertilize before and after flowering; allow foliage to ripen; self-seeds
ALTERNATIVE: *Scilla sibirica* (Siberian squill)

Clematis AND *Malus*

LESLEY REYNOLDS

From spring to late summer, lovely prairie-hardy clematis species and cultivars lend spectacular color to walls, trellises, and arbors, enhancing all neighboring perennials. It's easy to find friends for summer-blooming clematis, but coming up with spring pairings requires a bit more imagination. One of the most enchanting clematis partnerships of the year is the spring-blooming *Clematis macropetala* 'Blue Bird' winding through the blossom-laden branches of a 'Red Jade' weeping crabapple. Bred by Dr. Frank Skinner, 'Blue Bird' bears lavender-blue, open bell-shaped blooms. The fragrant, single, white to pink blossoms of 'Red Jade' shine brightly against the dusky clematis flowers, while the tree's unusual weeping habit makes it a fine choice for small spaces or rock gardens.

'BLUE BIRD' CLEMATIS
Clematis macropetala 'Blue Bird' (top)
(*klem*-ah-tiss or klem-*ah*-tiss ma-krow-*pe*-ta-lah)

TYPE: perennial vine
HEIGHT: 3 m (10 ft.)
WIDTH: 1.2 m (4 ft.)
SOIL: fertile, moist, well drained
LIGHT: full to part sun
FLOWERING TIME: mid to late spring
GROWING TIPS: plant with 15 cm (6 in.) of stem below soil line; use organic mulch for moisture retention and winter protection; fertilize in spring; if necessary, prune lightly soon after blooming
ALTERNATIVE: *Clematis alpina*

'RED JADE' WEEPING CRABAPPLE
Malus x *purpurea* 'Red Jade' (bottom)
(*ma*-luss x purr-*purr*-ree-ah)

TYPE: deciduous tree
HEIGHT: 1 to 3 m (3.3 to 10 ft.)
WIDTH: 6 m (20 ft.)
SOIL: average, well drained
LIGHT: full to part sun
FLOWERING TIME: mid-spring
GROWING TIPS: drought tolerant once established; prune after flowering and once leaves have fully emerged; prune young trees lightly to achieve desired shape; water well in fall
ALTERNATIVES: *Malus* x *adstringens* 'Morning Princess', *M.* x *purpurea* 'Rosy Glo', 'Royal Beauty'

Crocus AND *Iris*

LESLEY REYNOLDS

Delightful and diminutive snow crocuses and reticulata irises are sure to be the first perfect partners of the prairie growing season, often appearing by the end of March or early April. Each 'Romance' crocus corm produces up to four cupped, lemon yellow flowers, in bright contrast to the slightly taller, deep blue 'Harmony' irises. Plant this pretty pair where they are easy to view—in a rock garden, among low-growing groundcovers along pathways or at the front of a border, or naturalized in drifts under deciduous trees or in turf. Charming *Crocus chrysanthus* cultivars include 'Cream Beauty' (cream with greenish base and golden yellow throat), 'E. A. Bowles' (yellow with purple marks on outside), 'Ladykiller' (white with deep violet marks on outside), and 'Snow Bunting' (white).

'ROMANCE' SNOW CROCUS
Crocus chrysanthus 'Romance' (bottom)
(*kro*-kus kri-*san*-thus)

TYPE: hardy corm
HEIGHT: 8 cm (3 in.)
WIDTH: 2.5 cm (1 in.)
SOIL: average, well drained
LIGHT: full sun
FLOWERING TIME: early spring
GROWING TIPS: plant corms in fall; use organic mulch for winter protection; fertilize before and after flowering; allow foliage to ripen
ALTERNATIVES: *Crocus ancyrensis* (golden bunch), *C. vernus* 'Yellow Mammoth' (Dutch crocus)

'HARMONY' RETICULATA IRIS
Iris 'Harmony' (top)
(*eye*-riss)

TYPE: hardy true bulb
HEIGHT: 10 cm (4 in.)
WIDTH: 2.5 cm (1 in.)
SOIL: average to fertile, well drained
LIGHT: full to part sun
FLOWERING TIME: early spring
GROWING TIPS: plant bulbs in fall; use organic mulch for winter protection; fertilize before and after flowering; allow foliage to ripen
ALTERNATIVES: *Iris histrioides* 'Major', *I.* 'Joyce', *I. reticulata* 'Cantab'

Dianthus AND *Gentiana*

LLYN STRELAU

If you're crying the blues for more blues in the garden, dry your eyes and indulge in collecting gentians, which put on a spectacular show in the rockery or at the front of well-drained borders. The spring gentian is a low-growing, evergreen alpine plant that produces basal rosettes of dark green foliage smothered in magnificent solitary blossoms, each with five rounded, sky blue petals and a touch of white at the throat. For a winning combination, pair spring gentian with *Dianthus microlepis*. Although somewhat slow to establish, this species pink mimics the gentian with its single, pink, purple, or white, slightly ragged, five-petaled blossoms. Even without the benefit of flowers, the silvery or blue-green grassy tufts of dianthus foliage always bring out the best in their neighbors.

PINK
Dianthus microlepis (right)
(die-*an*-thuss my-kro-*lep*-iss)

TYPE: perennial
HEIGHT: 5 cm (2 in.)
WIDTH: 15 cm (6 in.)
SOIL: average to fertile, well drained
LIGHT: full sun
FLOWERING TIME: late spring to early summer
GROWING TIPS: provide shade from hot afternoon sun; requires excellent drainage; to prevent winter drying of evergreen foliage, cover with mulch or evergreen boughs; deadhead
ALTERNATIVES: *Dianthus alpinus* (alpine pink), *D. gratianopolitanus* 'Tiny Rubies' (cheddar pink), *D. pavonius*

SPRING GENTIAN
Gentiana verna (left)
(jen-tee-*ah*-na *ver*-nah)

TYPE: perennial
HEIGHT: 4 cm (1.5 in.)
WIDTH: 10 cm (4 in.)
SOIL: fertile, moist, well drained
LIGHT: full sun
FLOWERING TIME: late spring to early summer
GROWING TIPS: in areas with hot, dry summers, provide shade from afternoon sun; requires excellent drainage; deadhead
ALTERNATIVES: *Veronica liwanensis* (Turkish speedwell), *V. pectinata* (comb speedwell), *V. prostrata* (harebell speedwell)

Dianthus AND *Ranunculus*

LIESBETH LEATHERBARROW

The sparkling yellow buttercup is a familiar wildflower that, perhaps surprisingly, earns its keep in prairie gardens. An unmistakable winner, 'Flore Pleno' produces dozens of little, multi-petaled, golden orbs that hover aloft like a fleet of wee spaceships on thin, rigid, branching stems. Blooming for weeks on end, 'Flore Pleno' is an interesting companion for many plants in mixed or perennial borders, including pinks, whose low mounds of grassy, blue-green foliage contrast effectively with the deeply cut, medium green leaves of 'Flore Pleno'. Lovely pinks' blossoms have elegant, up-facing petals that are as flat as 'Flore Pleno's are curved. They come in an extensive palette of white, pinks, and reds, and many are bicolored, with a central zone or eye of a contrasting color.

PINK
Dianthus (bottom)
(die-*an*-thuss)

TYPE: perennial
HEIGHT: 30 to 45 cm (12 to 18 in.)
WIDTH: 30 cm (12 in.)
SOIL: average to fertile, well drained
LIGHT: full to part sun
FLOWERING TIME: late spring to mid-summer
GROWING TIPS: to prevent winter drying of evergreen foliage, cover with mulch or evergreen boughs; deadhead to maintain compact habit, prolong flowering, and prevent self-seeding
ALTERNATIVES: *Dianthus alpinus* (alpine pink), *D. deltoides* (maiden pink), *D. gratianopolitanus* (cheddar pink)

DOUBLE MEADOW BUTTERCUP
Ranunculus acris 'Flore Pleno' (top)
(ra-*nun*-kew-luss *ah*-kriss)

TYPE: perennial
HEIGHT: 20 to 90 cm (8 to 36 in.)
WIDTH: 23 cm (9 in.)
SOIL: fertile, moist, well drained
LIGHT: full sun to light shade
FLOWERING TIME: mid-spring to early summer
GROWING TIPS: avoid planting in hot, dry areas; deadhead; sap may irritate skin
ALTERNATIVES: *Trollius* x *cultorum* (globeflower)

Dicentra AND *Tulipa*

LESLEY REYNOLDS

Far from common in appearance, the common bleeding heart is better described as a classic, its eye-catching heart-shaped blossoms gracing many a prairie garden in late spring. In a true case of opposites attracting, the arching racemes of pendant, pink and white bleeding heart blooms against a background of lobed, light green foliage frame the vertical stems, and cup- or goblet-shaped flowers of single late tulips. Plant this lovely pair in a mixed border with morning sun, or a little shade from deciduous trees or shrubs during the hottest part of the day. There are also white cultivars of the common bleeding heart; 'Pantaloons' is the most robust. Look for the red single late tulip cultivars 'Balalaika', 'Baronesse', 'Halcro', 'Ile de France', 'Kingsblood', and 'Renown'.

COMMON BLEEDING HEART
Dicentra spectabilis (left)
(di-*ken*-trah speck-*ta*-bi-liss)

TYPE: perennial
HEIGHT: 90 cm (36 in.)
WIDTH: 60 cm (24 in.)
SOIL: fertile, moist
LIGHT: full sun to light shade
FLOWERING TIME: late spring to early summer
GROWING TIPS: avoid planting in hot, dry areas; use organic mulch for moisture retention and winter protection; may go dormant
ALTERNATIVES: *Dicentra eximia* (fringed bleeding heart), *D. formosa* (western or fernleaf bleeding heart), *D.* x 'Luxuriant'

SINGLE LATE TULIP
Tulipa (right)
(*tew*-lip-ah)

TYPE: hardy true bulb
HEIGHT: 45 to 76 cm (18 to 30 in.)
WIDTH: 10 cm (4 in.)
SOIL: fertile, moist, well drained
LIGHT: full sun
FLOWERING TIME: late spring
GROWING TIPS: plant bulbs in fall; mulch for winter protection; fertilize before and after flowering; deadhead; allow foliage to ripen
ALTERNATIVES: red lily-flowered, fringed, or double late tulips ('Abba', 'Akita', 'Burgundy Lace')

Dodecatheon AND *Primula*

LIESBETH LEATHERBARROW

Two plants with a shared passion for wiggling their toes in cool, moist soil are Siebold's primrose and shooting star. Happily, their pink and magenta blossoms also unfurl at the same time, making this duo a lovely tone-on-tone combination in woodland and bog gardens or moist borders. The exquisite magenta-pink shooting star blossoms that hang in the air atop arching stems are deserving of their common name—their reflexed petals sweep back from the blossom center, creating the illusion of a gaseous comet tail burning through the atmosphere. In perfect harmony with its galactic neighbor, the dainty primrose blossoms have widely flared, frilled petals and are pink, lilac-purple, or crimson, with a white eye. 'Dancing Ladies' and 'Geisha Girl' are beautiful Siebold's primrose cultivars.

SHOOTING STAR
Dodecatheon meadia (top)
(doe-deh-*kath*-ee-on *mee*-dee-ah)

TYPE: perennial
HEIGHT: 40 cm (16 in.)
WIDTH: 25 cm (10 in.)
SOIL: fertile, moist, well drained
LIGHT: full sun to light shade
FLOWERING TIME: late spring
GROWING TIPS: avoid planting in hot, dry areas; use organic mulch for moisture retention and winter protection; deadhead; may go dormant
ALTERNATIVES: *Erythronium dens-canis* (dog's-tooth violet); *Fritillaria meleagris* (checkered lily)

PRIMROSE
Primula sieboldii (bottom)
(*prim*-you-lah see-*bold*-ee-ee)

TYPE: perennial
HEIGHT: 30 cm (12 in.)
WIDTH: 45 cm (18 in.)
SOIL: fertile, moist, well drained
LIGHT: part sun to light shade
FLOWERING TIME: late spring
GROWING TIPS: avoid planting in hot, dry areas; tolerates full sun if soil kept moist at all times; use organic mulch for moisture retention and winter protection; deadhead
ALTERNATIVES: *Primula auricula*, *P. cortusoides*, *P. denticulata* (drumstick primrose), *P.* x *juliae*, *P. veris* (cowslip), *P. vulgaris* (common primrose)

Doronicum AND *Primula*

LIESBETH LEATHERBARROW

Prairie gardeners with a penchant for English cottage gardens will delight in the carefree combination of sunny leopard's bane and rose-pink *Primula cortusoides*, perfect choices for a partly shaded perennial border. Appearing in mid-spring, the single, daisylike blossoms of leopard's bane wave in the breeze above mounds of attractive heart-shaped, toothed leaves. Although not as bold as its cheerful daisy companion, *Primula cortusoides* also puts on a splendid show, bearing umbels of up to fifteen dainty flowers that are set off beautifully against the vivid green leopard's bane foliage. Each little primrose blossom has a yellow eye, echoing the bright yellow blooms of leopard's bane. The leopard's bane cultivar 'Miss Mason' is recommended for its long-lasting foliage.

LEOPARD'S BANE

Doronicum columnae (top)
(do-*ron*-i-kum ko-*lum*-neye)

TYPE: perennial
HEIGHT: 60 cm (24 in.)
WIDTH: 60 cm (24 in.)
SOIL: fertile, moist, well drained
LIGHT: light shade to full sun
FLOWERING TIME: mid to late spring
GROWING TIPS: avoid planting in hot, dry areas; use organic mulch for moisture retention and winter protection; deadhead
ALTERNATIVES: *Doronicum orientale*; *Trollius* x *cultorum* 'Canary Bird', 'Yellow Queen' (globeflower)

PRIMROSE

Primula cortusoides (bottom)
(*prim*-you-lah kor-too-*soy*-dees)

TYPE: perennial
HEIGHT: 30 cm (12 in.)
WIDTH: 30 cm (12 in.)
SOIL: average to fertile, moist, well drained
LIGHT: part sun to light shade
FLOWERING TIME: mid to late spring
GROWING TIPS: avoid planting in hot, dry areas; use organic mulch for moisture retention and winter protection; deadhead
ALTERNATIVES: *Primula auricula*, *P. denticulata* (drumstick primrose), *P. frondosa, P. saxatilis*

Erysimum AND *Prunus*

CALGARY ZOO

If the astonishing and unexpected are welcome in your garden, try introducing purpleleaf sand cherry and showy, light orange Siberian wallflower into the mixed border. A bold and brazen partnership from late spring through late summer, it sizzles with heat and hints at the wild color extravaganzas that will grace our gardens in fall. The fragrant Siberian wallflower is a biennial or short-lived perennial with long-lasting clusters of small, four-petaled blossoms typical of members of the mustard family. The flowers grow on short stems above mounded, lance-shaped, toothed foliage. The purpleleaf sand cherry, with its fabulous red-purple leaf color, creates an effective backdrop for most flowering plants, but it is never more dramatic than when paired with the perky wallflower.

SIBERIAN WALLFLOWER

Erysimum x *allionii* (bottom)
(er-*rih*-see-mum x all-ee-*oh*-nee-ee)

TYPE: biennial, short-lived perennial
HEIGHT: 60 cm (24 in.)
WIDTH: 30 cm (12 in.)
SOIL: average to fertile, well drained
LIGHT: full sun
FLOWERING TIME: late spring to late summer
GROWING TIPS: use organic mulch for winter protection; trim lightly after flowering to keep plant compact; drought tolerant once established
ALTERNATIVES: *Calendula officinalis* (pot marigold); *Eschscholzia californica* (California poppy)

PURPLELEAF SAND CHERRY

Prunus x *cistena* (top)
(*proo*-nuss x siss-*tee*-nah)

TYPE: deciduous shrub
HEIGHT: 2 m (6.5 ft.)
WIDTH: 1.5 m (5 ft.)
SOIL: fertile, moist, well drained
LIGHT: full sun
FLOWERING TIME: mid-spring
GROWING TIPS: prefers a sheltered location; prune when dormant as it flowers on previous or current year's growth; may suffer tip-kill after severe or dry winters; water well in fall
ALTERNATIVE: *Physocarpus opulifolius* 'Diablo' (purple ninebark)

Euphorbia AND *Muscari*

LIESBETH LEATHERBARROW

Yellow and violet make a winning combination in the garden, as exemplified by the springtime pairing of grape hyacinth and cushion spurge. Not only do these outstanding plants come in complementary colors, each offsetting the bold effect of the other, but their contrasting shapes and forms also work well together. Grape hyacinth may be small in stature, but it makes a big impact in perennial and mixed borders. Its spiky clusters of nodding, bell-shaped flowers that resemble upside-down bunches of lilliputian grapes can hold their own, even when planted beside bright yellow cushion spurge. The spurge's horizontal flower arrangement, which consists of flat, up-facing collars of chartreuse bracts enclosing dense clusters of small, yellow flowers, is a pleasant contrast to the vertical grape hyacinth.

CUSHION SPURGE

Euphorbia polychroma (top)
(ew-*for*-bee-ah paw-lee-*krow*-mah)

TYPE: perennial
HEIGHT: 40 cm (16 in.)
WIDTH: 60 cm (24 in.)
SOIL: average to fertile, moist, well drained
LIGHT: full sun to light shade
FLOWERING TIME: mid to late spring
GROWING TIPS: in areas with hot, dry summers, provide shade from afternoon sun; drought tolerant once established; sap in stems may irritate skin
ALTERNATIVES: *Aurinia saxatilis* (basket-of-gold); *Doronicum columnae*, *D. orientale* (leopard's bane)

GRAPE HYACINTH

Muscari armeniacum (bottom)
(moose-*kah*-ree ar-men-ee-*ah*-kum)

TYPE: hardy true bulb
HEIGHT: 10 to 20 cm (4 to 8 in.)
WIDTH: 2.5 cm (1 in.)
SOIL: average, well drained
LIGHT: full to part sun
FLOWERING TIME: mid-spring
GROWING TIPS: plant bulbs in fall; use organic mulch for moisture retention and winter protection; fertilize before and after flowering; allow foliage to ripen; leaves may emerge aboveground in fall and winter, flowers appear the following spring
ALTERNATIVES: *Muscari botryoides*, *M. comosum*, *M. latifolium*

Festuca AND *Potentilla*

LIESBETH LEATHERBARROW

The very effective and practical water-wise plant partnership of potentilla and blue fescue ornamental grass works wonders in out-of-the-way, sunny, dry corners of the garden. Potentillas are wiry, little, dark green or blue-green shrubs that bear a profusion of cheerful buttercuplike flowers from late spring to late summer. Although originally only available in bright yellow, potentilla cultivars now boast a range of blossom colors, including white ('Abbotswood'), orange ('Mango Tango'), pink ('Pink Beauty'), and red ('Red Robin'). The cool blue-green, fine-textured foliage and flower spikelets of clump-forming blue fescue grasses form a soft carpet around potentilla, showing it off to advantage. 'Elijah Blue' and 'Skinner's Blue' are excellent fescue cultivars.

BLUE FESCUE
Festuca glauca (bottom)
(fess-*too*-ka *glau*-ka)

TYPE: perennial
HEIGHT: 15 to 45 cm (6 to 18 in.)
WIDTH: 25 cm (10 in.)
SOIL: poor to average, well drained
LIGHT: full sun
FLOWERING TIME: early to mid summer
GROWING TIPS: use organic mulch for moisture retention; cut leaves back to form tight bun in spring to encourage neat new growth; drought tolerant once established
ALTERNATIVE: *Helictotrichon sempervirens* (blue oat grass)

POTENTILLA
Potentilla fruticosa (top)
(po-ten-*till*-ah froo-ti-*ko*-sah)

TYPE: deciduous shrub
HEIGHT: 90 cm (36 in.)
WIDTH: 90 cm (36 in.)
SOIL: average, well drained
LIGHT: full to part sun
FLOWERING TIME: late spring to fall
GROWING TIPS: use organic mulch for moisture retention; prune when dormant, removing dead or weak growth at ground level; thin out older branches at soil level to prevent crowding; water well in fall
ALTERNATIVES: *Caragana frutex* 'Globosa' (globe caragana), *C. pygmaea* (pygmy caragana)

Fritillaria AND *Lamium*

LESLEY REYNOLDS

The pendant, square bells of the checkered lily, patterned in shades of reddish purple, pink, or creamy to pure white, show to perfection nodding in the breeze above a silver-splashed carpet of lamium. Undeserving of the ugly common name "spotted dead nettle," lamium boasts small flower clusters and attractive toothed, silver and green leaves that camouflage the ripening checkered lily foliage and provide a superb summer-long groundcover under deciduous trees or around shrubs in partly shaded borders. Checkered lily aficionados should hunt for *Fritillaria meleagris* var. *alba* (white) and named varieties: 'Adonis', 'Aphrodite', 'Artemis', 'Charon', and 'Saturnis'. Excellent *Lamium maculatum* cultivars include 'Beacon Silver', 'Chequers', and 'White Nancy'.

CHECKERED LILY
Fritillaria meleagris (top)
(fri-ti-*lay*-ree-yah may-lee-*ah*-griss)

TYPE: hardy true bulb
HEIGHT: 45 cm (18 in.)
WIDTH: 5 cm (2 in.)
SOIL: fertile, moist, well drained
LIGHT: full sun to light shade
FLOWERING TIME: late spring
GROWING TIPS: plant bulbs in fall; bulbs should not dry out before planting; fertilize before and after flowering; allow foliage to ripen
ALTERNATIVES: *Fritillaria camschatcensis* (black sarana), *F. michailovskyi* (Michael's flower), *F. pallidiflora* (Siberian fritillary), *F. pudica* (yellow fritillary)

LAMIUM
Lamium maculatum (bottom)
(*lay*-mee-um ma-kue-*la*-tum)

TYPE: perennial groundcover
HEIGHT: 30 cm (12 in.)
WIDTH: 30 to 90 cm (12 to 36 in.)
SOIL: fertile, moist, well drained
LIGHT: part sun to full shade
FLOWERING TIME: late spring
GROWING TIPS: avoid planting in hot, dry areas; use organic mulch for moisture retention and winter protection; deadhead; excellent for hiding dying bulb foliage
ALTERNATIVES: *Lamium galeobdolon* (yellow archangel); *Ajuga genevensis*, *A. reptans* (bugleweed)

Galium AND *Hosta*

LESLEY REYNOLDS

Hostas are a hot commodity in prairie garden centers these days as they bring an unsurpassed diversity of leaf color, shape, and texture to shaded or partly shaded gardens. A living mulch for the moisture-loving hosta, sweet woodruff carpets the ground with whorls of lance-shaped, shiny, emerald-green leaves, in a delightful counter-point to the substantial hosta foliage. As a bonus to their fascinating foliage, hostas also produce scapes of white or lavender, lilylike flowers in summer, whereas the starry, pure white, fragrant flowers of sweet woodruff appear in mid to late spring and last for several weeks. Underplant any medium-sized to large hosta with sweet woodruff; try the readily available hosta cultivars 'Elegans', 'Frances Williams', 'Gold Standard', 'Krossa Regal', and 'Sum and Substance'.

SWEET WOODRUFF
Galium odoratum (bottom)
(*gal*-ee-yum oh-dor-*a*-tum)

TYPE: perennial groundcover
HEIGHT: 25 cm (10 in.)
WIDTH: indefinite
SOIL: fertile, moist, well drained
LIGHT: full shade to part sun
FLOWERING TIME: late spring to early summer
GROWING TIPS: avoid planting in hot, dry areas; may be invasive, but is easy to control
ALTERNATIVES: *Convallaria majalis* (lily-of-the-valley); white-flowered *Vinca minor* (common periwinkle)

HOSTA
Hosta (top)
(*hoss*-tah)

TYPE: perennial
HEIGHT: 30 to 120 cm (12 to 48 in.)
WIDTH: 50 to 120 cm (20 to 48 in.)
SOIL: fertile, moist, well drained
LIGHT: part sun to full shade
FLOWERING TIME: early summer to fall
GROWING TIPS: avoid planting in hot, dry areas; plant in sheltered area; use organic mulch for moisture retention and winter protection; excellent for hiding dying bulb foliage
ALTERNATIVE: *Bergenia* (elephant ears)

Gentiana AND *Tulipa*

For those who treasure "true blue" in the garden, the dramatic blossoms of the trumpet gentian are a must. A star performer in its own right, this mat-forming alpine perennial, with its rosettes of fleshy, dark green leaves, produces large, solitary, trumpet-shaped flowers in shades of brilliant ultramarine blue. Despite the trumpet gentian's theatrical ability to "go it alone" in the late-spring rock garden, its appearance can be enhanced by the species tulip *Tulipa batalinii* 'Bright Gem'. Also of alpine origin, the low-growing 'Bright Gem' produces blue-gray foliage and delightful lightly scented, soft golden yellow blossoms flushed in apricot—a perfect foil for the intensely blue gentians. Other lovely *Tulipa batalinii* hybrids include 'Apricot Jewel', 'Red Gem', and 'Yellow Jewel'.

TRUMPET GENTIAN
Gentiana acaulis (top)
(jen-tee-*ah*-na a-*kaw*-liss)

TYPE: perennial
HEIGHT: 8 to 10 cm (3 to 4 in.)
WIDTH: 30 cm (12 in.)
SOIL: fertile, moist, well drained
LIGHT: full to part sun
FLOWERING TIME: late spring to early summer
GROWING TIPS: in areas with hot, dry summers, provide shade from afternoon sun; requires excellent drainage; deadhead
ALTERNATIVE: *Gentiana verna* (spring gentian)

'BRIGHT GEM' SPECIES TULIP
Tulipa batalinii 'Bright Gem' (bottom)
(*tew*-lip-ah bah-ta-*lin*-ee-ee)

TYPE: hardy true bulb
HEIGHT: 20 to 25 cm (8 to 10 in.)
WIDTH: 25 cm (10 in.)
SOIL: fertile, moist, well drained
LIGHT: full sun
FLOWERING TIME: late spring
GROWING TIPS: plant bulbs in fall; use organic mulch for winter protection; fertilize before and after flowering; allow foliage to ripen; drought tolerant once established
ALTERNATIVE: *Tulipa acuminata, T. clusiana* var. *chrysantha* (lady tulip)

Geranium AND *Phlox*

LIESBETH LEATHERBARROW

From early-blooming, dainty denizens of the rock garden to impressive perennials for the late-summer border, *Geranium* and *Phlox* are among the most versatile genera for prairie gardens. 'Ballerina' cranesbill and moss phlox are fine examples, a showy pair of perennials for a sunny rock garden or the front of the border. 'Ballerina' bears lilac-pink, crimson-veined flowers with dark crimson centers, held on delicate stems above mounded, finely cut, gray-green leaves. In contrast, moss phlox forms mats of dense, needlelike foliage smothered with small flowers. Although available in a profusion of colors, including white, pink, and purple, it is the dark pink to red shades of moss phlox that really make 'Ballerina' dance by highlighting the crimson veins and centers of the saucer-shaped blooms.

'BALLERINA' CRANESBILL

Geranium cinereum 'Ballerina' (right)
(jer-*ane*-ee-um kin-*air*-ee-um)

TYPE: perennial
HEIGHT: 15 cm (6 in.)
WIDTH: 30 cm (12 in.)
SOIL: average, well drained
LIGHT: full to part sun
FLOWERING TIME: late spring to early summer
GROWING TIPS: use organic mulch for moisture retention and winter protection; deadhead to encourage reblooming
ALTERNATIVES: *Geranium endressii* (Endres cranesbill), *G. sanguineum* var. *striatum* (bloody cranesbill)

MOSS PHLOX

Phlox subulata (left)
(flocks sub-you-*lah*-tah)

TYPE: perennial
HEIGHT: 15 cm (6 in.)
WIDTH: 50 cm (20 in.)
SOIL: fertile, well drained
LIGHT: full to part sun
FLOWERING TIME: late spring to early summer
GROWING TIPS: to prevent winter drying of evergreen foliage, cover with mulch or evergreen boughs; shear after flowering to keep plant compact; drought tolerant once established
ALTERNATIVES: *Arabis caucasica* 'Compinkie' (rock cress); *Saponaria ocymoides* (rock soapwort)

Geum AND *Hemerocallis*

LIESBETH LEATHERBARROW

The first daylily to bloom each year is the species lemon daylily, *Hemerocallis lilio-asphodelus*. As luck would have it, its bloom time overlaps with that of three-flowered avens, a native prairie plant that begins its flirtation with prairie gardeners in mid-spring and continues into summer. The much smaller, more intricately shaped blossoms of three-flowered avens mimic in triplicate the elegant nodding, trumpetlike daylily flowers. Each avens flower stem rises from a basal rosette of finely cut leaves and is topped by three nodding flowers shaped like rose hips, with narrow, smoky pink sepals and yellowish petals. Once they have been fertilized, three-flowered avens' blossoms transform into silken, feathery plumes that persist long after the flowers have faded.

THREE-FLOWERED AVENS

Geum triflorum (bottom)
(*gay*-um try-*flor*-um)

TYPE: perennial
HEIGHT: 30 cm (12 in.)
WIDTH: 30 cm (12 in.)
SOIL: average, well drained
LIGHT: full sun to light shade
FLOWERING TIME: mid-spring to early summer
GROWING TIPS: drought tolerant once established; very low maintenance
ALTERNATIVE: *Geum rivale* (purple avens)

LEMON DAYLILY

Hemerocallis lilioasphodelus (top)
(hem-er-oh-*kal*-iss lil-ee-oh-ass-fo-*dell*-iss)

TYPE: perennial
HEIGHT: 90 cm (36 in.)
WIDTH: 90 cm (36 in.)
SOIL: average to fertile, well drained
LIGHT: full to part sun
FLOWERING TIME: late spring to early summer
GROWING TIPS: plant with crowns just below soil level; blooms last one day; deadhead daily; drought tolerant once established
ALTERNATIVES: *Doronicum columnae*, *D. orientale* (leopard's bane); *Trollius* x *cultorum* (globeflower)

Gymnocarpium AND *Omphalodes*

LIESBETH LEATHERBARROW

For a richly textured tapestry of green and blue in the mid-spring shaded border or woodland garden, plant blue-eyed Mary and oak ferns in close proximity. Groundcovers such as these inhabit shady glades in the wild and also lend a natural aspect to prairie shade gardens. Looking every bit the part of creeping forget-me-nots, blue-eyed Mary inches across the woodland floor by rhizomes, creating a river of sky blue flowers with white centers, nestled in a backdrop of medium green, heart-shaped leaves. Short oak ferns also populate the woodland floor through rhizomes and develop into a cool carpet of finely divided, feathery foliage that emerges pale yellow-green and transforms to vivid dark green. The obviously strong contrast in foliage form makes this an effective plant partnership.

OAK FERN
Gymnocarpium dryopteris (left)
(jim-no-*kar*-pee-um dry-*op*-terr-iss)

TYPE: perennial groundcover
HEIGHT: 20 cm (8 in.)
WIDTH: indefinite
SOIL: fertile, moist, well drained
LIGHT: light to full shade
FLOWERING TIME: not applicable
GROWING TIPS: avoid planting in hot, dry areas; plant with crowns just below soil level; use organic mulch for moisture retention; excellent for hiding dying bulb foliage
ALTERNATIVES: *Gymnocarpium robertianum*; *Athyrium filix-femina* 'Minutissimum' (lady fern), *A. niponicum* var. *pictum* (Japanese painted fern)

BLUE-EYED MARY
Omphalodes verna (right)
(om-fah-*lo*-deez *ver*-nah)

TYPE: perennial groundcover
HEIGHT: 20 cm (8 in.)
WIDTH: 30 cm (12 in.)
SOIL: fertile, moist, well drained
LIGHT: light shade
FLOWERING TIME: mid-spring
GROWING TIPS: avoid planting in hot, dry areas; use organic mulch for moisture retention and winter protection; very low maintenance
ALTERNATIVES: *Brunnera macrophylla* (Siberian bugloss); *Myosotis sylvatica* (forget-me-not)

Hemerocallis AND *Iris*

LIESBETH LEATHERBARROW

For a splash of color at the back of sunny borders, why not establish co-mingling clumps of vivid purple-blue Siberian iris and the yellow species daylily *Hemerocallis lilioasphodelus.* The purple and yellow blossoms of this duo complement each other perfectly, resulting in a pleasing alliance. Fragrant, trumpetlike daylily blossoms last but one day, but established clumps are very floriferous, providing an extended show of color. Siberian iris blossoms are daintier and are etched in an intricate pattern of white, brown, and yellow at the center. Both plants have strappy foliage, but whereas iris foliage maintains an erect stance, daylily foliage arches at the tips, creating fountains of greenery in the border. 'Caesar's Brother' and 'Silver Edge' are excellent purple Siberian iris cultivars.

LEMON DAYLILY

Hemerocallis lilioasphodelus (top)
(hem-er-oh-*kal*-iss li-lee-oh-ass-fo-*dell*-uss)

TYPE: perennial
HEIGHT: 90 cm (36 in.)
WIDTH: 90 cm (36 in.)
SOIL: average to fertile, well drained
LIGHT: full to part sun
FLOWERING TIME: late spring to early summer
GROWING TIPS: plant with crowns just below soil level; blooms last one day; deadhead daily; drought tolerant once established; excellent for hiding dying bulb foliage
ALTERNATIVES: *Doronicum columnae*, *D. orientale* (leopard's bane); *Trollius* x *cultorum* (globeflower)

SIBERIAN IRIS

Iris sibirica (bottom)
(*eye*-riss seye-*beer*-ih-ka)

TYPE: hardy rhizome
HEIGHT: 76 cm (30 in.)
WIDTH: 60 cm (24 in.)
SOIL: fertile, moist, well drained
LIGHT: full to part sun
FLOWERING TIME: mid-spring to early summer
GROWING TIPS: avoid planting in hot, dry areas; use organic mulch for moisture retention and winter protection; will not require staking if it receives adequate sunlight; deadhead
ALTERNATIVE: *Iris ensata* (Japanese iris)

Hepatica AND *Scilla*

LIESBETH LEATHERBARROW

A glorious blue-on-blue duo for a partly shaded woodland or rock garden, hepatica and Siberian squill are among the first plants to welcome spring to the prairies. Bright blue hepatica blossoms consist of five to seven petal-like sepals surrounding a cluster of very visible, light-colored stamens. The upward-facing flowers grow on long stems atop tidy, dome-shaped mounds of leaves. By contrast, up to six intensely blue, nodding bells adorn each Siberian squill flower spike. Unlike the pretty hepatica foliage, which enhances the woodland garden all summer, the lance- or strap-shaped, emerald green basal leaves of the squill die back soon after flowering. Squill will spread and bloom happily for many years and is among the best small bulbs for naturalizing in prairie woodland gardens or lawns.

HEPATICA
Hepatica nobilis (right)
(heh-*pa*-ti-kah *no*-bill-is)

TYPE: perennial
HEIGHT: 20 cm (8 in.)
WIDTH: 13 cm (5 in.)
SOIL: fertile, moist, well drained
LIGHT: light shade to part sun
FLOWERING TIME: early to mid spring
GROWING TIPS: avoid planting in hot, dry areas; use organic mulch for moisture retention and winter protection
ALTERNATIVES: *Hepatica americana*, *H. transsilvanica*; *Brunnera macrophylla* (Siberian bugloss)

SIBERIAN SQUILL
Scilla sibirica (left)
(*skee*-lah sy-*bee*-ri-kah)

TYPE: hardy true bulb
HEIGHT: 15 cm (6 in.)
WIDTH: 2.5 cm (1 in.)
SOIL: average to fertile, well drained
LIGHT: full sun to light shade
FLOWERING TIME: early to mid spring
GROWING TIPS: plant bulbs in fall; use organic mulch for winter protection; fertilize before and after flowering; allow foliage to ripen; self-seeds; drought tolerant once established
ALTERNATIVES: *Scilla bifolia*, *S. mischtschenkoana* (milk squill); *Chionodoxa forbesii*, *C. luciliae* (glory-of-the-snow)

Iberis AND *Myosotis*

One of the pleasures of self-seeding, sky blue forget-me-nots is that they emerge in the most unexpected places, pairing cheerfully with whatever plant they happen to land beside. However, one springtime combination worth planning for is that of dainty forget-me-nots and bold perennial candytuft. The brilliant white of candytuft's flat-topped flower clusters intensifies the true blue shade of forget-me-not petals and ties in perfectly with forget-me-not's white or yellow flower centers. Even after its blossoms have faded, candytuft's dark green foliage is a handsome accessory to later-blooming perennials. Several candytuft cultivars are available, including *Iberis sempervirens* 'Little Gem' and 'Snowflake'. Two others, 'Autumn Beauty' and 'Autumn Snow', may bloom in fall as well as spring.

PERENNIAL CANDYTUFT

Iberis sempervirens (bottom)
(eye-*bee*-riss sem-per-*vee*-renz)

TYPE: perennial
HEIGHT: 30 cm (12 in.)
WIDTH: 60 cm (24 in.)
SOIL: average to fertile, well drained
LIGHT: full sun
FLOWERING TIME: mid to late spring
GROWING TIPS: to prevent winter drying of evergreen foliage, cover with mulch or evergreen boughs; trim lightly after flowering
ALTERNATIVES: *Iberis saxatilis* (rock candytuft); *Arabis caucasica* (rock cress); *Cerastium tomentosum* (snow-in-summer)

FORGET-ME-NOT

Myosotis sylvatica (top)
(mee-oh-*so*-tiss sil-*vah*-ti-kah)

TYPE: biennial, short-lived perennial
HEIGHT: 15 to 20 cm (6 to 8 in.)
WIDTH: 15 to 20 cm (6 to 8 in.)
SOIL: average to fertile, moist, well drained
LIGHT: full sun to part shade
FLOWERING TIME: spring to fall
GROWING TIPS: self-seeds freely, but is easy to control; very low maintenance
ALTERNATIVES: *Omphalodes verna* (blue-eyed Mary); *Brunnera macrophylla* (Siberian bugloss)

Iris AND *Tanacetum*

LESLEY REYNOLDS

Deep purple, golden-throated bearded irises are the true stars of the late-spring perennial border, particularly when backed with a supporting cast of brilliant magenta painted daisies. This successful collaboration features striking differences in flower form and foliage characteristics. Sophisticated iris blooms are composed of six petals—three that point upward and three that curve downward. The beard is a fuzzy strip that runs down the center of the falls. Each flower stem bears multiple blooms, held above fans of broad, sword-shaped leaves. Cheerful chorus girls to the diva, painted daisies have pink ray florets and yellow disks, dancing on slim stems above mounded, ferny foliage. Purple irises show best with resplendent painted daisy cultivars like 'Brenda' and 'Robinson Rose'.

BEARDED IRIS
Iris hybrids (top)
(*eye*-riss)

TYPE: hardy rhizome
HEIGHT: 40 to 120 cm (16 to 48 in.)
WIDTH: 30 to 45 cm (12 to 18 in.)
SOIL: average to fertile, well drained
LIGHT: full sun
FLOWERING TIME: late spring to early summer
GROWING TIPS: plant in spring or summer, leaving top of rhizome exposed; fertilize in late spring; deadhead
ALTERNATIVES: *Iris laevigata, I. pallida* (sweet iris), *I. sibirica* (Siberian iris), *I. versicolor* (blue flag iris)

PAINTED DAISY
Tanacetum coccineum (bottom)
(ta-na-*see*-tum ko-chin-*ee*-um)

TYPE: perennial
HEIGHT: 60 cm (24 in.)
WIDTH: 45 cm (18 in.)
SOIL: average, well drained
LIGHT: full sun
FLOWERING TIME: late spring to early summer
GROWING TIPS: may require staking; deadhead; may irritate skin
ALTERNATIVES: *Hesperis matronalis* (sweet rocket); *Leucanthemum* x *superbum* (Shasta daisy)

Lamium AND *Pulmonaria*

LESLEY REYNOLDS

Even on a cloudy day, the silver-streaked and spotted foliage of lamium and pulmonaria mimics the effect of dappled sunlight on the forest floor. These shade-lovers not only are prized for their decorative leaves, which combine beautifully throughout the growing season, but they also bring long-lasting flowers to the spring garden. Lamium produces toothed, medium green leaves marked with silver, and small spikes of pink or white flowers. Pulmonaria's hairy, medium green leaves are frequently spotted with silver; its nodding, clustered flowers may be vibrant blue, violet, pink, or white. Pink-flowered *Lamium maculatum* cultivars include 'Beacon Silver' and 'Chequers'. Recommended blue-flowered, spotted-leaved *Pulmonaria saccharata* cultivars are 'Frühlingshimmel' and 'Mrs. Moon'.

LAMIUM

Lamium maculatum (left)
(*lay*-mee-um ma-kue-*la*-tum)

TYPE: perennial groundcover
HEIGHT: 30 cm (12 in.)
WIDTH: 30 to 90 cm (12 to 36 in.)
SOIL: fertile, moist, well drained
LIGHT: part sun to full shade
FLOWERING TIME: late spring
GROWING TIPS: avoid planting in hot, dry areas; use organic mulch for moisture retention and winter protection; deadhead
ALTERNATIVES: *Lamium galeobdolon* (yellow archangel); *Ajuga genevensis*, *A. reptans* (bugleweed)

LUNGWORT

Pulmonaria saccharata (right)
(pull-mon-*air*-ee-ah sa-kar-*ra*-tah)

TYPE: perennial groundcover
HEIGHT: 30 cm (12 in.)
WIDTH: 60 cm (24 in.)
SOIL: fertile, moist, well drained
LIGHT: light shade to part sun
FLOWERING TIME: mid to late spring
GROWING TIPS: avoid planting in hot, dry areas; use organic mulch for moisture retention and winter protection; deadhead
ALTERNATIVES: *Pulmonaria angustifolia* (blue lungwort), *P. longifolia* (longleaf lungwort), *P. officinalis* (Jerusalem cowslip); *Vinca minor* (common periwinkle)

Larix AND *Pinus*

LIESBETH LEATHERBARROW

'Pendula' European larch, a deciduous conifer, and evergreen mugo pine are year-round winners in a mixed or shrub border. A dependable backdrop to the larch's seasonal costume changes, the mugo pine is immutably green and solid. In spring, the flexible, soft green needles of the larch emerge along slender, weeping, light brown branches and are highlighted against the stiff, darker green pine needles. The larch retains its airy texture all summer long, in pleasing contrast to the densely branched pine. As autumn nights grow chilly, the contrast intensifies when the larch needles transform into fiery shades of yellow and orange before dropping. 'Pendula' may be staked and grown as a cascading, small tree, used as a spreading groundcover, or allowed to trail over walls or rockeries.

WEEPING EUROPEAN LARCH
Larix decidua 'Pendula' (right)
(*lair*-ix dee-*kid*-you-ah)

TYPE: deciduous tree
HEIGHT: variable, depending on how it is grown
WIDTH: 3 to 9 m (10 to 30 ft.)
SOIL: average to fertile, well drained
LIGHT: full sun
FLOWERING TIME: not applicable
GROWING TIPS: avoid planting in hot, dry areas; use organic mulch for moisture retention and winter protection; requires staking to grow as an erect tree; water well in fall
ALTERNATIVES: *Larix laricina* (tamarack), *L. sibirica* (Siberian larch)

MUGO PINE
Pinus mugo (left)
(*pee*-nus or *py*-nus *moo*-go)

TYPE: evergreen tree
HEIGHT: 1 to 3.7 m (3.3 to 12 ft.)
WIDTH: 1 to 2.5 m (3.3 to 8 ft.)
SOIL: average to fertile, well drained
LIGHT: full sun
FLOWERING TIME: not applicable
GROWING TIPS: to keep compact, remove half of new growth on each growing tip in late spring; water well in fall
ALTERNATIVES: *Pinus aristata* (bristlecone pine), *P. cembra* (Swiss stone pine), *P. flexilis* (limber pine), *P. sylvestris* (Scots pine)

Malus AND *Prunus*

LESLEY REYNOLDS

For spring romance in the prairie garden, nothing surpasses the profusion of pink offered by the lovely duet of rosybloom crabapples and double-flowering plums. Sized to suit any garden, rosybloom crabapples sweetly perfume the spring air, and their attractive foliage, often bronze-green or purple, turns orange in the fall. Red or purple ornamental fruits adorn the fall and winter garden, providing welcome sustenance for the birds. Smaller in scale, but big in impact, the double-flowering plum is an upright shrub that is smothered every spring with glorious clusters of fully double flowers. Three-lobed leaves appear after flowering. Select rosybloom crabapple cultivars, such as 'Kelsey' or 'Thunderchild', that are moderately to extremely resistant to fireblight.

ROSYBLOOM CRABAPPLE

Malus x *adstringens* (top)
(*ma*-luss x ad-*strin*-jenz)

TYPE: deciduous tree
HEIGHT: 5 to 7 m (16 to 23 ft.)
WIDTH: 5 m (16 ft.)
SOIL: average, well drained
LIGHT: full to part sun
FLOWERING TIME: mid-spring
GROWING TIPS: drought tolerant once established; prune after flowering and once leaves have fully emerged; prune young trees lightly to achieve desired shape; water well in fall
ALTERNATIVES: white-flowered crabapples, such as 'Dolgo', 'Kerr', and 'Snowcap'

DOUBLE-FLOWERING PLUM

Prunus triloba 'Multiplex' (bottom)
(*proo*-nuss try-*low*-bah)

TYPE: deciduous tree
HEIGHT: 3 m (10 ft.)
WIDTH: 3 m (10 ft.)
SOIL: fertile, moist, well drained
LIGHT: full sun to light shade
FLOWERING TIME: mid-spring
GROWING TIPS: prefers a sheltered location; prune after flowering; does not set fruit; water well in fall
ALTERNATIVES: *Prunus* x *cistena* (purpleleaf sand cherry), *P. tenella* (Russian or flowering almond), *P. tomentosa* (Nanking cherry)

Narcissus AND *Primula*

LIESBETH LEATHERBARROW

The conspicuous simplicity and bold colors of daffodils and drumstick primroses make them an outstanding combination in the mid-spring border. Perfect, densely packed spheres of pink, blue, lilac, or white primrose flowers are supported on relatively thick, straight stems and hover invitingly next to rich yellow blossoms of 'Fortune'. Whereas primrose flowers, flower clusters, and foliage come with rounded edges, daffodils are more angular, from the ring of individual petal-like segments (perianth) of their blossoms to the clumps of strappy foliage found at the base of their sturdy, bare stems. The juxtaposition of distinctly rounded and more angular shapes provides visual interest in this cheerful pair of spring beauties. Good substitutes for 'Fortune' include 'Carlton' and 'Ceylon'.

'FORTUNE' DAFFODIL

Narcissus 'Fortune' (left)
(nar-*siss*-us)

TYPE: hardy true bulb
HEIGHT: 20 to 60 cm (8 to 24 in.)
WIDTH: 10 cm (4 in.)
SOIL: fertile, moist, well drained
LIGHT: full sun to light shade
FLOWERING TIME: mid-spring
GROWING TIPS: plant bulbs in fall (before September 15); use organic mulch for winter protection; fertilize before and after flowering; deadhead; allow foliage to ripen
ALTERNATIVES: mid- to late-spring daffodils, such as 'Barrett Browning', 'Cassata', and 'Ice Follies'

DRUMSTICK PRIMROSE

Primula denticulata (right)
(*prim*-you-lah den-tick-yew-*la*-tah)

TYPE: perennial
HEIGHT: 30 cm (12 in.)
WIDTH: 20 cm (8 in.)
SOIL: average to fertile, moist, well drained
LIGHT: part sun to light shade
FLOWERING TIME: mid-spring
GROWING TIPS: avoid planting in hot, dry areas; use organic mulch for moisture retention and winter protection; deadhead
ALTERNATIVES: *Primula auricula, P.* x *juliae* 'Wanda'

Narcissus AND *Pulmonaria*

Most bulbs prefer a sunny to partly sunny location, but this should not deter gardeners from planting bulbs amidst shade-loving perennials in woodland gardens. Because most bulbs grow vigorously and bloom before deciduous trees have fully leafed out, ample sunlight reaches the plants. The woodland garden is the ideal setting for the delightful yellow and blue floral duet of daffodils and pulmonaria. Daffodils have the knack of making any plant companion look good, and pulmonaria is no exception, returning the favor by hiding dying daffodil leaves in its mounds of silver-spotted foliage. Whether they are bright or soft yellow, white, pink, or a combination of colors, long-stemmed daffodils draw attention to the tubular, blue pulmonaria flowers that nod above its decorative leaves.

DAFFODIL

Narcissus cultivars (bottom)
(nar-*siss*-us)

TYPE: hardy true bulb
HEIGHT: 20 to 60 cm (8 to 24 in.)
WIDTH: 10 cm (4 in.)
SOIL: fertile, moist, well drained
LIGHT: full sun to light shade
FLOWERING TIME: early to late spring
GROWING TIPS: plant bulbs in fall (before September 15); use organic mulch for winter protection; fertilize before and after flowering; deadhead; allow foliage to ripen
ALTERNATIVES: mid- to late-spring daffodils, such as 'Barrett Browning', 'Cassata', and 'Ice Follies'

LUNGWORT

Pulmonaria saccharata (top)
(pull-mon-*air*-ee-ah sa-kar-*ra*-tah)

TYPE: perennial groundcover
HEIGHT: 30 cm (12 in.)
WIDTH: 60 cm (24 in.)
SOIL: fertile, moist, well drained
LIGHT: light shade to part sun
FLOWERING TIME: mid to late spring
GROWING TIPS: avoid planting in hot, dry areas; use organic mulch for moisture retention and winter protection; deadhead
ALTERNATIVES: *Pulmonaria angustifolia* (blue lungwort), *P. longifolia* (longleaf lungwort), *P. officinalis* (Jerusalem cowslip); *Vinca minor* (common periwinkle)

Narcissus AND *Tulipa*

As colorful as a carnival, cheeky red and yellow 'Pinocchio' tulips are a delightful sight teamed with an array of mixed daffodils in shades of creamy white to bright yellow. The upward-facing, striped tulip flowers open like harlequin stars in the spring sunshine beneath the graceful, slightly nodding daffodils. Like other Greigii tulips, 'Pinocchio' has attractive purple-striped, wavy-edged leaves that add to its festive appeal and are a pleasing contrast to the strappy, solid green daffodil foliage. Whereas single daffodil cultivars always make attractive tulip partners, the variety of color and flower form achieved by combining several types is particularly appealing. Purchase bags of mixed daffodil bulbs, or create your own collection of favorite early- to mid-spring blooming cultivars.

DAFFODIL CULTIVARS

Narcissus (right)
(nar-*siss*-us)

TYPE: hardy true bulb
HEIGHT: 20 to 60 cm (8 to 24 in.)
WIDTH: 10 cm (4 in.)
SOIL: fertile, moist, well drained
LIGHT: full sun to part shade
FLOWERING TIME: early to mid spring
GROWING TIPS: plant bulbs in fall (before September 15); use organic mulch for winter protection; fertilize before and after flowering; deadhead; allow foliage to ripen
ALTERNATIVES: early- to mid-spring daffodils, such as trumpet types

'PINOCCHIO' GREIGII TULIP

Tulipa greigii 'Pinocchio' (left)
(*tew*-lip-ah *gree*-gee-ee)

TYPE: hardy true bulb
HEIGHT: 30 cm (12 in.)
WIDTH: 15 cm (6 in.)
SOIL: fertile, moist, well drained
LIGHT: full to part sun
FLOWERING TIME: early to mid spring
GROWING TIPS: plant bulbs in fall; mulch for winter protection; fertilize before and after flowering; deadhead; allow foliage to ripen
ALTERNATIVES: *Tulipa kaufmanniana* 'Guiseppe Verdi', 'Heart's Delight', 'Stressa', *T. kolpakowskiana*

Opuntia AND *Penstemon*

LIESBETH LEATHERBARROW

Sculptural and spiny, cacti are intriguing plants that can appear misplaced amidst lush, profusely flowering garden perennials. However, far from being alien, some species of prickly pear cacti are native to the prairies of Canada and the northern United States. Naturals for a sloping rock garden, prickly pear cacti have flattened, round to oval, gray-green stems with small clusters of spines. Yellow flowers grow from the stem tips and sides, followed by edible red fruit.

Also native to North America, beardtongues have an unpretentious wildflower appeal that suits the prickly pear's sparse appearance. They bear tubular flowers in shades of blue, purple, pink, red, or white. Choose small rock garden species and cultivars, such as *Penstemon fruticosus* 'Purple Haze', for cactus companions.

COMPRESSED PRICKLY PEAR CACTUS

Opuntia compressa (bottom)
(oh-*pun*-tee-ah kom-*press*-ah)

TYPE: perennial
HEIGHT: 15 to 30 cm (6 to 12 in.)
WIDTH: 90 cm (36 in.)
SOIL: poor to average, gritty, well drained
LIGHT: full sun
FLOWERING TIME: late spring to early summer
GROWING TIPS: plant in sheltered area; requires excellent drainage; mulch with layer of grit to prevent rotting at soil level
ALTERNATIVES: *Opuntia fragilis* (brittle prickly pear cactus), *O. polyacantha* (plains prickly pear cactus)

BEARDTONGUE

Penstemon (top)
(*pen*-ste-mon)

TYPE: perennial
HEIGHT: 5 to 30 cm (2 to 12 in.)
WIDTH: 30 to 60 cm (12 to 24 in.)
SOIL: average to fertile, gritty, well drained
LIGHT: full sun
FLOWERING TIME: late spring to fall
GROWING TIPS: requires excellent drainage; to prevent winter drying of semi-evergreen or evergreen foliage, cover with mulch or evergreen boughs; deadhead
ALTERNATIVES: *Penstemon caesius*, *P. fruticosus* (bush beardtongue), *P. hirsutus* 'Pygmaeus', *P. pinifolius* (pineleaf beardtongue)

Papaver AND *Polemonium*

LIESBETH LEATHERBARROW

In the quest for the new and unusual in our gardens, it's easy to overlook the value of plants that have been prairie residents for generations. Familiar, well loved, and fully prairie hardy, Jacob's ladder and oriental poppy make a perfect combination, despite their differences in deportment. Whereas Jacob's ladder is a reserved but "at attention" kind of plant, with its masses of purplish blue, bell-shaped flowers atop strongly vertical stems, the oriental poppy is exactly the opposite—flamboyant and "at ease." Red oriental poppies such as 'Allegro' and 'Prince of Orange' are the belles of the late-spring border, producing showy bowl-shaped flowers that dance in the breeze on slightly lax, wiry stems. 'Album', 'Blue Bell', and variegated 'Brise d'Anjou' are good Jacob's ladder choices.

ORIENTAL POPPY

Papaver orientale (top)
(pa-*pah*-ver or-ee-en-*tal*-eh)

TYPE: perennial
HEIGHT: 90 cm (36 in.)
WIDTH: 60 cm (24 in.)
SOIL: average to fertile, well drained
LIGHT: full sun
FLOWERING TIME: late spring to early summer
GROWING TIPS: plant in protected area; may require staking; deadhead to prolong bloom period and prevent self-seeding; drought tolerant once established; may go dormant
ALTERNATIVE: *Papaver croceum* (Iceland poppy)

JACOB'S LADDER

Polemonium caeruleum (bottom)
(paw-li-*moh*-nee-um kai-*roo*-lee-um)

TYPE: perennial
HEIGHT: 60 cm (24 in.)
WIDTH: 30 cm (12 in.)
SOIL: average to fertile, moist, well drained
LIGHT: light shade to full sun
FLOWERING TIME: late spring to early summer
GROWING TIPS: use organic mulch for moisture retention; may require staking; deadhead to prevent self-seeding; trim lightly after flowering
ALTERNATIVES: *Iris sibirica* (Siberian iris); *Penstemon strictus* (stiff beardtongue)

Penstemon AND *Sempervivum*

Although a mat of hen and chicks or cobweb houseleeks, with their unique succulent foliage, enhances just about any alpine plant partnership, one can't help but be impressed when cobweb houseleek is paired with the beardtongue *Penstemon davidsonii*, an easy-to-grow alpine treasure. The evergreen foliage of this little beardtongue virtually disappears in late spring under a cascade of showy pink or purple, funnel-shaped, two-lipped blossoms that beckon to hummingbirds. Anchoring this plant combination are the exquisite rosettes of 'Yukon Snow' cobweb houseleek, which is festooned with fine, white filaments that soften the bold lines of its fleshy, silvery green leaves. Attractive to the local bee population, the reddish pink, star-shaped flowers of the cobweb houseleek are a bonus.

BEARDTONGUE

Penstemon davidsonii (top)
(*pen*-ste-mon day-vid-*sow*-nee-ee)

TYPE: perennial
HEIGHT: 20 cm (8 in.)
WIDTH: 40 cm (16 in.)
SOIL: poor to average, well drained
LIGHT: full sun
FLOWERING TIME: late spring
GROWING TIPS: requires excellent drainage; to prevent winter drying of evergreen foliage, cover with mulch or evergreen boughs; deadhead
ALTERNATIVES: *Penstemon fruticosus* (bush beardtongue) 'Purple Haze', *P. pinifolius* (pineleaf beardtongue)

COBWEB HOUSELEEK

Sempervivum arachnoideum (bottom)
(sem-per-*veev*-um a-rak-*noi*-dee-um)

TYPE: perennial
HEIGHT: 8 cm (3 in.)
WIDTH: 2.5 cm (1 in.)
SOIL: poor to average, well drained
LIGHT: full sun
FLOWERING TIME: early to mid summer
GROWING TIPS: requires excellent drainage, resents winter moisture; to prevent winter drying of evergreen foliage, cover with mulch or evergreen boughs; deadhead; drought tolerant once established
ALTERNATIVES: *Sempervivum tectorum* (hen and chicks); *Sedum* (stonecrop)

Phlox AND *Primula*

LIESBETH LEATHERBARROW

For a study in opposites, tuck a carpet of ground-hugging moss phlox around the base of auricula primroses. Despite their differences in flower form and foliage texture, or perhaps because of them, this duo has much to commend it. Whereas moss phlox has mounds of delicate, needlelike foliage and thin, wiry flower stems, auricula primrose has bold, fleshy, paddle-shaped leaves and thick, sturdy flower stems. Moss phlox has dainty flowers with five small, lobed petals in shades of purple, red, pink, or white, with an "eye" of contrasting color; the species auricula primrose bears prominent yellow flowers with eight or nine overlapping, velvety petals. Auricula hybrids come in a range of unusual colors from deep plum purple, to burgundy, to beet red, with large, cream-colored or yellow "eyes."

MOSS PHLOX
Phlox subulata (bottom)
(flocks sub-you-*lah*-tah)

TYPE: perennial
HEIGHT: 15 cm (6 in.)
WIDTH: 50 cm (20 in.)
SOIL: fertile, well drained
LIGHT: full to part sun
FLOWERING TIME: late spring to early summer
GROWING TIPS: to prevent winter drying of evergreen foliage, cover with mulch or evergreen boughs; shear after flowering to keep plant compact; drought tolerant once established
ALTERNATIVES: *Arabis caucasica* 'Compinkie' (rock cress); *Saponaria ocymoides* (rock soapwort)

AURICULA PRIMROSE
Primula auricula (top)
(*prim*-you-lah or-*ik*-kew-lah)

TYPE: perennial
HEIGHT: 30 cm (12 in.)
WIDTH: 40 cm (16 in.)
SOIL: average to fertile, moist, well drained
LIGHT: part sun to light shade
FLOWERING TIME: mid-spring to early summer
GROWING TIPS: avoid planting in hot, dry areas; use organic mulch for moisture retention and winter protection; deadhead
ALTERNATIVES: *Primula cortusoides*, *P. denticulata* (drumstick primrose), *P. x juliae*, *P. veris* (cowslip), *P. vulgaris* (common primrose)

Primula AND *Tiarella*

Gardeners intent on creating the serenity of a woodland garden under a shade tree or in a lightly shaded border will marvel at the quiet beauty of Allegheny foamflower in combination with *Primula cortusoides*. Delicate foamflower forms spreading mounds of hairy, heart-shaped leaves, topped by short, airy spikes of soft white flowers. Planted in close proximity to foamflower, the small umbels of dainty, rose-pink primrose blossoms, borne on fine, wiry stems above small rosettes of wrinkled leaves, seem to float gently just above their frothy companions. *Primula cortusoides* will self-seed modestly when in tune with its surroundings, and Allegheny foamflower spreads by underground stolons; together, they form a luxuriant groundcover that carpets the woodland floor in spring and early summer.

PRIMROSE
Primula cortusoides (left)
(*prim*-you-la kor-too-*soy*-dees)

TYPE: perennial
HEIGHT: 30 cm (12 in.)
WIDTH: 30 cm (12 in.)
SOIL: average to fertile, moist, well drained
LIGHT: part sun to light shade
FLOWERING TIME: mid to late spring
GROWING TIPS: avoid planting in hot, dry areas; use organic mulch for moisture retention and winter protection; deadhead
ALTERNATIVES: *Primula auricula*, *P. denticulata* (drumstick primrose), *P. frondosa, P. saxatilis, P. veris* (cowslip), *P. vulgaris* (common primrose)

ALLEGHENY FOAMFLOWER
Tiarella cordifolia (right)
(tee-ah-*rell*-ah kor-dih-*foe*-lee-ah)

TYPE: perennial groundcover
HEIGHT: 10 to 30 cm (4 to 12 in.)
WIDTH: 30 cm (12 in.)
SOIL: fertile, moist, well drained
LIGHT: light to full shade
FLOWERING TIME: mid-spring to mid-summer
GROWING TIPS: avoid planting in hot, dry areas; use organic mulch for moisture retention and winter protection; tolerates competition from shallow tree roots
ALTERNATIVES: *Tiarella wherryi* 'Inkblot', 'Oakleaf'; x *Heucherella alba* (foamy bells), *H.* x 'Bridget Bloom', 'Snow White'

Prunus AND *Tulipa*

LESLEY REYNOLDS

The genus *Prunus* offers several showy, spring-flowering shrubs for the mixed border. Among them, the vase-shaped Nanking cherry is a sure winner, bearing delightful blooms in spring and delicious edible fruit in summer. Nanking cherry blossoms are bowl-shaped, pale pink, and fragrant. After the flowers fade, dull green, wrinkled, softly hairy, and distinctly toothed leaves emerge on branches covered in peeling, shiny, reddish brown bark. By late summer, shiny red cherries adorn the shrub, a tasty treat for gardeners and birds alike. Nanking cherry is a superb companion for many hardy spring-flowering bulbs, especially single late hybrid tulips. Bright red tulips, such as 'Balalaika', 'Kingsblood', or 'Renown', glow in cheerful contrast to the light pink cherry blossoms.

NANKING CHERRY

Prunus tomentosa (right)
(*proo*-nuss toe-men-*toe*-sah)

TYPE: deciduous shrub
HEIGHT: 3 m (10 ft.)
WIDTH: 5 m (16 ft.)
SOIL: fertile, moist, well drained
LIGHT: full sun
FLOWERING TIME: mid-spring
GROWING TIPS: prefers a sheltered location; fruit yield increases when shrub is cross-pollinated by another Nanking cherry in close proximity; prune after flowering; water well in fall
ALTERNATIVES: *Prunus* x *cistena* (purpleleaf sand cherry), *P. tenella* (Russian or flowering almond), *P. triloba* 'Multiplex' (double-flowering plum)

SINGLE LATE TULIP

Tulipa (left)
(*tew*-lip-ah)

TYPE: hardy true bulb
HEIGHT: 45 to 76 cm (18 to 30 in.)
WIDTH: 10 cm (4 in.)
SOIL: fertile, moist, well drained
LIGHT: full to part sun
FLOWERING TIME: late spring
GROWING TIPS: plant bulbs in fall; use organic mulch for winter protection; fertilize before and after flowering; deadhead; allow foliage to ripen; drought tolerant once established
ALTERNATIVES: red lily-flowered, fringed, or double late tulips ('Abba', 'Akita', 'Burgundy Lace')

Rheum AND *Trollius*

LIESBETH LEATHERBARROW

The only way to describe ornamental rhubarb is big, bold, and beautiful! Worth growing for its immense, deeply lobed foliage alone, it also produces tall, purplish red flower stalks topped with panicles of small, greenish white or red, star-shaped flowers in early summer. Ornamental rhubarb is an architectural plant, ideal for creating a focal point in perennial borders or at the edge of a water feature, where it teams naturally with the smaller but equally lovely globeflower. Globeflower's blossoms come in a range of deep yellows and oranges and resemble giant buttercup buds that never quite unfurl. Its finely divided, deeply lobed leaves mimic the much larger rhubarb leaves. 'Atrosanguineum' is a popular rhubarb cultivar, whereas 'Cheddar' and 'Lemon Queen' are good globeflower choices.

ORNAMENTAL RHUBARB

Rheum palmatum (right)
(*ree*-um paul-*mah*-tum)

TYPE: perennial
HEIGHT: 1.5 to 2.1 m (5 to 7 ft.)
WIDTH: 1.2 to 1.8 m (4 to 6 ft.)
SOIL: fertile, moist, well drained
LIGHT: full sun to light shade
FLOWERING TIME: late spring to early summer
GROWING TIPS: use organic mulch for moisture retention and winter protection; deadhead
ALTERNATIVES: *Rheum* x *cultorum* (garden rhubarb); *Ligularia dentata*, *L. przewalskii*, *L. stenocephala* 'The Rocket' (rayflower)

GLOBEFLOWER

Trollius x *cultorum* (left)
(*tro*-lee-us x kul-*to*-rum)

TYPE: perennial
HEIGHT: 90 cm (36 in.)
WIDTH: 45 cm (18 in.)
SOIL: average to fertile, moist, well drained
LIGHT: full sun to light shade
FLOWERING TIME: mid-spring to early summer
GROWING TIPS: use organic mulch for moisture retention and winter protection; trim vigorously after flowering
ALTERNATIVES: *Trollius chinensis*, *T. europaeus*, *T. pumilus*

Rhodiola AND *Tulipa*

LESLEY REYNOLDS

Every prairie gardener should celebrate spring's arrival with tarda species tulips in the rock garden or at the front of a mixed border. Native to dry mountainous regions, these quintessential little bulbous plants have shiny, lance-shaped leaves and star-shaped, yellow blossoms edged in white. One good companion for tarda tulips is roseroot, a stonecrop relative that is also native to dry, rocky habitats. Roseroot produces a fleshy, rose-scented rootstock and multiple stems clothed in small, fleshy, gray-green leaves. Terminal clusters of tiny, yellow, star-shaped flowers with protruding stamens are produced from late spring to early summer. Used for more than 3,000 years in traditional folk medicine, roseroot is a popular herbal remedy for enhancing mental and physical performance.

ROSEROOT

Rhodiola rosea (right)
(ro-*dee*-o-lah ro-*zee*-ah)

TYPE: perennial
HEIGHT: 30 cm (12 in.)
WIDTH: 20 cm (8 in.)
SOIL: average, well drained
LIGHT: full sun
FLOWERING TIME: late spring to early summer
GROWING TIPS: requires excellent drainage; deadhead; drought tolerant once established; raw rootstock can cause skin irritation; very low maintenance
ALTERNATIVES: *Rhodiola rosea* subsp. *integrifolia*; *Sedum* (stonecrop)

TARDA TULIP

Tulipa tarda (left)
(*tew*-lip-ah *tar*-dah)

TYPE: hardy true bulb
HEIGHT: 15 cm (6 in.)
WIDTH: 15 cm (6 in.)
SOIL: fertile, well drained
LIGHT: full sun
FLOWERING TIME: mid-spring
GROWING TIPS: plant bulbs in fall; use organic mulch for winter protection; fertilize before and after flowering; allow foliage to ripen; self-seeds; drought tolerant once established
ALTERNATIVES: *Tulipa clusiana* var. *chrysantha* (lady tulip), *T. kaufmanniana* 'Stressa', *T. turkestanica*, *T. urumiensis*

Scilla AND *Tulipa*

LESLEY REYNOLDS

It's easy to fall in love with species tulips, those little natives of mountainous terrains that, once established, develop into sizeable colonies, becoming lovelier every year. Although they are much shorter than the familiar Dutch hybrids, their flowers are every bit as lovely. Waterlily tulips bear simple gray-green leaves with slightly wavy margins and open bowl-shaped blossoms in shades of creamy yellow and red. Interestingly, their hybrids, which also come in combinations of yellow and red, have unique purple-brown, striped or mottled foliage that looks great long after the blossoms fade. For a dynamite look in the rock garden or at the front of mixed borders, float waterlily tulips in a pool of blue Siberian squill, prized for its little racemes of dainty, bell-shaped blossoms.

SIBERIAN SQUILL

Scilla sibirica (blue)
(*skee*-lah sy-*bee*-ri-kah)

TYPE: hardy true bulb
HEIGHT: 15 cm (6 in.)
WIDTH: 2.5 cm (1 in.)
SOIL: average to fertile, well drained
LIGHT: full sun to light shade
FLOWERING TIME: early to mid spring
GROWING TIPS: plant bulbs in fall; use organic mulch for winter protection; fertilize before and after flowering; allow foliage to ripen; self-seeds; drought tolerant once established
ALTERNATIVES: *Scilla bifolia, S. mischtschenkoana* (milk squill); *Chionodoxa forbesii, C. luciliae* (glory-of-the-snow)

WATERLILY TULIP

Tulipa kaufmanniana (cream and red)
(*tew*-lip-ah kauf-man-ee-*ah*-nah)

TYPE: hardy true bulb
HEIGHT: 15 cm (6 in.)
WIDTH: 15 cm (6 in.)
SOIL: fertile, well drained
LIGHT: full sun
FLOWERING TIME: mid-spring
GROWING TIPS: plant bulbs in fall; use organic mulch for winter protection; fertilize before and after flowering; deadhead; allow foliage to ripen; drought tolerant once established
ALTERNATIVES: *Tulipa clusiana* var. *chrysantha* (lady tulip), *T. tarda, T. turkestanica, T. urumiensis*

Sempervivum AND *Veronica*

Alpine rock gardens are an excellent source of inspiration for exceptional plant combinations. Two of these striking alpine partners are Turkish speedwell and cobweb houseleek. Whether this duo inhabits a crevice or a scree garden, the cracks between paving stones, or the front of a very well-drained flower bed, it is a study in contrasting textures. Turkish speedwell, with its ground-hugging, draping habit, has waxy, teardrop-shaped leaves and shimmering, cobalt blue blossoms, each with a white center. Cobweb houseleek forms mats of tight rosettes of thick, succulent, perfectly formed leaves with cobweblike filaments that stretch from leaf tip to leaf tip. In summer, it produces upright, leafy stems topped by bright red, star-shaped flowers that attract bees from miles around.

COBWEB HOUSELEEK
Sempervivum arachnoideum (top)
(sem-per-*veev*-um a-rak-*noi*-dee-um)

TYPE: perennial
HEIGHT: 8 cm (3 in.)
WIDTH: 2.5 cm (1 in.)
SOIL: poor to average, well drained
LIGHT: full sun
FLOWERING TIME: early to mid summer
GROWING TIPS: requires excellent drainage, resents winter moisture; to prevent winter drying of evergreen foliage, cover with mulch or evergreen boughs; deadhead; drought tolerant once established
ALTERNATIVES: *Sempervivum tectorum* (hen and chicks); *Sedum* (stonecrop)

TURKISH SPEEDWELL
Veronica liwanensis (bottom)
(ver-*on*-ih-kah lee-one-*en*-sis)

TYPE: perennial
HEIGHT: 2.5 cm (1 in.)
WIDTH: 45 cm (18 in.)
SOIL: average, well drained
LIGHT: full to part sun
FLOWERING TIME: late spring
GROWING TIPS: requires excellent drainage; resents winter moisture; spent flower spikes disappear on their own; drought tolerant once established
ALTERNATIVES: *Veronica pectinata* (comb speedwell), *V. prostrata* (harebell speedwell)

Sorbus AND *Syringa*

LIESBETH LEATHERBARROW

Some of the best plant pairs, like mountain ash and common lilac, result from the combination of two plants that have achieved such enduring popularity that we take them for granted. In spring, the mountain ash offers clusters of white blossoms, enhancing the sweetly fragrant panicles of blue-purple lilac blossoms. The compound leaves of mountain ash, which blaze in fiery hues in fall, relieve the solidity of the large, oval lilac leaves. In addition, the mountain ash boasts clusters of red or orange berries to brighten the winter garden. Because mountain ash trees may be susceptible to fireblight, choose the most fireblight-resistant species or cultivars, such as *Sorbus decora* 'Grootendorst'. Select from many fine hybrids of the common lilac, such as 'President Grévy' or 'Wedgwood'.

MOUNTAIN ASH

Sorbus (right)
(*sore*-bus)

TYPE: deciduous tree
HEIGHT: 8 m (26 ft.)
WIDTH: 5 m (16 ft.)
SOIL: average to fertile, well drained
LIGHT: full to part sun
FLOWERING TIME: late spring
GROWING TIPS: use organic mulch for moisture retention and winter protection; prune after flowering, once leaves have fully emerged; may suffer sunscald in winter if planted in extremely sunny locations; water well in fall
ALTERNATIVES: *Sorbus americana* (American mountain ash), *S. decora* (showy mountain ash)

COMMON LILAC

Syringa vulgaris (left)
(sih-*ring*-gah vul-*gair*-iss)

TYPE: deciduous shrub
HEIGHT: 5 m (16 ft.)
WIDTH: 3 m (10 ft.)
SOIL: average to fertile, well drained
LIGHT: full to part sun
FLOWERING TIME: mid to late spring
GROWING TIPS: deadhead and prune immediately after flowering; water well in fall
ALTERNATIVES: *Syringa* x *hyacinthiflora* (Skinner lilacs or American hybrids)

Spiraea AND *Tulipa*

LIESBETH LEATHERBARROW

Garland spirea and medium-height 'Barcelona' Triumph tulips make a stunning combination in mid-spring. The generously proportioned, bright pink, cup-shaped flowers of 'Barcelona' top strong stems and strike an unmistakably vertical pose in the garden. As such they seem to reach towards the unbranched, arching shoots of garland spirea, which are covered their entire length with flat clusters of small, white flowers and bright green, lance-shaped leaves. An image of graceful spirea branches swooping down to greet the elegant tulips paints a very welcoming portrait in the garden. If garden space is limited, try 'Compacta', a dwarf cultivar of garland spirea. Other pink or red Triumph tulips that partner well with the bright white spirea include 'Don Quichotte', 'Frankfurt', and 'Passionale'.

GARLAND SPIREA
Spiraea x *arguta* (top)
(spy-*ree*-ah x ar-*goo*-tah)

TYPE: deciduous shrub
HEIGHT: 1.8 m (6 ft.)
WIDTH: 1.8 m (6 ft.)
SOIL: fertile, moist, well drained
LIGHT: full sun to light shade
FLOWERING TIME: mid to late spring
GROWING TIPS: prune after flowering, once leaves have fully emerged; can prune 20 percent of existing shoots to base to promote replacement growth; water well in fall
ALTERNATIVES: *Spiraea* x 'Snowhite', *S.* x *vanhouttei*

'BARCELONA' TRIUMPH TULIP
Tulipa 'Barcelona' (bottom)
(*tew*-lip-ah)

TYPE: hardy true bulb
HEIGHT: 60 cm (24 in.)
WIDTH: 10 cm (4 in.)
SOIL: fertile, moist, well drained
LIGHT: full sun
FLOWERING TIME: mid-spring
GROWING TIPS: plant bulbs in fall; use organic mulch for moisture retention and winter protection; fertilize before and after flowering; deadhead; allow foliage to ripen; drought tolerant once established
ALTERNATIVES: pink or red Darwin Hybrid tulips ('Apeldoorn', 'Elizabeth Arden', 'Parade', 'Renown')

Tulipa AND *Viola*

LESLEY REYNOLDS

Annuals may seem unlikely companions for tulips in the frost-prone spring prairie garden, but pansies, hybrids of several viola species, thrive in cool temperatures. Pansies offer an incredible range of colors to complement late-blooming lily-flowered tulips. Choose brilliant or soft yellows, vibrant reds and purples, cool blues, and pastel pinks and peaches, or mix and match for a kaleidoscope of shades. Also available in many bright or subtle hues, aristocratic long-petaled, lily-flowered tulips rise serenely above the cheeky gaze of the upfacing pansies in a perfect balance of elegance and enthusiasm. There are many other superb lily-flowered tulip cultivars, including 'Akita', 'Ballerina', 'Marilyn', 'Maytime', 'Temple of Beauty', 'White Triumphator', and 'West Point'.

'MARIETTE'
LILY-FLOWERED TULIP
Tulipa 'Mariette' (top)
(*tew*-lip-ah)

TYPE: hardy true bulb
HEIGHT: 45 cm (18 in.)
WIDTH: 10 cm (4 in.)
SOIL: fertile, moist, well drained
LIGHT: full sun
FLOWERING TIME: late spring
GROWING TIPS: plant bulbs in fall; use organic mulch for winter protection; fertilize before and after flowering; deadhead; allow foliage to ripen; drought tolerant once established
ALTERNATIVES: other late-spring-blooming tulips, including single late, fringed, viridiflora, Rembrandt, parrot, and double late

PANSY
Viola x *wittrockiana* (bottom)
(*vie*-oh-lah or *vee*-oh-lah x wih-trok-ee-*ah*-nah)

TYPE: annual
HEIGHT: 15 to 23 cm (6 to 9 in.)
WIDTH: 23 to 30 cm (9 to 12 in.)
SOIL: fertile, moist, well drained
LIGHT: part to full sun in spring, part sun to light shade in summer
FLOWERING TIME: early spring to late summer
GROWING TIPS: avoid planting in hot, dry areas; fertilize biweekly; deadhead; pinch back growing tips
ALTERNATIVES: *Viola tricolor* (Johnny-jump-up), *V. labradorica*, *V. pedatifida*, *V. sororia* (violets)

This delightful informal perennial border features strong vertical accent plants and hot colors against a cool spruce background. LIESBETH LEATHERBARROW

CHAPTER THREE

Summer

No single garden could ever be large enough to hold the entire bounty of summer-flowering hardy perennials, bulbs, trees, and shrubs available to prairie gardeners (not to mention the profusion of annuals and tender bulbs now spilling from nursery and garden center shelves). This leads to some difficult choices for those of us whose heads are easily turned by a bold leaf, a comely bloom, or a graceful stem. More variety is not always better and can be disruptive to overall garden esthetics. Fortunately, when it comes to creating plant partnerships, the artistic benefits of all these choices far outweigh the drawbacks. Start with plants that you can't live without, then decide which other plants will bring out the best in them. This should help to eliminate impulse buying and discordant, unflattering plant neighbors.

As summer dawns on the prairies and we luxuriate in the long, sunny days, our gardens are at their best. Perennial borders are filled with an abundance of bloom, but are not yet messy or overgrown. Foliage is still fresh, green, and flawless, undamaged by

A few carefully placed flowering perennials accent the superb foliage texture, form, and color displayed in this tranquil prairie garden. LESLEY REYNOLDS

Bright hues of rudbeckia, pinks, and flowering tobacco are punctuated by cool gray dusty miller in this eye-catching tapestry of annuals. LIESBETH LEATHERBARROW

insects, wind, hail, or drought. Shrubs have leafed out in hedges and borders, and deciduous trees fulfill their promise of cool shade from the hot afternoon sun. In early summer, prairie gardeners welcome tall bearded and Siberian irises, roses, and peonies, many of them old favorites passed on from generation to generation, or from friend to friend.

The early-summer garden is filled with the romance and nostalgia of fragrance: the orange-blossom spice of mock orange; the lovely old-fashioned scent of late-blooming dwarf Korean or Japanese tree lilacs; and the evocative perfume of roses. Many hardy shrub roses begin to bloom in June and continue to flower until frost, forming the basis of evolving summer-long partnerships as adjacent perennials flower and fade in turn. Early summer also sees the dawning of our love affair with vines, as clematis scramble up trellises or trees and open their exquisite blooms.

On the prairies, mid-summer means delphiniums, the backbone of many perennial gardens. The cool blues and whites of delphiniums flatter almost any other color, making them among the most companionable perennials in the border. Daylilies and lilies are perhaps even more useful partners; the proliferation of hybrids and cultivars of these phenomenally popular and stunningly beautiful plants allows gardeners much creative leeway. Other perennials, such as hostas, monarda, loosestrife, bellflowers, coral bells, and pincushion flowers, provide a host of intriguing flower and foliage forms and sizes sure to inspire imaginative gardeners in their quest for perfect partnerships. Mid-summer is also a good time for gardeners to evaluate which partners aren't getting along and to make notes on plant relocation for late summer or the following spring.

Gardeners should not overlook the ornamental possibilities of vegetable and herb partners in the mid- to late-summer garden. Many culinary plants contribute colorful and texturally interesting foliage to borders or containers. Consider golden, silver, and variegated thyme and sages, feathery dill and fennel, golden oregano, curly or flat-leaved parsley, various basils, red or green lettuce in all its forms, carrot tops, rainbow Swiss chard, ornamental peppers, and cherry tomatoes.

By late summer, the prairie garden can be declining and disheveled as fading perennials flop and go to seed. However, many bold and bright perennials are just hitting their stride by mid-August, promising several more weeks of floral color in the border. Chief among these are Asteraceae family members, including rudbeckia, sneezeweed, and false sunflower. In keeping with the maturing crops in prairie fields, they are clad in the harvest colors of yellow, gold, orange, red, and bronze. Pairing up your favorites of these hot-colored, daisylike plants is one of the best ways to add more sunshine to the waning summer. September brings summer's end to prairie schoolchildren, but not to the garden, as snapdragons shake off the light frost that settles on their blooms during chilly nights, ornamental grasses whisper above the comforting hum of late-summer bees, and asters and hardy mums set the scene for the garden's glorious finale.

A carnival of brightly colored annuals and perennials makes this exuberant mixed border a pleasure to behold. Winston Goretsky

Achillea AND *Gaillardia*

Gaillardia, a cheerful, drought-tolerant prairie native, is one of those perennials that blooms until hard frost, making it indispensable in the late fall garden. Most of the gaillardia cultivars grown today sport eye-catching, multicolored flowers in rich shades of yellow, orange, burgundy, red, and bronze, the colors used in blankets woven by Natives of the American Southwest, hence the common name "blanket flower." 'Goblin' is a choice gaillardia cultivar; its orange-red petals are tipped in yellow and arranged around a dark red and yellow center. To avoid detracting from 'Goblin's brilliant display, plant it beside a cool white perennial such as sneezewort. This yarrow relative produces a succession of large sprays of pure white, double flowers from early summer to fall.

SNEEZEWORT

Achillea ptarmica (top)
(ah-*kill*-ee-ah *tar*-mi-kah)

TYPE: perennial
HEIGHT: 30 to 90 cm (12 to 36 in.)
WIDTH: 60 cm (24 in.)
SOIL: average, well drained
LIGHT: full to part sun
FLOWERING TIME: early to late summer
GROWING TIPS: may spread rapidly and flop if soil is too rich, but is easy to control; deadhead to encourage continuous bloom; drought tolerant once established
ALTERNATIVES: *Achillea* Galaxy Series 'Snow Taler'; *Phlox paniculata* 'David' (garden phlox)

'GOBLIN' GAILLARDIA

Gaillardia x *grandiflora* 'Goblin' (bottom)
(gah-*lar*-dee-ah x gran-di-*flor*-ah)

TYPE: perennial
HEIGHT: 30 cm (12 in.)
WIDTH: 45 cm (18 in.)
SOIL: average, well drained
LIGHT: full sun
FLOWERING TIME: mid-summer to fall
GROWING TIPS: avoid planting in overly rich soil or plants will become floppy; deadhead to prevent self-seeding; drought tolerant once established
ALTERNATIVES: *Gaillardia aristata*, annual *G. pulchella*; annual *Rudbeckia hirta* (gloriosa daisy)

Achillea AND *Leucanthemum*

LIESBETH LEATHERBARROW

Two common perennials that strike an uncommonly lovely pose in sunny borders are Shasta daisy and yarrow. Perfectly suited for cottage, wildflower, and cutting gardens, their carefree nature is also not out of place in more formal plantings. Yarrow comes in many colors, including red, pink, terra cotta, yellow, and white. Beneficial as well as beautiful, its broad, flat-topped flowerheads attract butterflies, predatory wasps, and other helpful garden insects. Although the colors fade as flowers mature, yarrow continues to bloom all summer, providing superb cut flowers for both fresh and dried arrangements. Popular Shasta daisies also bloom all summer, producing rosettes of dark green foliage and the pure white, yellow-centered flowers of "he loves me, he loves me not" fame.

YARROW
Achillea (right)
(ah-*kill*-ee-ah)

TYPE: perennial
HEIGHT: 60 to 90 cm (24 to 36 in.)
WIDTH: 60 cm (24 in.)
SOIL: poor to average, well drained
LIGHT: full sun
FLOWERING TIME: early summer to fall
GROWING TIPS: requires excellent drainage; requires very little fertilizer, too much nitrogen encourages floppy growth; deadhead; may require staking; may irritate skin
ALTERNATIVES: *Achillea* 'Anthea', *A.* 'Coronation Gold', *A. filipendulina* (fernleaf yarrow), *A.* Galaxy Series, *A. millefolium* (common yarrow)

SHASTA DAISY
Leucanthemum x *superbum* (left)
(loo-*kan*-the-mum x soo-*per*-bum)

TYPE: perennial
HEIGHT: 60 cm (24 in.)
WIDTH: 30 to 45 cm (12 to 18 in.)
SOIL: average to fertile, well drained
LIGHT: full sun
FLOWERING TIME: early summer to fall
GROWING TIPS: requires excellent drainage; may require staking; pinch back growing tips; deadhead to encourage reblooming
ALTERNATIVES: *Anthemis tinctoria* (golden marguerite); *Tanacetum parthenium* (feverfew)

Achillea AND *Nicotiana*

LIESBETH LEATHERBARROW

Gardeners can sometimes create interesting effects by juxtaposing plant species of significantly different forms but of similar colors. One such pairing that works very well is Summer Pastels yarrow and Merlin Series flowering tobacco. The yarrow has fine, fernlike, gray-green foliage clothing tallish stems that are topped by large, flat clusters of tiny, daisylike flowers. In contrast, the shorter flowering tobacco produces sticky, hairy, spoon-shaped leaves and elegant tubular blossoms that flare into five flat, elliptic petals. Summer Pastels yarrow comes in a pleasant blend of white, cream, pink, magenta, lavender, and pale apricot. A similar suite of colors is echoed in the Merlin Series flowering tobacco, thus creating a strong visual link in this plant partnership.

SUMMER PASTELS YARROW
Achillea Summer Pastels (top)
(ah-*kill*-ee-ah)

TYPE: perennial
HEIGHT: 60 to 90 cm (24 to 36 in.)
WIDTH: 60 cm (24 in.)
SOIL: average, well drained
LIGHT: full sun
FLOWERING TIME: early summer to fall
GROWING TIPS: requires excellent drainage; requires very little fertilizer, too much nitrogen encourages floppy growth; deadhead; may require staking; may irritate skin
ALTERNATIVES: *Achillea* Debutante Hybrids, *A. millefolium* (common yarrow)

MERLIN SERIES FLOWERING TOBACCO
Nicotiana x *sanderae*
Merlin Series (bottom)
(nick-oh-shee-*ah*-na x *san*-der-eye)

TYPE: annual
HEIGHT: 25 cm (10 in.)
WIDTH: 30 cm (12 in.)
SOIL: average to fertile, moist, well drained
LIGHT: full to part sun
FLOWERING TIME: early summer to fall
GROWING TIPS: fertilize biweekly; deadhead to encourage continuous bloom; contact with foliage may irritate skin; very low maintenance
ALTERNATIVES: *Nicotiana* Domino Series, Havana Series, Sensation Mix, Starship Series, *N. alata* Nicki Series

Achillea AND *Phlox*

LIESBETH LEATHERBARROW

Gardeners no longer need to give elegant garden phlox a wide berth because of its susceptibility to powdery mildew. Many new introductions, such as 'David', 'Dusterlohe', 'Julyfest', and 'Redividus', are very mildew-resistant, making them stalwarts of informal mixed borders and cottage gardens. Delighting gardeners with its ornate flower clusters and delicious fragrance, phlox has the advantage of giving height to borders without requiring staking. Yarrow is a standout among the many suitable partners for phlox. Its horizontal clusters of small, daisylike blossoms come in a wide range of colors and last all summer long. Popular yarrow choices include the Galaxy Series, Summer Pastels, and many named *Achillea millefolium* cultivars. Both phlox and yarrow make excellent cut flowers.

YARROW
Achillea (right)
(ah-*kill*-ee-ah)

TYPE: perennial
HEIGHT: 60 to 90 cm (24 to 36 in.)
WIDTH: 60 cm (24 in.)
SOIL: average, well drained
LIGHT: full sun
FLOWERING TIME: early summer to fall
GROWING TIPS: requires excellent drainage; requires very little fertilizer, too much nitrogen encourages floppy growth; deadhead; may require staking; may irritate skin
ALTERNATIVES: *Achillea* 'Anthea', *A.* 'Coronation Gold', *A. filipendulina* (fernleaf yarrow)

GARDEN PHLOX
Phlox paniculata (left)
(flocks pan-ick-you-*lah*-tah)

TYPE: perennial
HEIGHT: 90 cm (36 in.)
WIDTH: 90 cm (36 in.)
SOIL: fertile, moist, well drained
LIGHT: full to part sun
FLOWERING TIME: mid-summer to fall
GROWING TIPS: use organic mulch for moisture retention and winter protection; thin multi-stemmed clumps to encourage good air circulation; pinch back growing tips; deadhead to prevent self-seeding
ALTERNATIVES: *Dictamnus alba* (gas plant); *Hesperis matronalis* (sweet rocket)

Ajuga AND *Lysimachia*

WINSTON GORETSKY

Glossy, dark-leaved creeping bugleweed and bright golden creeping Jenny are appealing groundcovers that strike a perfect color balance in the shade garden; they also provide a beautiful, maintenance-free carpet in any shaded area where grass will not thrive. Creeping bugleweed has rounded, somewhat spoon-shaped leaves that grow in clustered rosettes and spread by means of stolons. Tiny spikes of violet-blue flowers rise above the leaves, which may be dark green, bronze, purple, or even variegated, depending on the cultivar. Golden creeping Jenny is even more vigorous, quickly spreading to clothe the ground with small, chartreuse leaves that darken to lime green in the summer. The stems, which will root along their entire length, are covered with bright yellow, star-shaped flowers.

CREEPING BUGLEWEED
Ajuga reptans (left)
(ah-*jew*-gah *rep*-tans)

TYPE: perennial groundcover
HEIGHT: 15 cm (6 in.)
WIDTH: 90 cm (36 in.)
SOIL: average to fertile, moist, well drained
LIGHT: full shade to full sun
FLOWERING TIME: late spring to early summer
GROWING TIPS: avoid planting in hot, dry areas; deadhead; excellent for hiding dying bulb foliage
ALTERNATIVES: *Ajuga genevensis, A. pyramidalis*; *Omphalodes verna* (blue-eyed Mary)

GOLDEN CREEPING JENNY
Lysimachia nummularia 'Aurea' (right)
(li-si-*mak*-ee-ah num-ewe-*lair*-ee-ah)

TYPE: perennial groundcover
HEIGHT: 10 cm (4 in.)
WIDTH: indefinite
SOIL: fertile, moist, well drained
LIGHT: full sun to light shade
FLOWERING TIME: early to late summer
GROWING TIPS: avoid planting in hot, dry areas; may be invasive, but is easy to control; excellent for hiding dying bulb foliage
ALTERNATIVE: *Origanum vulgare* 'Aureum' (golden oregano)

Alchemilla AND *Digitalis*

LIESBETH LEATHERBARROW

Foxglove and lady's mantle are two of many ornamental plants with a fascinating folk history as medicinal or magic plants. At home in lightly shaded woodlands or a tangled border, the yellow foxglove is the quintessential English cottage garden flower. Reputedly favored by fairies, the foxglove produces one-sided flower spikes of pale yellow, tubular flowers veined with brown on the insides. Its pointed, oval leaves are glossy and medium green, growing in basal rosettes. Since 1768, foxglove has been recognized as the source of digitalis, a cardiac stimulant. Used by medieval alchemists, lovely lady's mantle is one of the most versatile plants in the perennial border, with a rounded form and velvety soft foliage that provide textural contrast to the upright foxglove.

LADY'S MANTLE
Alchemilla mollis (bottom)
(al-ke-*mil*-ah *maw*-lis)

TYPE: perennial
HEIGHT: 45 cm (18 in.)
WIDTH: 60 cm (24 in.)
SOIL: fertile, moist, well drained
LIGHT: full to part sun
FLOWERING TIME: late spring to mid-summer
GROWING TIPS: avoid planting in hot, dry areas; use organic mulch for moisture retention and winter protection; deadhead to prevent self-seeding; excellent for hiding dying bulb foliage
ALTERNATIVES: *Alchemilla alpina, A. erythropoda, A. glaucescens*

YELLOW FOXGLOVE
Digitalis grandiflora (top)
(di-ji-*tal*-iss gran-di-*flor*-ah)

TYPE: biennial or short-lived perennial
HEIGHT: 90 cm (36 in.)
WIDTH: 45 cm (18 in.)
SOIL: average to fertile, moist, well drained
LIGHT: full sun to light shade
FLOWERING TIME: early to mid summer
GROWING TIPS: avoid planting in hot, dry areas; use organic mulch for moisture retention and winter protection; deadhead
ALTERNATIVES: *Digitalis* x *mertonensis, D. purpurea* (common foxglove)

Alchemilla AND *Rosa*

LESLEY REYNOLDS

Lady's mantle is the bridesmaid of the perennial and mixed border, its velvety, gray-green leaves intensifying the colors of brighter neighbors, who tend to garner most of the attention. The blooms of lady's mantle are usually regarded as secondary to the mounds of exquisite pleated foliage; however, the frothy sprays of small, chartreuse flowers unite effortlessly with the vivid 'Morden Fireglow' rose to create one of the most striking partnerships of the summer mixed border.

In the border or in a vase, the clusters of glowing, scarlet-red blooms show superbly against the delicate lady's mantle flowers. 'Morden Fireglow' is a stunning Parkland Series hardy shrub rose, introduced in 1989. Small enough to fit into any garden, it blooms recurrently throughout the growing season.

LADY'S MANTLE
Alchemilla mollis (bottom)
(al-ke-*mil*-ah *maw*-lis)

TYPE: perennial
HEIGHT: 45 cm (18 in.)
WIDTH: 60 cm (24 in.)
SOIL: fertile, moist, well drained
LIGHT: full to part sun
FLOWERING TIME: late spring to mid-summer
GROWING TIPS: avoid planting in hot, dry areas; use organic mulch for moisture retention and winter protection; deadhead to prevent self-seeding; excellent for hiding dying bulb foliage
ALTERNATIVES: *Alchemilla alpina*, *A. erythropoda*, *A. glaucescens*

'MORDEN FIREGLOW' ROSE
Rosa 'Morden Fireglow' (top)
(*roh*-zah)

TYPE: deciduous shrub
HEIGHT: 76 cm (30 in.)
WIDTH: 76 cm (30 in.)
SOIL: fertile, moist, well drained
LIGHT: full sun
FLOWERING TIME: early summer; some repeat blooming from mid to late summer
GROWING TIPS: use organic mulch for moisture retention and winter protection; fertilize regularly; deadhead; prune in spring to remove tip kill and old, woody canes; water well in fall
ALTERNATIVES: *Rosa* 'Adelaide Hoodless', 'John Franklin', 'Morden Cardinette', 'Winnipeg Parks'

Allium AND *Artemisia*

LIESBETH LEATHERBARROW

The prairie gardeners' love affair with ornamental onions continues to grow, and it isn't only the large, showy cultivars that are winning our hearts. Increasingly, the shorter species are being naturalized or massed at the front of mixed borders or tucked into rock gardens. *Allium oreophilum* is one such little gem; it produces loose clusters of bell-shaped, rose-purple flowers above linear, medium green leaves in early summer. A lovely partner for this onion is 'Boughton Silver' artemisia, with its deeply lobed, silver-gray foliage. An excellent foil for the rosy onion blossoms, it also provides an effective disguise for the maturing bulb foliage. Even after 'Boughton Silver' has finished serving double duty with the little onions, it continues its stellar performance until summer's end.

ORNAMENTAL ONION
Allium oreophilum (pink)
(*al*-ee-um o-ray-*o*-fi-lum)

TYPE: hardy true bulb
HEIGHT: 20 cm (8 in.)
WIDTH: 20 cm (8 in.)
SOIL: fertile, moist, well drained
LIGHT: full sun
FLOWERING TIME: late spring to early summer
GROWING TIPS: plant bulbs in fall; use organic mulch for winter protection; fertilize before and after flowering; allow foliage to ripen
ALTERNATIVES: *Allium flavum*, *A. moly* (golden garlic)

'BOUGHTON SILVER'
ARTEMISIA
Artemisia stelleriana
'Boughton Silver' (silver)
(ar-tay-*mis*-ee-ah stel-la-ree-*ah*-nah)

TYPE: perennial
HEIGHT: 15 cm (6 in.)
WIDTH: 30 to 45 cm (12 to 18 in.)
SOIL: poor to average, well drained
LIGHT: full sun
FLOWERING TIME: late summer to early fall
GROWING TIPS: requires excellent drainage; drought tolerant once established; excellent for hiding dying bulb foliage; very low maintenance
ALTERNATIVES: *Artemisia schmidtiana* 'Silver Mound'; *Arabis caucasica* (rock cress); *Cerastium tomentosum* (snow-in-summer)

Anagallis AND *Calibrachoa*

WINSTON GORETSKY

There is no better recipe for a spectacular container or hanging basket than blue pimpernel and Million Bells *Calibrachoa*. Blue pimpernel has branching, trailing stems with small, lance-shaped leaves and a profusion of flowers of the purest, most intense azure blue this side of gentians. Each five-petaled, saucer-shaped pimpernel flower has a rosy red center. Million Bells are equally dependable, long blooming, and easy to grow, quickly spreading to fill containers with mounded, trailing plants covered with masses of colorful blossoms that resemble diminutive petunias. Although Million Bells come in several outstanding colors, the peachy bronze to orange 'Terra Cotta' and the apricot-throated 'Yellow' Million Bells are the liveliest partners for blue pimpernel.

BLUE PIMPERNEL
Anagallis monellii (blue)
(an-ah-*gal*-iss mo-*nell*-ee-ee)

TYPE: annual
HEIGHT: 10 to 20 cm (4 to 8 in.)
WIDTH: 40 cm (16 in.)
SOIL: average to fertile, well drained
LIGHT: full sun
FLOWERING TIME: early summer to fall
GROWING TIPS: fertilize biweekly; pinch back growing tips; drought tolerant once established
ALTERNATIVES: *Lobelia erinus* (lobelia); *Nemophila menziesii* (baby blue-eyes); *Phacelia campanularia* (Californian bluebell)

MILLION BELLS
Calibrachoa (terra cotta)
(kal-ih-bra-*ko*-ah)

TYPE: annual
HEIGHT: 10 to 15 cm (4 to 6 in.)
WIDTH: 45 to 60 cm (18 to 24 in.)
SOIL: fertile, moist, well drained
LIGHT: full to part sun
FLOWERING TIME: early to late summer
GROWING TIPS: avoid planting in hot, dry areas; fertilize biweekly; pinch back growing tips
ALTERNATIVES: small trailing petunias, such as Fantasy Series and Dream Series Petitunias

Anagallis AND *Eschscholzia*

LIESBETH LEATHERBARROW

Flamboyant California poppies and brilliant blue pimpernels are two amazing annuals that make an irresistible pair. Even in their native golden orange form, the shimmering, paper-thin, cupped petals of California poppies are a pleasure to view when interwoven with branching pimpernel stems laden with electric gentian-blue blossoms. However, recent California poppy introductions in shades of rosy red and pink, or white flushed with rosy red, make even better partners for pimpernel, whose blossoms are dabbed rosy red at the center. The finely divided, bluish California poppy foliage forges an even stronger color tie with blue-flowered pimpernels. Fine California poppy cultivars include 'Thai Silk Mixed', 'Carmine King', and 'Pink Chiffon'.

BLUE PIMPERNEL

Anagallis monellii (blue)
(an-ah-*gal*-iss mo-*nell*-ee-ee)

TYPE: annual
HEIGHT: 10 to 20 cm (4 to 8 in.)
WIDTH: 40 cm (16 in.)
SOIL: average to fertile, well drained
LIGHT: full sun
FLOWERING TIME: early summer to fall
GROWING TIPS: fertilize biweekly; pinch back growing tips; drought tolerant once established
ALTERNATIVES: *Lobelia erinus* (lobelia); *Nemophila menziesii* (baby blue-eyes); *Phacelia campanularia* (Californian bluebell)

CALIFORNIA POPPY

Eschscholzia californica (pink)
(esh-*sholts*-ee-ah ka-li-*for*-ni-kah)

TYPE: annual
HEIGHT: 25 cm (10 in.)
WIDTH: 25 cm (10 in.)
SOIL: poor to average, well drained
LIGHT: full sun
FLOWERING TIME: early summer to fall
GROWING TIPS: sow directly into ground or containers; do not fertilize; deadhead to prevent self-seeding; when flowering ceases, cut back by half to encourage reblooming; drought tolerant once established
ALTERNATIVES: *Eschscholzia caespitosa* 'Sundew'; *Papaver commutatum* (Flanders poppy), *P. rhoeas* (corn or Shirley poppy)

Anthemis AND *Centaurea*

For gardeners enamored with the casual, carefree look of a cottage garden, what plants are more welcome than brilliant blue bachelor's buttons and sunny golden marguerites? Originally a European cornfield weed, annual bachelor's buttons are accommodated just as easily in modern gardens as they were in the Tudor gardens of centuries ago. The spherical, mop-top, intensely blue flowerheads of bachelor's buttons have a knack for populating sunny flower beds with ease, giving birth to the "volunteers" that are the essence of cottage gardens. More two-dimensional in nature, the flat, daisylike golden marguerite blossoms positively shine when enveloped in a sea of cornflower blue. Pleasing marguerite cultivars include 'E. C. Buxton', 'Beauty of Grallagh', 'Kelwayi', and 'Moonlight'.

GOLDEN MARGUERITE
Anthemis tinctoria (right)
(*an*-them-iss tink-*to*-ree-ah)

TYPE: perennial
HEIGHT: 45 to 90 cm (18 to 36 in.)
WIDTH: 30 to 60 cm (12 to 24 in.)
SOIL: poor to average, well drained
LIGHT: full to part sun
FLOWERING TIME: early summer to fall
GROWING TIPS: do not fertilize; may require staking; deadhead to prevent self-seeding; drought tolerant once established
ALTERNATIVES: *Leucanthemum* x *superbum* (Shasta daisy); annual *Rudbeckia hirta* (gloriosa daisy); *Tanacetum parthenium* (feverfew)

BACHELOR'S BUTTON
Centaurea cyanus (left)
(kent-*ow*-ree-ah kee-*an*-us)

TYPE: annual
HEIGHT: 20 to 76 cm (8 to 30 in.)
WIDTH: 15 cm (6 in.)
SOIL: poor to average, moist, well drained
LIGHT: full sun
FLOWERING TIME: early summer to fall
GROWING TIPS: deadhead to prevent self-seeding and to encourage reblooming; drought tolerant once established
ALTERNATIVES: *Consolida ajacis* (larkspur); *Nigella damascena* (love-in-a mist); *Salvia* x *superba* (violet sage)

Anthemis AND *Erigeron*

LIESBETH LEATHERBARROW

Mid-summer is daisy season on the prairies; peek over almost any fence and you'll see substantial clumps of shining Shastas or bright marguerites. Golden marguerite daisies are easy to naturalize in an informal setting; indeed, in borders they should be deadheaded to prevent rampant self-seeding! The single golden yellow, orange, or cream flowers grow on branching stems clad with deeply divided, aromatic foliage. Create a daisy duo for the cutting garden by adding the golden marguerite's more sophisticated cousin 'Pink Jewel' fleabane. 'Pink Jewel' is a clump-forming plant with lance-shaped leaves and semi-double, pale to rose pink flowers with finely textured petals and yellow centers to match its golden companion. 'Darkest of All' and 'Double Beauty' are violet-blue fleabane cultivars.

GOLDEN MARGUERITE
Anthemis tinctoria (top)
(*an*-them-iss tink-*to*-ree-ah)

TYPE: perennial
HEIGHT: 45 to 90 cm (18 to 36 in.)
WIDTH: 30 to 60 cm (12 to 24 in.)
SOIL: poor to average, well drained
LIGHT: full to part sun
FLOWERING TIME: early summer to fall
GROWING TIPS: do not fertilize; may require staking; deadhead to prevent self-seeding; drought tolerant once established
ALTERNATIVES: *Leucanthemum* x *superbum* (Shasta daisy); annual *Rudbeckia hirta* (gloriosa daisy); *Tanacetum parthenium* (feverfew)

'PINK JEWEL' FLEABANE
Erigeron 'Pink Jewel' (bottom)
(eh-*rig*-ur-on)

TYPE: perennial
HEIGHT: 60 cm (24 in.)
WIDTH: 45 cm (18 in.)
SOIL: poor to average, well drained
LIGHT: full sun
FLOWERING TIME: early to late summer
GROWING TIPS: do not fertilize; may require staking; deadhead; drought tolerant once established; prone to powdery mildew, ensure good air circulation around plants
ALTERNATIVES: *Erigeron caespitosus* (tufted fleabane); *Coreopsis rosea* (pink tickseed)

Antirrhinum AND *Pennisetum*

Prairie gardeners seeking annuals that don't swoon at the first hint of frost are well advised to fill their containers and flower beds with robust, colorful snapdragons. 'Ribbon Crimson' is an intermediate snapdragon with a bushy, branching habit and upright flower spikes that are smothered with velvety red, tubular, two-lipped blossoms well into autumn. Ornamental grasses provide a perfect textural counterpoint to sturdy snapdragons, which benefit from companions with a more delicate aspect. Fountain grass, an annual on the prairies, forms elegant clumps of slender, medium green foliage topped with feathery, bottlebrush flower spikes in soft tones of pink and purple. For a change, try some of the six other colors of snapdragons in the Ribbon Series, or a mix.

'RIBBON CRIMSON'
SNAPDRAGON
Antirrhinum majus
'Ribbon Crimson' (red)
(an-tee-*ree*-num *may*-uss)

TYPE: annual
HEIGHT: 45 to 56 cm (18 to 22 in.)
WIDTH: 30 cm (12 in.)
SOIL: fertile, moist, well drained
LIGHT: full sun to light shade
FLOWERING TIME: early summer to fall
GROWING TIPS: remove first bloom spike at time of planting to encourage branching and multiple flower spikes; fertilize biweekly; deadhead
ALTERNATIVES: *Salpiglossis sinuata* Royale Series (painted tongue)

FOUNTAIN GRASS
Pennisetum setaceum (green)
(pen-ih-*see*-tum set-*eh*-see-um)

TYPE: annual
HEIGHT: 90 cm (36 in.)
WIDTH: 45 cm (18 in.)
SOIL: average to fertile, well drained
LIGHT: full sun
FLOWERING TIME: early to late summer
GROWING TIPS: very low maintenance
ALTERNATIVES: *Pennisetum alopecuroides*, *P. a.* 'Moudry', *P. orientale*, *P. villosum* (feathertop); *Stipa calamagrostis* (feather grass), *S. tenuissima* (Mexican feather grass)

Arrhenatherum AND *Artemisia*

For a touch of class in the garden, add a touch of silver. Many silver-leaved plants, such as variegated bulbous oat grass and artemisia, are grown for their appealing foliage color and texture alone. Serving a practical as well as an esthetic function, they enhance the blues, pinks, magentas, and yellows of neighboring plants, and even mediate between plants with clashing colors. 'Silver Mound' artemisia, a fragrant mound of soft feathery foliage, shows to advantage when planted beside variegated bulbous oat grass, which forms short vertical clumps of foliage, variegated in cream and silver-green. Together, these plants form a quiet partnership at the front of mixed borders, a welcome visual break from the vivid colors of annuals and perennials.

VARIEGATED BULBOUS OAT GRASS

Arrhenatherum elatius subsp. *bulbosum* 'Variegatum' (right)
(a-ren-*a*-the-rum ay-*lah*-tee-us subsp. bul-*bo*-sum)

TYPE: perennial
HEIGHT: 60 cm (24 in.)
WIDTH: 30 cm (12 in.)
SOIL: average to fertile, moist, well drained
LIGHT: full sun to light shade
FLOWERING TIME: early summer
GROWING TIPS: drought tolerant once established; cut back foliage in early spring before new growth emerges
ALTERNATIVES: *Festuca glauca* (blue fescue); *Helictotrichon sempervirens* (blue oat grass)

'SILVER MOUND' ARTEMISIA

Artemisia schmidtiana 'Silver Mound' (left)
(ar-tay-*mis*-ee-ah shmit-ee-*ah*-nah)

TYPE: perennial
HEIGHT: 30 cm (12 in.)
WIDTH: 45 cm (18 in.)
SOIL: poor to average, well drained
LIGHT: full sun
FLOWERING TIME: late summer
GROWING TIPS: requires excellent drainage; drought tolerant once established; fertilizing and overwatering cause it to flop; cut back mid-season to maintain bushy growth
ALTERNATIVES: *Artemisia stelleriana* 'Boughton Silver'; *Cerastium tomentosum* (snow-in-summer)

Artemisia AND *Pelargonium*

LIESBETH LEATHERBARROW

A standout among tender plants, 'Oriental Limelight' artemisia is a recent introduction with unusual, variegated, maplelike foliage in shades of creamy yellow and bold lime green. Gardeners who dare to experiment with the new and curious will enjoy planning plant partners for 'Oriental Limelight'. Although it shows to advantage against a backdrop of dark-leaved foliage in mixed borders or containers, another bold treatment consists of combining 'Oriental Limelight' with plants of contrasting variegations. The rounded foliage of many zonal geraniums comes in distinctly bicolor and tricolor forms, in combinations of gold, red, green, brown, or cream that are not always appealing to the faint of heart. Working in tandem with the artemisia, it creates an absorbing tapestry effect in containers.

'ORIENTAL LIMELIGHT' ARTEMISIA

Artemisia vulgaris
'Oriental Limelight' (left)
(ar-tay-*mis*-ee-ah vul-*gair*-iss)

TYPE: annual
HEIGHT: 30 cm (12 in.)
WIDTH: 30 cm (12 in.)
SOIL: average to fertile, moist, well drained
LIGHT: full sun to light shade
FLOWERING TIME: late summer
GROWING TIPS: fertilize biweekly; deadhead; may develop tall stalks which can be cut back to maintain a mounded form
ALTERNATIVES: *Artemisia ludoviciana* 'Valerie Finnis'; *Arrhenatherum elatius* subsp. *bulbosum* 'Variegatum' (variegated bulbous oat grass)

ZONAL GERANIUM

Pelargonium x *hortorum* (right)
(pell-are-*go*-nee-um x hor-*tor*-um)

TYPE: annual
HEIGHT: 30 to 90 cm (12 to 36 in.)
WIDTH: 30 to 45 cm (12 to 18 in.)
SOIL: fertile, moist, well drained
LIGHT: full to part sun
FLOWERING TIME: early summer to fall
GROWING TIPS: fertilize biweekly; deadhead; pinch back growing tips
ALTERNATIVES: *Pelargonium* x *domesticum* (Martha Washington geranium), *P. peltatum* (ivy-leaved geranium)

Artemisia AND *Physocarpus*

LIESBETH LEATHERBARROW

'Diablo' purple ninebark is a unique shrub that is making a big splash in prairie gardens. Adorned with pinkish white, buttonlike flowers in early summer, rich chocolate-burgundy foliage fading to copper in fall, a broadly upright form, and shredding bark, 'Diablo' creates unique landscaping opportunities for adventuresome gardeners. Choice enough to be grown alone as a specimen plant, it also brings out the best in green-leaved, shrubby neighbors and is an excellent foil for silver and gold foliage plants. 'Oriental Limelight', a recent annual artemisia introduction, is another attention seeker and the perfect companion for 'Diablo'. Beautifully marked with variegations of creamy yellow and lime green, its jagged-edged leaves glow against the backdrop of dramatic 'Diablo' foliage.

'ORIENTAL LIMELIGHT' ARTEMISIA

Artemisia vulgaris
'Oriental Limelight' (bottom)
(ar-tay-*mis*-ee-ah vul-*gair*-iss)

TYPE: annual
HEIGHT: 30 cm (12 in.)
WIDTH: 30 cm (12 in.)
SOIL: average to fertile, moist, well drained
LIGHT: full sun to light shade
FLOWERING TIME: late summer
GROWING TIPS: fertilize biweekly; deadhead; may develop tall stalks which can be cut back to maintain a rounded form
ALTERNATIVES: *Artemisia ludoviciana* 'Valerie Finnis'; *Arrhenatherum elatius* subsp. *bulbosum* 'Variegatum' (variegated bulbous oat grass)

'DIABLO' PURPLE NINEBARK

Physocarpus opulifolius 'Diablo' (top)
(fie-zo-*kar*-pus op-ew-li-*fo*-lee-us)

TYPE: deciduous shrub
HEIGHT: 1.5 to 2.5 m (5 to 8 ft.)
WIDTH: 2.5 m (8 ft.)
SOIL: fertile, moist, well drained
LIGHT: full sun to light shade
FLOWERING TIME: early summer
GROWING TIPS: use organic mulch for moisture retention; after flowering, prune 20 percent of old shoots to base to promote replacement growth; may suffer winter die-back; water well in fall
ALTERNATIVE: *Prunus* x *cistena* (purpleleaf sand cherry)

Astilbe AND *Hosta*

LIESBETH LEATHERBARROW

Unsurpassed for enlivening a shady corner, colorful astilbes absolutely glow in the company of cool, white-edged hostas. The deeply divided, toothed foliage of most astilbes emerges from the ground a dark bronze-green in early spring, transforming to pure green during the growing season. From early to late summer, depending on the hybrid or cultivar, airy plumes of tiny, red, magenta, pink, lavender, salmon, or white flowers appear on tall stems. The substantial leaves of variegated hostas, staples of the prairie shade garden, provide a serene contrast to the lacy astilbe foliage and its vibrantly colored flowers. There's an astilbe to suit every taste and circumstance; try the notable pink and red *Astilbe* x *arendsii* hybrids 'Bressingham Beauty', 'Elizabeth Bloom', 'Fanal', and 'Glow'.

ASTILBE

Astilbe (top)
(ah-*still*-bee)

TYPE: perennial
HEIGHT: 30 to 90 cm (12 to 36 in.)
WIDTH: 30 to 45 cm (12 to 18 in.)
SOIL: fertile, moist, well drained
LIGHT: part sun to light shade
FLOWERING TIME: early to late summer
GROWING TIPS: avoid planting in hot, dry areas; use organic mulch for moisture retention and winter protection
ALTERNATIVES: *Astilbe* x *arendsii*, *A. chinensis*, *A. japonica*, *A. simplicifolia*, *A. thunbergii*

VARIEGATED HOSTA

Hosta (bottom)
(*hoss*-tah)

TYPE: perennial
HEIGHT: 25 to 60 cm (10 to 24 in.)
WIDTH: 45 cm (18 in.)
SOIL: fertile, moist, well drained
LIGHT: part sun to full shade
FLOWERING TIME: early summer to fall
GROWING TIPS: avoid planting in hot, dry areas; plant in sheltered area; use organic mulch for moisture retention and winter protection; excellent for hiding dying bulb foliage
ALTERNATIVES: *Hosta* 'Francee', 'Ground Master', 'Patriot', 'Regal Splendor'

Astrantia AND *Astrantia*

LESLEY REYNOLDS

Sometimes the most delightful plant partnerships are between very similar plants, particularly members of the same species. In these pairings the foliage affinity adds coherence to the union, while the dissimilarities, usually flower color or size, are highlighted. This is the case with the delightful marriage of the masterworts 'Rubra' and 'Shaggy' (also sold as 'Margery Fish'). Both feature mounds of lobed, toothed leaves and long-stemmed, long-lasting flower clusters prized in dried flower arrangements. Papery bracts encircle each rounded masterwort bloom. 'Rubra' bears maroon-pink flowers, whereas 'Shaggy' has striking, ivory-white flowers shaded with green and surrounded by long, green-tipped bracts. 'Ruby Wedding' and 'Claret' are other fine red-flowered companions for 'Shaggy'.

'RUBRA' MASTERWORT

Astrantia major 'Rubra' (right)
(as-*stran*-tee-yah *ma*-jor)

TYPE: perennial
HEIGHT: 90 cm (36 in.)
WIDTH: 60 cm (24 in.)
SOIL: fertile, moist, well drained
LIGHT: part sun to light shade
FLOWERING TIME: early to mid summer
GROWING TIPS: use organic mulch for moisture retention and winter protection; deadhead; excellent for hiding dying bulb foliage
ALTERNATIVES: *Astilbe* x *arendsii*, *A. chinensis, A. japonica, A. simplicifolia, A. thunbergii*

'SHAGGY' MASTERWORT

Astrantia major 'Shaggy' (left)
(as-*stran*-tee-yah *ma*-jor)

TYPE: perennial
HEIGHT: 90 cm (36 in.)
WIDTH: 60 cm (24 in.)
SOIL: fertile, moist, well drained
LIGHT: part sun to light shade
FLOWERING TIME: early to mid summer
GROWING TIPS: use organic mulch for moisture retention and winter protection; deadhead; excellent for hiding dying bulb foliage
ALTERNATIVES: *Astrantia major* subsp. *involucrata; Astilbe* x *arendsii, A. chinensis, A. japonica, A. simplicifolia, A. thunbergii*

Astrantia AND *Hosta*

LIESBETH LEATHERBARROW

A stellar combination of unusual, long-lasting flowers and fabulous foliage, 'Rubra' masterwort and 'Sum and Substance' hosta excel in the woodland garden. Masterwort bears long-stemmed umbels of bristly, maroon-pink flowers, each bloom surrounded by papery bracts. Against the mounds of deeply lobed, matte green masterwort foliage, 'Sum and Substance' is all curves and high polish, boasting shiny, golden green leaves that are puckered when mature and tough enough to resist hungry slugs. These leaves require some sun to achieve their best golden color. Graceful scapes of pale lavender, lilylike flowers are the jewels in the crown of this fine specimen plant. 'Hadspen Blood' is a darker red masterwort cultivar. Other king-sized hostas include 'Elegans', 'Krossa Regal', and 'Royal Standard'.

'RUBRA' MASTERWORT

Astrantia major 'Rubra' (bottom)
(as-*stran*-tee-yah *ma*-jor)

TYPE: perennial
HEIGHT: 90 cm (36 in.)
WIDTH: 60 cm (24 in.)
SOIL: fertile, moist, well drained
LIGHT: part sun to light shade
FLOWERING TIME: early to mid summer
GROWING TIPS: use organic mulch for moisture retention and winter protection; deadhead; excellent for hiding dying bulb foliage
ALTERNATIVES: *Astilbe* x *arendsii*, *A. chinensis*, *A. japonica*, *A. simplicifolia*, *A. thunbergii*

'SUM AND SUBSTANCE' HOSTA

Hosta 'Sum and Substance' (top)
(*hoss*-tah)

TYPE: perennial
HEIGHT: 90 cm (36 in.)
WIDTH: 1.5 m (5 ft.)
SOIL: fertile, moist, well drained
LIGHT: part sun to light shade
FLOWERING TIME: early summer to fall
GROWING TIPS: avoid planting in hot, dry areas; plant in sheltered area; use organic mulch for moisture retention and winter protection; excellent for hiding dying bulb foliage
ALTERNATIVE: *Bergenia* (elephant ears)

Athyrium AND *Gymnocarpium*

LESLEY REYNOLDS

Most people associate ferns with moist, gentle climates; however, several lovely species are perfectly hardy in prairie gardens, given the proper growing conditions. Because of their widely varying sizes, colors, and textures, different species of ferns may be combined with fabulous results, their graceful form and intricate foliage enhancing the woodland garden or any cool, shady corner that needs a lift. The most strikingly colored of all the hardy ferns, the Japanese painted fern has red-purple stems and feathery, arching fronds marked with metallic gray and burgundy. 'Plumosum' oak fern, smaller in stature and more delicate in aspect, bears triangular fronds of leaf blades that are bright yellow-green in spring, darkening to emerald green as they mature.

JAPANESE PAINTED FERN
Athyrium niponicum var. *pictum* (top)
(a-*thi*-ree-um nih-*pon*-ih-kum var. *pik*-tum)

TYPE: perennial
HEIGHT: 30 cm (12 in.)
WIDTH: 60 cm (24 in.)
SOIL: fertile, moist, well drained
LIGHT: light shade
FLOWERING TIME: not applicable
GROWING TIPS: avoid planting in hot, dry areas; plant with crowns just below soil level; use organic mulch for moisture retention; slow to emerge in spring
ALTERNATIVES: *Matteuccia struthiopteris* (ostrich fern); *Osmunda cinnamomea* (cinnamon fern), *O. claytoniana* (interrupted fern), *O. regalis* (royal fern)

'PLUMOSUM' OAK FERN
Gymnocarpium dryopteris
'Plumosum' (bottom)
(jim-no-*kar*-pee-um dry-*op*-terr-iss)

TYPE: perennial groundcover
HEIGHT: 20 cm (8 in.)
WIDTH: indefinite
SOIL: fertile, moist, well drained
LIGHT: light to full shade
FLOWERING TIME: not applicable
GROWING TIPS: avoid planting in hot, dry areas; use organic mulch for moisture retention; excellent for hiding dying bulb foliage
ALTERNATIVES: *Gymnocarpium robertianum*; *Athyrium filix-femina* 'Minutissimum' (lady fern)

Athyrium AND *Primula*

LESLEY REYNOLDS

The rainbow hues of dainty primroses and the cool, unfurling greenery of hardy ferns are synonymous with spring, a fleeting season on the prairies. However, gardeners can create the illusion of spring in the summer woodland garden with the remarkable Himalayan cowslip, a late-blooming primrose, and the lady fern, one of the loveliest ferns for prairie gardens. A true giant among primroses, Himalayan cowslip is a statuesque beauty bearing umbels of up to forty fragrant, funnel-shaped, yellow flowers atop long, sturdy stems. The basal foliage is deep green and toothed, with heart-shaped bases. The lady fern's light green fronds, divided into many small leaflets with graceful, downward-curving tips, provide a welcome change in texture from the substantial Himalayan cowslip foliage.

LADY FERN

Athyrium filix-femina (top)
(a-*thi*-ree-um fih-liks-*fay*-mee-nah)

TYPE: perennial
HEIGHT: 90 cm (36 in.)
WIDTH: 60 cm (24 in.)
SOIL: fertile, moist, well drained
LIGHT: light shade
FLOWERING TIME: not applicable
GROWING TIPS: avoid planting in hot, dry areas; plant with crowns just below soil level; use organic mulch for moisture retention
ALTERNATIVES: *Matteuccia struthiopteris* (ostrich fern); *Osmunda cinnamomea* (cinnamon fern), *O. claytoniana* (interrupted fern), *O. regalis* (royal fern)

HIMALAYAN COWSLIP

Primula florindae (bottom)
(*prim*-you-lah *flor*-in-die)

TYPE: perennial
HEIGHT: 60 to 90 cm (24 to 36 in.)
WIDTH: 30 to 60 cm (12 to 24 in.)
SOIL: fertile, moist, well drained
LIGHT: part sun to light shade
FLOWERING TIME: early to late summer
GROWING TIPS: avoid planting in hot, dry areas; tolerates full sun if soil is kept moist; use organic mulch for moisture retention and winter protection; deadhead
ALTERNATIVE: *Corydalis lutea* (golden corydalis)

Bacopa AND *Calibrachoa*

LIESBETH LEATHERBARROW

In recent years prairie gardeners have benefited from the introduction of a host of fabulous new annuals for container plantings. Two of the most exciting of this crop of "basket-stuffers" are bacopa and Million Bells *Calibrachoa*. Made to trail from hanging containers, these fast-growing annuals bloom profusely all summer. 'Snowstorm' bacopa has trailing stems clad with small, rounded and toothed, deep green leaves and diminutive, starry, white flowers. Like all white flowers, bacopa makes the lively colors of Million Bells appear even more intense. More mounded in habit, Million Bells produces bright blossoms like perfect miniature petunias tumbling over the edges of containers, mingling with the dainty bacopa. 'Lavender Showers' is a mauve-pink bacopa cultivar.

'SNOWSTORM' BACOPA
Bacopa 'Snowstorm' (right)
(ba-*ko*-pah)

TYPE: annual
HEIGHT: 8 cm (3 in.)
WIDTH: 45 to 60 cm (18 to 24 in.)
SOIL: fertile, moist
LIGHT: full to part sun
FLOWERING TIME: early to late summer
GROWING TIPS: avoid planting in hot, dry areas; fertilize biweekly; pinch back growing tips
ALTERNATIVES: white *Lobelia erinus* cultivars, such as 'Paper Moon', 'Regatta White', and 'White Cascade'

MILLION BELLS
Calibrachoa (left)
(kal-ih-bra-*ko*-ah)

TYPE: annual
HEIGHT: 10 to 15 cm (4 to 6 in.)
WIDTH: 45 to 60 cm (18 to 24 in.)
SOIL: fertile, moist, well drained
LIGHT: full to part sun
FLOWERING TIME: early to late summer
GROWING TIPS: avoid planting in hot, dry areas; fertilize biweekly; pinch back growing tips
ALTERNATIVES: small trailing petunias, such as Fantasy Series and Dream Series Petitunias

Begonia AND *Begonia*

LIESBETH LEATHERBARROW

For dazzling color in the shade or container garden, you can't go wrong with combining tuberous begonias and their fibrous-rooted cousins, the wax begonias. Resplendent in brilliant hues of red, orange, pink, yellow, and white, adaptable tuberous begonias produce large, showy blossoms in single, ruffled, double, or camellia forms above bold foliage. Interestingly, this begonia's dark green leaves point in the direction the blossoms will face, so plant accordingly! Whereas "big" describes most aspects of tuberous begonias, the opposite is true of wax begonias, which produce tidy mounds of small, shiny, semi-succulent leaves ranging from green, to bronze, to burgundy in color. Little, rounded, single or double blossoms in shades of pink, red, or white smother the plants all summer long.

WAX BEGONIA
Begonia semperflorens (small)
(bee-*goh*-nyah sem-per-*flor*-enz)

TYPE: annual
HEIGHT: 15 to 30 cm (6 to 12 in.)
WIDTH: 15 to 30 cm (6 to 12 in.)
SOIL: fertile, moist, well drained
LIGHT: light shade
FLOWERING TIME: early summer to fall
GROWING TIPS: plant outdoors after last expected frost date; fertilize biweekly; pinch back growing tips; very low maintenance
ALTERNATIVE: *Impatiens walleriana* (impatiens)

TUBEROUS BEGONIA
Begonia x *tuberhybrida* (large)
(bee-*goh*-nyah x tew-ber-*hib*-ri-dah)

TYPE: tender tuber
HEIGHT: 20 to 45 cm (8 to 18 in.)
WIDTH: 30 to 45 cm (12 to 18 in.)
SOIL: fertile, moist, well drained
LIGHT: light shade
FLOWERING TIME: early summer to fall
GROWING TIPS: start indoors three months before last expected frost date; fertilize biweekly; pinch out small female flowers to prolong bloom time; may need staking; deadhead; lift tubers in fall
ALTERNATIVE: none

Begonia AND *Lysimachia*

LESLEY REYNOLDS

Tuberous begonias live up to their tropical origins with gorgeous, richly colored blossoms and large, glossy leaves. Extensive hybridizing has produced begonias in an incredible range of flower forms and colors, including some of the most brilliant red, scarlet, and orange shades imaginable. Pair these hot begonias in a hanging basket with dense-flowered loosestrife, a vigorous, mat-forming plant with outstanding flower and foliage appeal. Dense-flowered loosestrife has small, medium green, oval leaves with pointed tips, and clusters of golden yellow, cup-shaped flowers. The simple, cheerful, and open flowers are the perfect complement to the full-blown lushness of the begonia blossoms. Try the cultivar 'Outback Sunset', which has variegated red, yellow, and green leaves.

TUBEROUS BEGONIA

Begonia x *tuberhybrida* (top)
(bee-*goh*-nyah x tew-ber-*hib*-ri-dah)

TYPE: tender tuber
HEIGHT: 20 to 45 cm (8 to 18 in.)
WIDTH: 30 to 45 cm (12 to 18 in.)
SOIL: fertile, moist, well drained
LIGHT: light shade
FLOWERING TIME: early summer to fall
GROWING TIPS: start indoors three months before last expected frost date; fertilize biweekly; pinch out small female flowers to prolong bloom time; may need staking; deadhead; lift tubers in fall
ALTERNATIVE: none

DENSE-FLOWERED LOOSESTRIFE

Lysimachia congestiflora (bottom)
(li-si-*mak*-ee-ah con-jest-ih-*flor*-ah)

TYPE: annual
HEIGHT: 10 cm (4 in.)
WIDTH: 30 cm (12 in.)
SOIL: fertile, moist, well drained
LIGHT: full sun to light shade
FLOWERING TIME: early to late summer
GROWING TIPS: avoid planting in hot, dry areas; fertilize biweekly; trim lightly after flowering
ALTERNATIVE: *Lysimachia nummularia* 'Aurea' (golden creeping Jenny)

Borago AND *Rudbeckia*

LESLEY REYNOLDS

Even on a cloudy day, 'Irish Eyes' gloriosa daisies and borage brighten the garden with the colors of sunshine and clear, unending prairie sky. Gloriosa daisies are aptly named, their golden, starry flowers shining in summer borders for several weeks. A magnet for bees and butterflies, they are untroubled by insect pests or deer. 'Irish Eyes' is a splendid cultivar, its unusual, vivid green centers an unexpected change from more common brown-eyed varieties. Like all of its kind, 'Irish Eyes' has rough, dark green leaves and stiff stems that rarely require staking. Much renowned in herbal lore, borage bears nodding clusters of small, star-shaped, bright blue flowers with prominent black stamens. The bristly stems are clad with gray-green leaves that are edible in salads when young.

BORAGE
Borago officinalis (left)
(bore-*a*-go o-fi-ki-*nah*-lis)

TYPE: annual
HEIGHT: 76 cm (30 in.)
WIDTH: 45 cm (18 in.)
SOIL: average to fertile, well drained
LIGHT: full to part sun
FLOWERING TIME: early to late summer
GROWING TIPS: deadhead to prevent self-seeding; very low maintenance
ALTERNATIVE: *Anchusa capensis* 'Blue Bird' (alkanet)

'IRISH EYES' GLORIOSA DAISY
Rudbeckia hirta 'Irish Eyes' (right)
(rude-*beck*-ee-ah *her*-tah)

TYPE: annual
HEIGHT: 60 to 76 cm (24 to 30 in.)
WIDTH: 30 cm (12 in.)
SOIL: average to fertile, well drained
LIGHT: full to part sun
FLOWERING TIME: mid-summer to fall
GROWING TIPS: fertilize biweekly; deadhead
ALTERNATIVES: *Rudbeckia fulgida* (black-eyed Susan), *R. f.* var. *sullivantii* 'Goldsturm'; *Heliopsis helianthoides* (false sunflower)

Brachyscome AND *Diascia*

LIESBETH LEATHERBARROW

The alliance of Swan River daisy and diascia is an inspired one, at its loveliest in containers and hanging baskets. Although there is no mistaking one for the other, the twosome presents a united front, generating decorative masses of delicate blossoms in equally delicate colors. Swan River daisies produce mounds of fine, dark green, lacy foliage smothered with sweetly scented, daisylike blossoms, in shades of white, rose, pink, lilac, or blue. Although most Swan River daisy cultivars are golden-eyed, many members of the Splendour Series have black centers. In contrast, dainty diascia blossoms are tubular, with five rounded lobes for petals. Two backward-facing spurs are located on the upper lobes. At present, diascia is available only in soft shades of pink and salmon pink.

SWAN RIVER DAISY

Brachyscome iberidifolia (lilac)
(bra-kees-*ko*-mee i-be-ri-di-*fo*-lee-ah)

TYPE: annual
HEIGHT: 45 cm (18 in.)
WIDTH: 35 cm (14 in.)
SOIL: fertile, moist, well drained
LIGHT: full sun
FLOWERING TIME: early summer to fall
GROWING TIPS: plant outdoors after last expected frost date; fertilize biweekly; deadhead to encourage reblooming; pinch back growing tips; drought tolerant once established
ALTERNATIVES: *Browallia speciosa* (bush violet); *Nigella damascena* (love-in-a-mist); *Scaevola aemula* (fairy fan-flower)

DIASCIA

Diascia (pink)
(dee-*a*-skee-ah)

TYPE: annual
HEIGHT: 25 cm (10 in.)
WIDTH: 50 cm (20 in.)
SOIL: fertile, moist, well drained
LIGHT: full sun
FLOWERING TIME: early summer to fall
GROWING TIPS: plant outdoors after last expected frost date; fertilize biweekly; deadhead; pinch back growing tips; blooms poorly in very hot summers
ALTERNATIVES: *Clarkia unguiculata* (clarkia); *Mimulus* x *hybridus* (monkey flower)

Brassica AND *Calendula*

WINSTON GORETSKY

Gardeners with a penchant for planting boldly should not hesitate to combine ornamental kale, distinguished for its multicolored foliage, and pot marigolds, renowned for their brilliant orange blossoms. This partnership might be too much of a good thing for some, but a blaze of unabashed color up front and center never fails to create a sense of joy in gardens. Used with discretion, the reds, pinks, purples, and greens of ruffled ornamental kale foliage juxtaposed with vivid orange pot marigolds make a strong statement without being overpowering. What's more, both annuals flaunt their colors well into the fall, surviving many degrees of frost for extended periods of time. Ornamental kale's colors actually intensify during cool days and nights, making it a standout in the autumn garden.

ORNAMENTAL KALE

Brassica oleracea (bottom)
(*bra*-si-kah o-le-*rah*-kee-ah)

TYPE: annual
HEIGHT: 30 cm (12 in.)
WIDTH: 45 cm (18 in.)
SOIL: fertile, moist, well drained
LIGHT: full to part sun
FLOWERING TIME: late summer
GROWING TIPS: use organic mulch for moisture retention; fertilize biweekly; remove lower leaves as they begin to fade
ALTERNATIVE: none

POT MARIGOLD

Calendula officinalis (top)
(ka-*len*-dew-lah o-fi-ki-*nah*-lis)

TYPE: annual
HEIGHT: 30 to 76 cm (12 to 30 in.)
WIDTH: 30 to 45 cm (12 to 18 in.)
SOIL: average to fertile, moist, well drained
LIGHT: full sun to light shade
FLOWERING TIME: early summer to fall
GROWING TIPS: deadhead to prevent self-seeding and to prolong blooming; drought tolerant once established
ALTERNATIVES: *Eschscholzia californica* (California poppy); *Rudbeckia hirta* 'Toto' (gloriosa daisy); *Tagetes* cultivars (marigold)

Brassica AND *Lobularia*

LIESBETH LEATHERBARROW

Imagine a flashy plant that thrives in cool weather and looks its best AFTER the first few serious frosts of the season. Although this sounds too good to be true, ornamental kale fits the bill perfectly. Grown as an annual for its magnificently colored foliage, its large, fancy rosettes of ruffled leaves develop in every imaginable combination of red, pink, purple, and green. Even simple green and white specimens add drama to the front of mixed borders or large containers. As night temperatures drop late in the summer, the foliage colors intensify, and moderate frosts enhance the brilliant coloring even more. Because ornamental kale is such a theatrical plant, one design approach is to give it a quiet but complementary partner such as sweet alyssum, the familiar, sweetly scented annual.

ORNAMENTAL KALE
Brassica oleracea (top)
(*bra*-si-kah o-le-*rah*-kee-ah)

TYPE: annual
HEIGHT: 30 cm (12 in.)
WIDTH: 45 cm (18 in.)
SOIL: fertile, moist, well drained
LIGHT: full to part sun
FLOWERING TIME: late summer
GROWING TIPS: use organic mulch for moisture retention; fertilize biweekly; remove lower leaves as they begin to fade
ALTERNATIVE: none

SWEET ALYSSUM
Lobularia maritima (bottom)
(lob-ew-*lah*-ree-ah ma-*ri*-ti-mah)

TYPE: annual
HEIGHT: 5 to 30 cm (2 to 12 in.)
WIDTH: 20 to 30 cm (8 to 12 in.)
SOIL: fertile, moist, well drained
LIGHT: full sun
FLOWERING TIME: early summer to fall
GROWING TIPS: fertilize biweekly; trim lightly after flowering to encourage reblooming and to keep plant compact
ALTERNATIVES: *Gypsophila repens* 'Alba' (creeping baby's breath); white *Lobelia erinus* cultivars

Calamintha AND *Mentha*

LIESBETH LEATHERBARROW

The aromatic duo of calamint and ginger mint is a natural for an old-fashioned herb garden, but it is also decorative enough to enhance any perennial border. Unlike other, more thuggish mint relatives, these pretty plants are never invasive. Carefree calamint forms dense clumps of stiff, square stems clothed with toothed, deep green leaves and tubular, two-lipped, rose-pink blossoms that are attractive to bees and hummingbirds. Low-growing ginger mint thrives in many sheltered prairie gardens; however, gardeners in colder areas of the prairie may need to grow it as an annual. It is valued primarily for its gold-splashed, ginger-flavored foliage and, where hardy, spreads slowly by underground rhizomes. Short spikes of tubular, lilac flowers mimic the showier calamint blossoms in miniature.

CALAMINT
Calamintha grandiflora (top)
(cal-ih-*min*-thah gran-di-*flor*-ah)

TYPE: perennial
HEIGHT: 45 cm (18 in.)
WIDTH: 45 cm (18 in.)
SOIL: average, moist, well drained
LIGHT: full sun to light shade
FLOWERING TIME: mid to late summer
GROWING TIPS: use organic mulch for moisture retention and winter protection
ALTERNATIVES: *Calamintha nepeta*; *Nepeta* x *faassenii*, *N. racemosa*, *N. sibirica* (catmint)

GINGER MINT
Mentha x *gracilis* 'Variegata' (bottom)
(*men*-thah x gra-*kill*-us)

TYPE: perennial
HEIGHT: 30 cm (12 in.)
WIDTH: 90 cm (36 in.)
SOIL: average to fertile, moist, well drained
LIGHT: full to part sun
FLOWERING TIME: mid to late summer
GROWING TIPS: use organic mulch for moisture retention and winter protection
ALTERNATIVES: *Mentha* x *piperita* 'Variegata' (variegated peppermint), *M. suaveolens* 'Variegata' (pineapple mint)

Campanula AND *Cornus*

LESLEY REYNOLDS

Whether used as a hedge or as a pleasing specimen in a shrub border, clump-forming 'Elegantissima' dogwood (also sold as 'Argenteo-marginata') offers year-round appeal to prairie gardeners. In addition, it is sufficiently well behaved to include in a mixed border as a silvery accent to hardy perennials, such as the unusual Korean bellflower. 'Elegantissima' has variegated silver and gray-green leaves and bright red winter stems that stand in bold contrast to the muted grays and browns of the season. Creamy white flowers appear in spring, followed by white berries. Like rosy pink chimes, the pendant blooms of the Korean bellflower harmonize with the dogwood foliage as naturally as if they belonged to that shrub. The Korean bellflower has heart-shaped, toothed leaves and spreads by rhizomes.

KOREAN BELLFLOWER

Campanula takesimana (bottom)
(kam-*pan*-you-lah tack-eh-sih-*ma*-na)

TYPE: perennial
HEIGHT: 50 cm (20 in.)
WIDTH: 90 cm (36 in.)
SOIL: fertile, moist, well drained
LIGHT: part to full sun
FLOWERING TIME: mid-summer
GROWING TIPS: avoid planting in hot, dry areas; use organic mulch for moisture retention and winter protection; deadhead; may be invasive, but is easy to control
ALTERNATIVE: *Campanula punctata*

'ELEGANTISSIMA' SILVER-LEAF DOGWOOD

Cornus alba 'Elegantissima' (top)
(*kore*-nuss *all*-bah)

TYPE: deciduous shrub
HEIGHT: 2 m (6.5 ft.)
WIDTH: 2 m (6.5 ft.)
SOIL: average to fertile, well drained
LIGHT: full sun to light shade
FLOWERING TIME: spring to early summer
GROWING TIPS: use organic mulch for moisture retention and winter protection; needs periodic rejuvenation pruning to maintain vivid stem and foliage coloration; water well in fall
ALTERNATIVE: *Cornus sericea* 'White Gold' (red osier dogwood)

Campanula AND *Scabiosa*

LIESBETH LEATHERBARROW

For many gardeners, the nodding blossoms of long-blooming bellflowers are an indispensable element of sunny mixed or perennial borders, invoking images of the ever-popular cottage garden. The same holds true for scabiosa, whose short alpine species make perfect partners for low-growing bellflowers and whose taller species make ideal mates for upright bellflowers. 'Chettle Charm', an especially lovely peach-leaved bellflower, produces tall, erect stems bearing pale porcelain blue flowers, each tinted purple and rimmed in a slightly darker blue. The large, flat, saucer-shaped flowers of 'Butterfly Blue' scabiosa with their pincushionlike centers come in a cool lavender-blue that echoes the delicate purple highlights of 'Chettle Charm'. As such, the two complement each other perfectly.

'CHETTLE CHARM'
PEACH-LEAVED BELLFLOWER
Campanula persicifolia
'Chettle Charm' (top)
(kam-*pan*-you-lah pur-sick-i-*foh*-lee-ah)

TYPE: perennial
HEIGHT: 1 m (3.3 ft.)
WIDTH: 30 cm (12 in.)
SOIL: fertile, moist, well drained
LIGHT: part to full sun
FLOWERING TIME: late spring to mid-summer
GROWING TIPS: avoid planting in hot, dry areas; use organic mulch for moisture retention and winter protection; deadhead to encourage continuous bloom
ALTERNATIVE: *Platycodon grandiflorus* (balloon flower)

'BUTTERFLY BLUE'
SMALL SCABIOUS
Scabiosa columbaria
'Butterfly Blue' (bottom)
(skab-ee-*oh*-sah ko-lum-*bear*-ee-ah)

TYPE: perennial
HEIGHT: 45 cm (18 in.)
WIDTH: 30 cm (12 in.)
SOIL: average to fertile, moist, well drained
LIGHT: full sun to light shade
FLOWERING TIME: early summer to fall
GROWING TIPS: requires excellent drainage; use organic mulch for moisture retention and winter protection; deadhead to encourage continuous bloom and prevent self-seeding
ALTERNATIVE: *Scabiosa caucasica* (pincushion flower)

Campanula AND *Tanacetum*

LESLEY REYNOLDS

Ethereal and romantic, white gardens are the stuff of dreams and perfect for busy people who love to slip outside at dusk to savor the quiet of the evening. There are many perennials suitable for a white border, but two of the finest are 'Alba' peach-leaved bellflower and feverfew. 'Alba' bears snowy white, bell-shaped flowers that face outward from tall stems. Plant it behind bushy feverfew, which has aromatic, deeply divided leaves and clusters of small, upward-facing, daisylike blossoms. Feverfew's white petals encircle golden yellow centers, which add just enough warmth and color to the partnership to prevent the abundance of white flowers from appearing stark and cold. For a double-flowered combo, try 'White Pearl' peach-leaved bellflower and 'Ball's Double White' feverfew.

'ALBA' PEACH-LEAVED BELLFLOWER
Campanula persicifolia 'Alba' (top)
(kam-*pan*-you-lah pur-sick-i-*foh*-lee-ah)

TYPE: perennial
HEIGHT: 1 m (3.3 ft.)
WIDTH: 30 cm (12 in.)
SOIL: fertile, moist, well drained
LIGHT: part to full sun
FLOWERING TIME: late spring to mid-summer
GROWING TIPS: avoid planting in hot, dry areas; use organic mulch for moisture retention and winter protection; deadhead
ALTERNATIVES: *Campanula alliariifolia* (ivory bells); *Platycodon grandiflorus* (balloon flower)

FEVERFEW
Tanacetum parthenium (bottom)
(ta-na-*see*-tum par-*thee*-nee-yum)

TYPE: perennial
HEIGHT: 45 to 60 cm (18 to 24 in.)
WIDTH: 30 cm (12 in.)
SOIL: poor to fertile, well drained
LIGHT: full to part sun
FLOWERING TIME: early summer to fall
GROWING TIPS: deadhead to encourage reblooming; short-lived perennial, but self-seeds readily if late-summer blooms are not deadheaded
ALTERNATIVES: *Leucanthemum* x *superbum* 'Little Miss Muffet', 'Silver Princess' (dwarf Shasta daisy)

Canna AND *Dahlia*

LESLEY REYNOLDS

For pure foliage drama, it's impossible to beat the rich hues of 'Tropicana' canna and 'Bishop of Llandaff' dahlia. These statuesque tender bulbs are a hot combination for large containers on a sheltered, sunny patio or deck. 'Tropicana' has broad, paddle-shaped leaves marked with jazzy stripes of red, pink, and gold on a background of the darkest green. The sheathed leaves unfurl slowly, eventually revealing reedlike flower stems that bear racemes of bright orange flowers similar in appearance to gladiolas. Flamboyant 'Tropicana' sizzles against the striking, black-red foliage of 'Bishop of Llandaff', a peony-flowered dahlia crowned with radiant red blooms with darker red centers. Other cannas with dazzling, variegated foliage include 'Pink Sunburst', 'Pretoria', and 'Striped Beauty'.

'TROPICANA' CANNA
Canna 'Tropicana' (bottom)
(*kah*-nah)

TYPE: tender rhizome
HEIGHT: 90 to 120 cm (36 to 48 in.)
WIDTH: 60 cm (24 in.)
SOIL: fertile, moist, well drained
LIGHT: full sun
FLOWERING TIME: late summer to early fall
GROWING TIPS: start rhizomes indoors six weeks before last expected frost; plant in sheltered area; fertilize before and after flowering; store bulbs indoors during winter
ALTERNATIVE: *Crinum* x *powellii* (crinum lily)

'BISHOP OF LLANDAFF' DAHLIA
Dahlia 'Bishop of Llandaff' (top)
(*dah*-lee-ah or *day*-lee-ah)

TYPE: tender tuberous root
HEIGHT: 90 cm (36 in.)
WIDTH: 30 cm (12 in.)
SOIL: fertile, moist, well drained
LIGHT: full sun
FLOWERING TIME: mid-summer to fall
GROWING TIPS: start tuberous roots indoors six weeks before last expected frost; plant in sheltered area; may require staking; fertilize before and after flowering; store bulbs indoors during winter
ALTERNATIVE: *Crocosmia* hybrids (montbretia)

Capsicum AND *Petroselinum*

LIESBETH LEATHERBARROW

Gardeners can design plantings that are both beautiful and practical by mingling edible and ornamental plants in the style of potager gardens. For example, parsley, which has culinary value as a flavoring or garnish, is also a notable foliage plant, perfect for incorporating into the front of mixed borders and container arrangements. It forms rounded clumps of dark green, crinkly, triangular leaves that introduce textural diversity no matter where you plant it. For a winning yet playful combination, pair parsley with one of the many little ornamental pepper plants available in garden centers. The deep green of the parsley leaves is an excellent foil for the colorful miniature hot pepper fruit, which starts out green and ripens to combinations of yellow, orange, red, and even purple.

ORNAMENTAL PEPPER

Capsicum annuum (bottom)
(*kap*-si-kum an-*ew*-um)

TYPE: annual
HEIGHT: 30 to 60 cm (12 to 24 in.)
WIDTH: 30 cm (12 in.)
SOIL: fertile, well drained
LIGHT: full sun
FLOWERING TIME: early summer
GROWING TIPS: for bushy plants, avoid overwatering and pinch growing tips; fertilize infrequently
ALTERNATIVES: *Beta vulgaris* var. *flavescens* 'Bright Lights' (multicolored Swiss chard); *Fragaria* cultivars (strawberry); *Lycopersicon esculentum* (tomato), small cultivars, such as 'Fargo', 'Orange Pixie'

PARSLEY

Petroselinum crispum (top)
(pet-ro-se-*leen*-um *kris*-pum)

TYPE: biennial, grown as annual
HEIGHT: 80 cm (32 in.)
WIDTH: 60 cm (24 in.)
SOIL: fertile, moist, well drained
LIGHT: full sun to light shade
FLOWERING TIME: summer, second year
GROWING TIPS: avoid planting in hot, dry areas; fertilize every four weeks; harvest leaves from the outside
ALTERNATIVES: *Petroselinum crispum* var. *neapolitanum* (Italian parsley), *P. c.* var. *tuberosum* (Hamburg parsley)

Centaurea AND *Papaver*

LIESBETH LEATHERBARROW

True blue bachelor's buttons and vivid red corn poppies are staple ingredients of wildflower mixes and easy annuals for the mixed border. Both are common in European grain fields, so it's not surprising that they enjoy prairie gardens, self-sowing abundantly. Bachelor's buttons have slender, silver-gray leaves and small, round flower heads composed of tubular florets. As well as the familiar deep blue shades, there are crimson, pink, and white, single and double cultivars.

A silky complement to raggedy bachelor's buttons, the original corn poppies are brilliant red with single, bowl-shaped flowers; however, Shirley poppies, a strain developed in the nineteenth century, may be single, semi-double, or double and have white-based petals in shades of pink, red, orange, white, and bicolors.

BACHELOR'S BUTTON

Centaurea cyanus (blue)
(kent-*ow*-ree-ah kee-*an*-us)

TYPE: annual
HEIGHT: 30 to 90 cm (12 to 36 in.)
WIDTH: 15 cm (6 in.)
SOIL: poor to average, well drained
LIGHT: full sun
FLOWERING TIME: early to late summer
GROWING TIPS: can be seeded directly outdoors; deadhead to encourage reblooming, but allow some late-season blooms to self-seed, if desired
ALTERNATIVES: *Helichrysum bracteatum* (strawflower); *Nigella damascena* (love-in-a-mist)

CORN POPPY

Papaver rhoeas (red)
(pa-*pah*-ver *ree*-as)

TYPE: annual
HEIGHT: 60 cm (24 in.)
WIDTH: 30 cm (12 in.)
SOIL: average to fertile, well drained
LIGHT: full sun
FLOWERING TIME: mid to late summer
GROWING TIPS: seed directly outdoors as poppies do not transplant well; deadhead, but allow a few seedpods to ripen to self-seed for the following year, if desired
ALTERNATIVES: *Papaver commutatum* (Flanders poppy), *P. somniferum* (opium poppy)

Cimicifuga AND *Lychnis*

LESLEY REYNOLDS

Never mind the blondes, the most desired siren of the shade garden is a dusky-leaved Russian 'Brunette'. Also known by the much more prosaic name of Kamchatka bugbane, 'Brunette' is prized for its lobed and toothed, chocolate-purple foliage, which makes a fine backdrop for fiery clusters of orange-scarlet Maltese cross blossoms. In fall, 'Brunette' produces tall spikes of pink-tinted white flowers; however, in areas of the prairies with short growing seasons it may not bloom before hard frost strikes. While 'Brunette' is a standout in the woodland garden, it also performs well in the partly sunny locations favored by Maltese cross. This hot bugbane companion is a prairie favorite, its rounded clusters of five-petaled flowers glowing atop erect stems clad with opposite leaves.

KAMCHATKA BUGBANE
Cimicifuga simplex 'Brunette' (right)
(ki-me-ki-*few*-gah *sim*-plex)

TYPE: perennial
HEIGHT: 1.2 m (4 ft.)
WIDTH: 60 cm (24 in.)
SOIL: fertile, moist
LIGHT: light shade to part sun
FLOWERING TIME: fall
GROWING TIPS: avoid planting in hot, dry locations; use organic mulch for moisture retention and winter protection
ALTERNATIVES: *Cimicifuga racemosa* 'Atropurpurea' (purple bugbane); *Ligularia dentata* 'Othello' (rayflower)

MALTESE CROSS
Lychnis chalcedonica (left)
(*lick*-niss kal-ky-*don*-i-ka)

TYPE: perennial
HEIGHT: 1.2 m (4 ft.)
WIDTH: 60 cm (24 in.)
SOIL: average to fertile, moist, well drained
LIGHT: full to part sun
FLOWERING TIME: early to mid summer
GROWING TIPS: avoid planting in hot, dry areas; use organic mulch for moisture retention and winter protection; may require staking; deadhead to encourage reblooming
ALTERNATIVES: *Lychnis* x *arkwrightii* 'Vesuvius', *L. haageana* (campion)

Cornus AND *Cornus*

LESLEY REYNOLDS

The secret to a successful shrub border frequently lies in the skillful juxtaposition of plants of varying size and foliage characteristics. However, similar plants with a single, striking dissimilarity can sometimes create impeccable vignettes. Such is the case with the marriage of silvery 'Elegantissima' and golden 'Spaethii' dogwoods. Of comparable stature and growth habit, these versatile shrubs suit both a casual suburban backyard or, with regular shaping, a formal Italian-style garden. Both have deeply veined, oval, pointed leaves and corymbs of creamy white flowers followed by clusters of white berries. The difference lies in the foliage color: 'Elegantissima' is clad with gray-green leaves edged with white, whereas the leaves of 'Spaethii' are bright green with sunny yellow margins.

'ELEGANTISSIMA' SILVER-LEAF DOGWOOD

Cornus alba 'Elegantissima' (left)
(*kore*-nuss *all*-bah)

TYPE: deciduous shrub
HEIGHT: 2 m (6.5 ft.)
WIDTH: 2 m (6.5 ft.)
SOIL: average to fertile, well drained
LIGHT: full sun to light shade
FLOWERING TIME: spring to early summer
GROWING TIPS: use organic mulch for moisture retention and winter protection; in late winter cut half of old stems to ground to encourage new, brilliant red growth; water well in fall
ALTERNATIVE: *Cornus sericea* 'White Gold' (red osier dogwood)

'SPAETHII' GOLDEN VARIEGATED DOGWOOD

Cornus alba 'Spaethii' (right)
(*kore*-nuss *all*-bah)

TYPE: deciduous shrub
HEIGHT: 2 m (6.5 ft.)
WIDTH: 2 m (6.5 ft.)
SOIL: average to fertile, well drained
LIGHT: full sun to light shade
FLOWERING TIME: spring to early summer
GROWING TIPS: use organic mulch for moisture retention and winter protection; needs periodic rejuvenation pruning to maintain vivid stem and foliage coloration; water well in fall
ALTERNATIVE: *Cornus sericea* 'Flaviramea' (red osier dogwood)

Cymbalaria AND *Senecio*

LIESBETH LEATHERBARROW

Ivies, grown as perennials elsewhere, are favored annuals on the prairies. You often see them trailing over the edges of pots and urns, their cool greenery supplementing arrangements that are otherwise ablaze with color. But ivies can be so much more than a basket stuffer. Because they are actually shade lovers and come in a variety of leaf forms and colors, they can be planted front and center in containers destined for the shade. For example, the combination of Kenilworth ivy with its small, kidney-shaped, scalloped foliage and German ivy with its much larger, pointy, triangular leaves is all you need in a wall-mounted pot for a lush display of textured foliage on a shaded wall or fence. You might also mix and match several different ivies to create a truly verdant tapestry.

KENILWORTH IVY
Cymbalaria muralis (left)
(sim-ba-*lar*-ee-ah mew-*rah*-liss)

TYPE: annual
HEIGHT: 60 cm (24 in.)
WIDTH: 60 cm (24 in.)
SOIL: fertile, moist, well drained
LIGHT: light shade to part sun
FLOWERING TIME: early summer to fall
GROWING TIPS: avoid planting in hot, dry areas; deadhead to prevent self-seeding; very low maintenance
ALTERNATIVES: *Hedera helix* (English ivy); *Senecio macroglossus* 'Variegatus' (wax ivy), *S. mikanioides* (German ivy); *Vinca major* 'Variegata' (vinca vine)

GERMAN IVY
Senecio mikanioides (right)
(se-*ne*-kee-oh mi-kah-nee-*oi*-deez)

TYPE: annual
HEIGHT: 90 cm (36 in.)
WIDTH: 60 cm (24 in.)
SOIL: fertile, moist, well drained
LIGHT: light shade to part sun
FLOWERING TIME: late summer to fall
GROWING TIPS: avoid planting in hot, dry areas; very low maintenance
ALTERNATIVES: *Senecio macroglossus* 'Variegatus' (wax ivy); *Cymbalaria muralis* (Kenilworth ivy); *Hedera helix* (English ivy); *Vinca major* 'Variegata' (vinca vine)

Delphinium AND *Ligularia*

LIESBETH LEATHERBARROW

Classic tall delphiniums are the backbone of many a prairie border. The color of the mid-summer sky, their scepters of brilliant blue flowers tower above nearby plants, attracting bees, butterflies, and humming-birds. The flower spikes are densely packed with single or double florets, each floret consisting of at least five colored, petal-like sepals; the top one sports a large recurved spur. At the center of each floret is the famous delphinium "bee," a cluster of true petals, often of a contrasting color. Complementing blue delphiniums with an explosion of black-stemmed, sunshine-gold spikes of daisylike flowers, 'The Rocket' is a bold perennial that produces sizeable clumps of large, finely toothed, triangular leaves that excel in screening tatty, late-summer delphinium foliage.

DELPHINIUM HYBRIDS

Delphinium x *elatum* (top)
(dell-*fin*-ee-um x ay-*lah*-tum)

TYPE: perennial
HEIGHT: 1.8 m (6 ft.)
WIDTH: 90 cm (36 in.)
SOIL: fertile, moist, well drained
LIGHT: full to part sun
FLOWERING TIME: mid-summer
GROWING TIPS: plant in sheltered areas; use organic mulch for moisture retention and winter protection; fertilize biweekly until blooming; prone to delphinium moth caterpillar, handpick in spring; may require staking; deadhead
ALTERNATIVES: *Delphinium* x *belladonna*, *D. elatum*

'THE ROCKET' LIGULARIA

Ligularia stenocephala 'The Rocket' (bottom)
(lig-ew-*lah*-ree-ah sten-o-*kef*-ah-lah)

TYPE: perennial
HEIGHT: 1.5 m (5 ft.)
WIDTH: 1.0 m (3.3 ft.)
SOIL: fertile, moist
LIGHT: light shade to part sun
FLOWERING TIME: mid to late summer
GROWING TIPS: avoid planting in hot, dry areas; use organic mulch for moisture retention and winter protection
ALTERNATIVES: *Ligularia dentata*, *L.* 'Gregynog Gold', *L. hodgsonii*, *L. przewalskii* (rayflower)

Delphinium AND *Monarda*

Made for the prairies, stately delphinium and shaggy monarda are adorned with some of the most enticing flowers in the mid-summer border. 'Gardenview Scarlet', a fine mildew-resistant monarda cultivar, is sure to attract bees and hummingbirds to its scarlet-red clusters of tubular flowers cupped in colorful modified leaves, called bracts. Whereas mop-headed monarda blooms are tousled and casual, the showy spires of delphinium lend height and elegance to the border. The densely packed flower spikes bear single or double florets, each centered with a cluster of petals called a "bee." Other mildew-resistant cultivars of monarda are 'Marshall's Delight' and 'Prairie Night'. The Pacific Giant Group of delphiniums includes 'Galahad', 'Guinevere', 'King Arthur', 'Lancelot', and 'Summer Skies'.

PACIFIC GIANT GROUP
DELPHINIUM HYBRIDS
Delphinium x *elatum*
Pacific Giant Group (top)
(dell-*fin*-ee-um x ay-*lah*-tum)

TYPE: perennial
HEIGHT: 1.8 m (6 ft.)
WIDTH: 90 cm (36 in.)
SOIL: fertile, moist, well drained
LIGHT: full to part sun
FLOWERING TIME: mid-summer
GROWING TIPS: plant in sheltered areas; use organic mulch for moisture retention and winter protection; prone to delphinium moth caterpillar, handpick in spring; may require staking; deadhead
ALTERNATIVES: *Delphinium* x *elatum* Magic Fountain Hybrids

'GARDENVIEW SCARLET'
MONARDA
Monarda didyma
'Gardenview Scarlet' (bottom)
(moh-*nar*-dah dih-*dih*-mah)

TYPE: perennial
HEIGHT: 90 cm (36 in.)
WIDTH: 60 cm (24 in.)
SOIL: average to fertile, moist, well drained
LIGHT: full sun to light shade
FLOWERING TIME: mid-summer to fall
GROWING TIPS: avoid planting in hot, dry areas; use organic mulch for moisture retention and winter protection; deadhead
ALTERNATIVE: *Monarda fistulosa* (wild bee balm)

Delphinium AND *Papaver*

A mixed border of perennials and annuals allows gardeners the luxury of experimenting with different flower bed designs each year without the labor of replanting the entire border. Hardy perennials provide a framework to be filled in with colorful annuals and hardy or tender bulbs. Statuesque delphiniums are among the best perennial choices for the mixed border, their erect spires forming an elegant backdrop for medium to tall annuals. Adding to their versatility, they are available in many colors, including soft to vibrant shades of blue, lilac, pink, and white. Annuals with rounded blossoms, such as lush and gorgeous peony-flowered opium poppies, effectively complement the delphinium's vertical floral feast. Some recommended cultivars are 'Pink Chiffon', 'White Cloud', and 'Black Peony'.

DELPHINIUM HYBRIDS

Delphinium x *elatum* (right)
(dell-*fin*-ee-um x ay-*lah*-tum)

TYPE: perennial
HEIGHT: 1.8 m (6 ft.)
WIDTH: 90 cm (36 in.)
SOIL: fertile, moist, well drained
LIGHT: full to part sun
FLOWERING TIME: mid-summer
GROWING TIPS: plant in sheltered areas; use organic mulch for moisture retention and winter protection; fertilize biweekly until blooming; prone to delphinium moth caterpillar, handpick in spring; may require staking; deadhead
ALTERNATIVES: *Delphinium* x *belladonna*, *D. elatum*

PEONY-FLOWERED OPIUM POPPY

Papaver somniferum var. *paeoniflorum* (left)
(pa-*pah*-ver som-*nif*-ur-um var. pay-own-ee-*flor*-um)

TYPE: annual
HEIGHT: 1.2 m (4 ft.)
WIDTH: 30 cm (12 in.)
SOIL: average to fertile, well drained
LIGHT: full sun
FLOWERING TIME: mid to late summer
GROWING TIPS: seed directly outdoors as poppies do not transplant well; deadhead to prevent self-seeding
ALTERNATIVES: *Papaver commutatum* (Flanders poppy), *P. rhoeas* (corn poppy, Shirley poppy)

Deschampsia AND *Veronica*

LIESBETH LEATHERBARROW

The dancing greens, whites, and pinks of the northern lights add a touch of magic to prairie nights. Gardeners who want to recreate that same magic at the front of mixed and perennial borders can now interplant 'Northern Lights' tufted hair grass with 'Heavenly Blue' harebell speedwell. 'Northern Lights', which has a bold, upright presence in the garden, is uniquely variegated in shades of gold that fade to cream tipped in pink as summer progresses—the same suite of pastels that color the aurora borealis. 'Heavenly Blue' harebell speedwell develops into spreading mats of tiny, brilliant blue flowers, forming an appropriately celestial backdrop for 'Northern Lights'. Although 'Northern Lights' may not be hardy everywhere on the prairies, it can be grown successfully as an annual.

'NORTHERN LIGHTS'
TUFTED HAIR GRASS
Deschampsia cespitosa
'Northern Lights' (left)
(day-*shomp*-see-ah keh-spi-*toe*-sah)

TYPE: perennial
HEIGHT: 45 cm (18 in.)
WIDTH: 45 cm (18 in.)
SOIL: average, moist, well drained
LIGHT: full sun to light shade
FLOWERING TIME: late summer
GROWING TIPS: avoid planting in hot, dry areas; use organic mulch for moisture retention and winter protection; cut back before new growth resumes in spring
ALTERNATIVE: *Arrhenatherum elatius* subsp. *bulbosum* 'Variegatum' (variegated bulbous oat grass)

'HEAVENLY BLUE'
HAREBELL SPEEDWELL
Veronica prostrata 'Heavenly Blue'
(right)
(ver-*on*-ih-kah pro-*stra*-tah)

TYPE: perennial
HEIGHT: 10 cm (4 in.)
WIDTH: 40 cm (16 in.)
SOIL: average to fertile, moist, well drained
LIGHT: full to part sun
FLOWERING TIME: early to mid summer
GROWING TIPS: use organic mulch for moisture retention and winter protection; shear after flowering to keep plant compact
ALTERNATIVES: *Veronica pectinata* (comb speedwell), *V. spicata* subsp. *nana* 'Blue Carpet'

Dianthus AND *Rosa*

LESLEY REYNOLDS

For many gardeners, summer arrives on the prairies when the first hardy shrub roses burst into bloom. Among the most noteworthy of the low-maintenance, prairie-bred roses is 'Morden Ruby', introduced in 1977. All summer long this vigorous rose produces abundant clusters of long-lasting, double, deep pink blossoms flecked with red and framed by glossy, dark green foliage. A perfect size for the middle border, 'Morden Ruby' is a jewel of a rose behind a carpet of mat-forming 'Arctic Fire' maiden pinks. 'Arctic Fire' bears single flowers with white, toothed petals and dark pink eyes that match 'Morden Ruby'. The narrow, dark green foliage remains attractive all summer. Other maiden pink cultivars include 'Albus' (white), 'Flashing Light' (bright pink), and 'Zing Rose' (deep rose red).

'ARCTIC FIRE' MAIDEN PINK

Dianthus deltoides 'Arctic Fire' (bottom)
(die-*an*-thuss dell-*toy*-dees)

TYPE: perennial
HEIGHT: 20 cm (8 in.)
WIDTH: 30 cm (12 in.)
SOIL: average to fertile, well drained
LIGHT: full to part sun
FLOWERING TIME: late spring to mid-summer
GROWING TIPS: to prevent winter drying of evergreen foliage, cover with mulch or evergreen boughs; shear after flowering to maintain compact habit and prolong flowering
ALTERNATIVES: *D. gratianopolitanus* (cheddar pink), *D. plumarius* (border pink)

'MORDEN RUBY' ROSE

Rosa 'Morden Ruby' (top)
(*roh*-zah)

TYPE: deciduous shrub
HEIGHT: 1.5 m (5 ft.)
WIDTH: 1.5 m (5 ft.)
SOIL: fertile, moist, well drained
LIGHT: full sun
FLOWERING TIME: early to late summer
GROWING TIPS: use organic mulch for moisture retention and winter protection; fertilize regularly; deadhead; prune in spring to remove tip kill and old canes; water well in fall
ALTERNATIVES: *Rosa* 'Adelaide Hoodless', 'Alexander Mackenzie', 'John Franklin', 'Winnipeg Parks'

Dianthus AND *Veronica*

LIESBETH LEATHERBARROW

Picking partners for low-growing plants in the rock garden or at the front of borders is a pleasurable task, simply because there are so many to choose from. For example, the vivid gentian blue of harebell speedwell never fails to impress, making it an excellent starting point for developing a small planting scheme. The cultivars 'Heavenly Blue', 'Lodden Blue', and 'Trehane', in particular, bring out the best in colorful neighbors such as 'Tiny Rubies', a cheddar pink that forms tidy, little mounds of grassy, blue-gray foliage smothered with small, double, rose-pink flowers. These rock garden treasures are also delightfully fragrant. Other cheddar pink cultivars of note include 'Blue Hills' (single rose pink), 'Bath's Pink' (fringed, single pink with a dark eye), or 'Badenia' (fringed red).

'TINY RUBIES' CHEDDAR PINK
Dianthus gratianopolitanus
'Tiny Rubies' (right)
(die-*an*-thuss gra-tee-an-oh-pol-i-*tah*-nuss)

TYPE: perennial
HEIGHT: 10 cm (4 in.)
WIDTH: 30 cm (12 in.)
SOIL: average to fertile, well drained
LIGHT: full to part sun
FLOWERING TIME: early to mid summer
GROWING TIPS: to prevent winter drying of evergreen foliage, cover with mulch or evergreen boughs; shear after flowering to maintain compact habit and prolong flowering
ALTERNATIVES: *Dianthus alpinus* (alpine pink), *D. deltoides* (maiden pink)

'HEAVENLY BLUE'
HAREBELL SPEEDWELL
Veronica prostrata 'Heavenly Blue' (left)
(ver-*on*-ih-kah pro-*stra*-tah)

TYPE: perennial
HEIGHT: 10 cm (4 in.)
WIDTH: 40 cm (16 in.)
SOIL: average to fertile, moist, well drained
LIGHT: full to part sun
FLOWERING TIME: early to mid summer
GROWING TIPS: use organic mulch for moisture retention and winter protection; shear after flowering to keep plant compact
ALTERNATIVES: *Veronica pectinata* (comb speedwell), *V. spicata* subsp. *nana* 'Blue Carpet'

Echeveria AND *Nicotiana*

For an annual version of the ever-popular hen and chicks, consider planting peacock echeveria, a compact, rosette-forming succulent well suited to containers, the front of mixed borders, and beds of annuals. Often grown as a houseplant, this echeveria has fleshy leaves that are frosty blue-green, triangular, and slightly tapered. The rosy color of each leaf edge and tip coordinates perfectly with the rosy blossoms of 'Avalon Bright Pink' flowering tobacco, making this an excellent, albeit unusual, plant combination. Tubular flowering tobacco blossoms flare into five flat petals that mimic the shape of echeveria foliage, thus adding to the appeal and strength of this partnership. Select short flowering tobacco series to combine with echeveria, such as Domino, Havana, and Merlin.

PEACOCK ECHEVERIA

Echeveria peacockii (bottom)
(e-kee-*ve*-ree-ah pee-*kok*-ee-ee)

TYPE: annual
HEIGHT: 15 cm (6 in.)
WIDTH: 25 cm (10 in.)
SOIL: average, moist, well drained
LIGHT: full sun
FLOWERING TIME: mid to late summer
GROWING TIPS: in areas with hot, dry summers, provide shade from afternoon sun; requires excellent drainage; deadhead; drought tolerant once established; very low maintenance
ALTERNATIVES: *Sedum* hybrids (stonecrop); *Sempervivum tectorum* hybrids (hen and chicks)

'AVALON BRIGHT PINK' FLOWERING TOBACCO

Nicotiana x *sanderae*
'Avalon Bright Pink' (top)
(nick-oh-shee-*ah*-na x *san*-der-eye)

TYPE: annual
HEIGHT: 25 cm (10 in.)
WIDTH: 30 cm (12 in.)
SOIL: average to fertile, moist, well drained
LIGHT: full to part sun
FLOWERING TIME: early summer to fall
GROWING TIPS: fertilize biweekly; deadhead to encourage continuous bloom; contact with foliage may irritate skin; very low maintenance
ALTERNATIVES: *Nicotiana alata* Nicki Series; *Petunia* Prism Series

Echinacea AND *Hemerocallis*

LIESBETH LEATHERBARROW

Although many late-summer bloomers belong to the Asteraceae family and thus sport composite blossoms in a wide range of colors, it is refreshing to discover cultivars of other plant species that overlap in bloom time with the ubiquitous daisy lookalikes. For example, mid- to late-season daylilies such as the russet-and-apricot bicolor 'Frans Hals' showcase elegant trumpet-like flowers and attractive, grassy foliage. The same russet color highlights the central burgundy cone of 'Bright Star' purple coneflower, making it a pleasing companion for 'Frans Hals'. With its daisylike blooms of rosy lavender-pink, borne from mid-summer to early fall, 'Bright Star' is compact, long-flowering, and a butterfly magnet! Other noteworthy coneflowers include 'Bravado', 'Crimson Star', and 'Magnus'.

'BRIGHT STAR' PURPLE CONEFLOWER

Echinacea purpurea 'Bright Star' (right)
(eck-in-*ay*-see-ah purr-*purr*-ee-ah)

TYPE: perennial
HEIGHT: 60 cm (24 in.)
WIDTH: 30 cm (12 in.)
SOIL: average, well drained
LIGHT: full to part sun
FLOWERING TIME: mid-summer to fall
GROWING TIPS: use organic mulch for moisture retention and winter protection; may require staking if soil is too rich; drought tolerant once established
ALTERNATIVES: *Leucanthemum* x *superbum* (Shasta daisy); *Rudbeckia fulgida* var. *sullivantii* 'Goldsturm'

'FRANS HALS' DAYLILY

Hemerocallis 'Frans Hals' (left)
(hem-er-oh-*kal*-iss)

TYPE: perennial
HEIGHT: 76 cm (30 in.)
WIDTH: 76 cm (30 in.)
SOIL: average to fertile, well drained
LIGHT: full to part sun
FLOWERING TIME: early to late summer
GROWING TIPS: plant crowns just below soil level; use organic mulch for moisture retention and winter protection; deadhead daily; remove entire flower stalk after last blossom is spent; excellent for hiding dying bulb foliage
ALTERNATIVE: *Iris sibirica* (Siberian iris)

Echinacea AND *Liatris*

LIESBETH LEATHERBARROW

A combination that brings untold beauty to the late-summer border consists of purple coneflower and gayfeather, both long-lived and low-maintenance perennials with their roots in the prairies. Purple coneflowers produce large, daisylike blooms composed of a dark, prickly center and purple-pink or white ray florets. They make excellent cut flowers and contrast effectively with the fuzzy purple wands of gayfeather. The dense spikes of gayfeather blossoms consist entirely of button-shaped clusters of seed-producing disk florets; petal-like ray florets are absent. These unusual flower heads open from the spike-top downward, a habit opposite to that of similar spiky flowers. 'White Swan', 'Bravado', 'Bright Star', and 'Magnus' are good coneflowers. 'Kobold' is a reliable gayfeather.

'WHITE SWAN' PURPLE CONEFLOWER

Echinacea purpurea
'White Swan' (bottom)
(eck-in-*ay*-see-ah purr-*purr*-ee-ah)

TYPE: perennial
HEIGHT: 90 cm (36 in.)
WIDTH: 45 cm (18 in.)
SOIL: average, well drained
LIGHT: full to part sun
FLOWERING TIME: mid-summer to fall
GROWING TIPS: use organic mulch for moisture retention and winter protection; may require staking if soil is too rich; drought tolerant once established
ALTERNATIVES: *Leucanthemum* x *superbum* (Shasta daisy); *Rudbeckia fulgida* var. *sullivantii* 'Goldsturm'

GAYFEATHER

Liatris spicata (top)
(lee-*ah*-tris spih-*ka*-tah)

TYPE: perennial
HEIGHT: 50 cm (20 in.)
WIDTH: 30 cm (12 in.)
SOIL: average to fertile, moist, well drained
LIGHT: full to part sun
FLOWERING TIME: late summer
GROWING TIPS: use organic mulch for moisture retention and winter protection; if desired, deadhead by trimming from the top; drought tolerant once established
ALTERNATIVES: *Liatris punctata* (snakeroot), *L. pycnostachya* (Kansas gayfeather)

Erigeron AND *Leontopodium*

When creating outstanding plant duos, what could be more apropos than combining the soft, violet-blue flower heads of 'Shining Sea' fleabane with the silvery white, starfishlike blossoms of edelweiss? Made famous by a popular number from *The Sound of Music*, edelweiss deserves praise in its own right. It makes a lovely addition to rock gardens or the front of mixed borders, where it happily produces a unique arrangement of lance-shaped, woolly leaves topped with clusters of insignificant, yellow-white flower heads, which in turn are supported by substantial, star-shaped bracts. In contrast, fleabane's delicate, asterlike blossoms comprise a double row of linear ray florets. Clustered in the background, they form a tidal pool of violet blue for the little edelweiss "starfish."

'SHINING SEA' FLEABANE

Erigeron 'Shining Sea' (top)
(eh-*rig*-ur-on)

TYPE: perennial
HEIGHT: 50 cm (20 in.)
WIDTH: 45 cm (18 in.)
SOIL: poor to average, well drained
LIGHT: full sun
FLOWERING TIME: early to late summer
GROWING TIPS: do not fertilize; may require staking if soil is too rich; deadhead; drought tolerant once established; prone to powdery mildew, ensure good air circulation around plants
ALTERNATIVES: *Erigeron caespitosus* (tufted fleabane); *Coreopsis rosea* (pink tickseed)

EDELWEISS

Leontopodium alpinum (bottom)
(lee-on-ti-*pod*-ee-um al-*peen*-um)

TYPE: perennial
HEIGHT: 20 cm (8 in.)
WIDTH: 10 cm (4 in.)
SOIL: average, well drained
LIGHT: full sun
FLOWERING TIME: late spring to early summer
GROWING TIPS: requires excellent drainage; in areas with hot, dry summers, provide shade from afternoon sun; drought tolerant once established
ALTERNATIVE: *Cerastium tomentosum* (snow-in-summer)

Eryngium AND *Lilium*

LESLEY REYNOLDS

Dependable Asiatic lilies combine effortlessly with many traditional prairie perennials, but if you want lilies like lovely 'Red Juanita' to really shine, introduce them to Zabel sea holly, a brash and beautiful accent plant that is sure to turn heads. For dramatic color and architectural effect in the garden, it's impossible to beat Zabel sea holly. Looking like a prickly metal sculpture, this thistlelike perennial has incredible, intensely blue-violet bracts and spiky, cone-shaped centers. The dark green foliage is spiny, toothed, and heart-shaped. A hot contrast to the cool, steely sea holly, 'Red Juanita' is an upward-facing Asiatic lily that bears a profusion of fiery red-orange flowers. Other superb red or orange-red Asiatic lilies include 'Marrakech', 'Milano', and 'Razzle Dazzle'.

ZABEL SEA HOLLY
Eryngium x *zabellii* (right)
(air-*in*-gee-um x za-*bell*-ee-ee)

TYPE: perennial
HEIGHT: 60 to 90 cm (24 to 36 in.)
WIDTH: 60 to 90 cm (24 to 36 in.)
SOIL: poor to average, well drained
LIGHT: full to part sun
FLOWERING TIME: mid to late summer
GROWING TIPS: deadhead to prevent self-seeding; drought tolerant once established
ALTERNATIVES: *Eryngium alpinum* (alpine sea holly), *E. amethystinum* (amethyst sea holly), *E. planum* (flat sea holly); *Echinops ritro* (globe thistle)

'RED JUANITA' ASIATIC LILY
Lilium x *hybridum* 'Red Juanita' (left)
(*lil*-ee-um x *hie*-bri-dum)

TYPE: hardy true bulb
HEIGHT: 90 cm (36 in.)
WIDTH: 30 to 45 cm (12 to 18 in.)
SOIL: fertile, moist, well drained
LIGHT: full to part sun
FLOWERING TIME: mid-summer
GROWING TIPS: plant bare bulbs in fall/spring, container-grown plants in spring; use organic mulch for moisture retention and winter protection; deadhead
ALTERNATIVES: Aurelian-Asiatic hybrids, Longiflorum-Asiatic hybrids, *Lilium martagon*, *L. monadelphum*

Euphorbia AND *Lavatera*

LIESBETH LEATHERBARROW

A rewarding annual, lavatera grows in just a few short weeks from seeds planted directly outside into statuesque, almost shrublike plants covered in a profusion of large, hibiscuslike flowers. The lustrous, rose-pink blossoms of 'Silver Cup', the best-known cultivar, are veined with a darker pink and display a silvery sheen between the veins. The lobed, dark green leaves resemble those of hollyhocks, to which lavatera is related. Lavatera has a decided penchant for white companions, but the showy, variegated, white-and-green foliage of snow-on-the-mountain is a particularly splendid accompaniment. Snow-on-the-mountain leaves have white margins that are widest on the upper leaves, which may be almost completely white. Inconspicuous, greenish white flowers appear in late summer.

SNOW-ON-THE-MOUNTAIN

Euphorbia marginata (bottom)
(yew-*for*-bee-yah mar-jin-*ah*-tah)

TYPE: annual
HEIGHT: 30 to 90 cm (12 to 36 in.)
WIDTH: 30 cm (12 in.)
SOIL: average, well drained
LIGHT: full sun
FLOWERING TIME: late summer
GROWING TIPS: fertilize biweekly; pinch back growing tips
ALTERNATIVES: *Arrenatherum elatium* subsp. *bulbosum* 'Variegatum' (variegated bulbous oat grass); *Tropaeolum* Alaska Series

'SILVER CUP' ROSE MALLOW

Lavatera trimestris 'Silver Cup' (top)
(la-vah-*tair*-ah tri-*mess*-triss)

TYPE: annual
HEIGHT: 60 to 120 cm (24 to 48 in.)
WIDTH: 45 cm (18 in.)
SOIL: average to fertile, well drained
LIGHT: full sun
FLOWERING TIME: mid to late summer
GROWING TIPS: plant in sheltered areas; fertilize biweekly; deadhead
ALTERNATIVES: *Alcea rosea* (hollyhock); *Malope trifida* (annual mallow); *Malva moschata* (musk mallow), *M. sylvestris* (high mallow)

Festuca AND *Solidago*

LIESBETH LEATHERBARROW

For lovers of blue and yellow, pair blue fescue grass and 'Crown of Rays' goldenrod in late-summer wildflower and xeriscape gardens. Although fescue is not a true blue, its distinctly blue-gray foliage is very effective combined with the intense yellow of goldenrod. Not only do the colors in this duo work well together, but the strong contrast in plant form is also eye-catching. The well-proportioned, urchinlike mounds of grassy fescue are handsome in front of erect, clump-forming goldenrods with their arching sprays of tiny blossoms. Named goldenrod cultivars such as 'Crown of Rays', 'Golden Baby', and 'Golden Wings' are well behaved compared to the parent species, which spreads too rapidly for garden use. 'Elijah Blue', 'Sea Urchin', and 'Skinner's Blue' are excellent fescue cultivars.

BLUE FESCUE
Festuca glauca (bottom)
(fess-*too*-ka *glau*-ka*)*

TYPE: perennial
HEIGHT: 15 to 45 cm (6 to 18 in.)
WIDTH: 25 cm (10 in.)
SOIL: poor to average, well drained
LIGHT: full sun
FLOWERING TIME: early to mid summer
GROWING TIPS: use organic mulch for moisture retention; cut leaves back to form tight bun in spring to encourage neat, new growth; drought tolerant once established
ALTERNATIVE: *Helictotrichon sempervirens* (blue oat grass)

'CROWN OF RAYS' GOLDENROD
Solidago 'Crown of Rays' (top)
(so-li-*dah*-go)

TYPE: perennial
HEIGHT: 60 cm (24 in.)
WIDTH: 45 cm (18 in.)
SOIL: average, moist, well drained
LIGHT: full to part sun
FLOWERING TIME: mid-summer to fall
GROWING TIPS: deadhead to prevent self-seeding; may require staking if soil is too rich; drought tolerant once established
ALTERNATIVES: *Helenium autumnale* (sneezeweed); *Heliopsis helianthoides* (false sunflower); *Verbascum chaixii* (nettle-leaved mullein)

Filipendula AND *Typha*

LIESBETH LEATHERBARROW

Ponds and bog gardens, the delight of many prairie gardeners, offer fascinating planting possibilities, including the pondside partners queen-of-the-prairie and common cattail. Like many moisture-loving plants, they grow to an impressive size and work best in large gardens. Stately queen-of-the-prairie is a clump-forming perennial with lobed and toothed, medium green leaves. Its feathery clusters of pink or rose flowers grow atop red stems. Queen-of-the-prairie is also a striking plant for the back of a moist, partly shaded border. An assertive exclamation mark beside its graceful, spreading companion, the common cattail is beloved by floral arrangers for its long stems topped with cigarlike, brown flower spikes. Long, strap-shaped leaves complete the vertical effect of this prairie native.

QUEEN-OF-THE-PRAIRIE
Filipendula rubra (pink)
(fill-ih-*pen*-dew-lah *roo*-brah)

TYPE: perennial
HEIGHT: 1.8 m (6 ft.)
WIDTH: 1.2 m (4 ft.)
SOIL: fertile, moist
LIGHT: light shade to full sun
FLOWERING TIME: mid-summer
GROWING TIPS: avoid planting in hot, dry locations; provide shade from hot afternoon sun; use organic mulch for moisture retention and winter protection
ALTERNATIVES: *Filipendula ulmaria* (queen-of-the-meadow); *Thalictrum aquilegifolium* (columbine meadow rue), *T. delavayi* (Yunnan meadow rue), *T. rochebrunianum* (lavender mist)

COMMON CATTAIL
Typha latifolia (medium green)
(*ty*-fah la-tih-*foe*-lee-ah)

TYPE: perennial
HEIGHT: 2 m (6.5 ft.)
WIDTH: indefinite
SOIL: boggy, or submerge in up to 30 cm (12 in.) of water
LIGHT: full to part sun
FLOWERING TIME: late summer
GROWING TIPS: very low maintenance; suitable for large gardens only; may be invasive
ALTERNATIVES: *Typha angustifolia* (narrow-leaved cattail), *T. minima* (dwarf cattail)

Geranium AND *Ixiolirion*

LIESBETH LEATHERBARROW

Tone-on-tone combinations are attractive additions to the garden. Instead of boldly announcing their presence, they await discovery as they impart subtle variations to the landscape. Interplanting showy cranesbills and Tatar lilies creates a lovely purple tone-on-tone partnership. The showy cranesbill lives up to its name, forming mounds of soft, hairy, deeply divided leaves topped with rich purple, saucer-shaped blossoms that are prominently veined in a darker purple and shimmer with iridescence. In contrast, the upright Tatar lily produces umbels of deep blue or violet, star-faced flowers. Each pointed petal is also marked lengthwise with a darker purple stripe. As a bonus for this pair, the cranesbill foliage works wonders at disguising the maturing Tatar lily foliage.

SHOWY CRANESBILL
Geranium x *magnificum* (left)
(jer-*ane*-ee-um x mag-*niff*-ih-kum)

TYPE: perennial
HEIGHT: 60 cm (24 in.)
WIDTH: 60 cm (24 in.)
SOIL: average, well drained
LIGHT: full to part sun
FLOWERING TIME: early summer
GROWING TIPS: use organic mulch for moisture retention and winter protection; cut back flowering stems after blooming; may require staking if soil is too rich; excellent for hiding dying bulb foliage
ALTERNATIVES: *Geranium* x 'Johnson's Blue', *G. pratense*

TATAR LILY
Ixiolirion tataricum (right)
(iks-ee-oh-*leer*-ee-on ta-*tar*-ih-kum)

TYPE: borderline true bulb
HEIGHT: 25 to 40 cm (10 to 16 in.)
WIDTH: 10 cm (4 in.)
SOIL: average to fertile, well drained
LIGHT: full sun
FLOWERING TIME: late spring to early summer
GROWING TIPS: plant bulbs in fall in a sheltered area; use organic mulch for winter protection; fertilize before and after flowering; allow foliage to ripen
ALTERNATIVE: *Scabiosa columbaria* 'Butterfly Blue' (small scabious)

Halimodendron AND *Potentilla*

Windswept, sun-drenched lots are a challenge, especially when it comes to selecting trees and shrubs that will survive relentless heat and drying winds. Native shrubs acclimatized to local conditions, such as popular potentillas, are always good choices for such difficult spots; imports from inhospitable Russian climes, such as the carefree salt tree, are also good bets. Combine the two and you have a partnership that is both practical and attractive. A member of the legume family, the salt tree is actually a shrub that has woolly, compound leaves and purple pink blossoms resembling pea flowers. With creative pruning, it may be shaped into a small, single-stemmed tree. Buttercuplike potentilla blossoms come in a range of colors, including yellow, orange, pink, white, and red.

SALT TREE
Halimodendron halodendron (top)
(ha-lim-o-*den*-dron ha-lo-*den*-dron)

TYPE: deciduous shrub
HEIGHT: 2 m (6.5 ft.)
WIDTH: 2 m (6.5 ft.)
SOIL: poor to average, well drained
LIGHT: full sun
FLOWERING TIME: early to mid summer
GROWING TIPS: requires excellent drainage; drought tolerant once established; may sucker; prune when dormant or in late summer after flowering; water well in fall
ALTERNATIVES: *Caragana arborescens* 'Sutherland', 'Walker' (fernleaf caragana); *Hippophae rhamnoides* (sea buckthorn); *Shepherdia argentia* (silver buffaloberry)

POTENTILLA
Potentilla fruticosa (bottom)
(po-ten-*till*-ah froo-ti-*ko*-sah)

TYPE: deciduous shrub
HEIGHT: 90 cm (36 in.)
WIDTH: 90 cm (36 in.)
SOIL: average, well drained
LIGHT: full to part sun
FLOWERING TIME: late spring to fall
GROWING TIPS: use organic mulch for moisture retention; prune in early spring, removing dead or weak growth at ground level; thin out older branches to prevent crowding; water well in fall
ALTERNATIVES: *Caragana frutex* 'Globosa' (globe caragana), *C. pygmaea* (pygmy caragana)

Helenium AND *Origanum*

LESLEY REYNOLDS

In late summer, prairie gardens are awash with sunny yellow drifts of sunflowers, false sunflowers, tickseed, and rudbeckia all valuable members of the Asteraceae family. Not so well known is the robust sneezeweed, another long-blooming, daisy-like perennial that adds rich hues of orange, red, brown, and gold to the late-summer and fall border. 'Moerheim Beauty' is a particularly dramatic sneezeweed cultivar; its large blooms feature deep copper-red petals tipped with gold, and dark brown centers. For a cottage garden effect, combine this dashing daisy with the subtler tones of aromatic oregano, a culinary herb that does double duty as an ornamental perennial. Available in upright or spreading forms, oregano has rounded leaves and clusters of tiny, tubular, pink or white flowers.

'MOERHEIM BEAUTY'
SNEEZEWEED
Helenium 'Moerheim Beauty' (right)
(hell-*en*-ee-um)

TYPE: perennial
HEIGHT: 90 cm (36 in.)
WIDTH: 60 cm (24 in.)
SOIL: fertile, moist, well drained
LIGHT: full sun
FLOWERING TIME: mid-summer to fall
GROWING TIPS: use organic mulch for moisture retention and winter protection; deadhead
ALTERNATIVES: *Heliopsis helianthoides* (false sunflower); *Rudbeckia fulgida* (black-eyed Susan), *R. f.* var. *sullivantii*, annual *R. hirta* (gloriosa daisy)

OREGANO
Origanum vulgare (left)
(or-*i*-ga-num vul-*gah*-ray)

TYPE: perennial
HEIGHT: 30 to 45 cm (12 to 18 in.)
WIDTH: 30 to 60 cm (12 to 24 in.)
SOIL: poor to average, well drained
LIGHT: full sun
FLOWERING TIME: mid to late summer
GROWING TIPS: mulch for winter protection; drought tolerant once established
ALTERNATIVE: *Origanum vulgare* subsp. *hirtum* (Greek oregano)

Helichrysum AND *Petunia*

LIESBETH LEATHERBARROW

With the introduction of dozens of new annuals every year, the possibilities for diverse container and mass plantings are endless. Two annuals that took gardeners by storm a few years ago, especially when planted together, are the silver-leaved licorice plant and vivacious Wave Series petunias. Licorice plant has a mounding or trailing habit, depending on whether it is pruned or left to ramble. Its slender, fuzzy stems are smothered in soft, velvety oval leaves of two-tone gray—dark on top and lighter gray below. 'Licorice', 'Petite', 'Variegatum', 'Roundhouse', and 'Limelight' are good choices. Wave Series petunias are dense, spreading plants that make an ideal groundcover or basket stuffer, producing mounds of blossoms all summer long. Try 'Purple', 'Pink', 'Rose', or 'Misty Lilac'.

LICORICE PLANT

Helichrysum petiolare (silver)
(hee-li-*kriss*-um pet-ee-oh-*lah*-ray)

TYPE: annual
HEIGHT: 20 cm (8 in.)
WIDTH: 90 cm (36 in.)
SOIL: fertile, moist, well drained
LIGHT: full sun to light shade
FLOWERING TIME: mid-summer to fall
GROWING TIPS: fertilize biweekly; pinch back growing tips to encourage bushy growth; very low maintenance
ALTERNATIVES: *Anagallis monellii* (blue pimpernel); *Bacopa*; *Bidens ferulifolia*; *Lobelia erinus*; *Sanvitalia procumbens* (creeping zinnia); *Scaevola aemula* (fairy fan-flower)

WAVE SERIES PETUNIA

Petunia Wave Series (pink)
(pe-*tewn*-ee-ah)

TYPE: annual
HEIGHT: 15 cm (6 in.)
WIDTH: 90 cm (36 in.)
SOIL: average to fertile, well drained
LIGHT: full to part sun
FLOWERING TIME: early summer to fall
GROWING TIPS: fertilize biweekly; pinch growing tips to encourage bushy growth; very low maintenance
ALTERNATIVES: *Petunia* Cascadia Series, Fantasy Series, Madness Series, Storm Series

Helictotrichon AND *Stachys*

LESLEY REYNOLDS

A study in textural contrast, spiky 'Sapphire' blue oat grass and velvety soft, yellow-tinted 'Primrose Heron' lambs' ears make a lovely foliage pair for the perennial border. 'Sapphire', which boasts the deepest blue of any of the blue oat grasses, forms tidy, rounded clumps that never threaten to overrun smaller neighbors and can be left undivided for several years. In spring, the woolly leaves of 'Primrose Heron' emerge golden yellow, maturing to gray with some hints of yellow remaining all summer long. Downy flower spikes appear in early summer, bearing small, magenta flowers that open over several weeks. Some gardeners remove the flowers, believing that they detract from the pleasing foliage effect. 'Big Ears', 'Margery Fish', and 'Silver Carpet' are silver-gray lambs' ears cultivars.

'SAPPHIRE' BLUE OAT GRASS

Helictotrichon sempervirens
'Sapphire' (top)
(hell-ick-toe-*try*-kon sem-per-*veer*-ens)

TYPE: perennial
HEIGHT: 90 cm (36 in.)
WIDTH: 60 cm (24 in.)
SOIL: poor to average, well drained
LIGHT: full sun
FLOWERING TIME: early to mid summer
GROWING TIPS: use organic mulch for moisture retention; cut leaves back to form tight bun in spring to encourage neat, new growth; drought tolerant once established
ALTERNATIVE: *Festuca glauca* (blue fescue)

'PRIMROSE HERON' LAMBS' EARS

Stachys byzantina
'Primrose Heron' (bottom)
(*sta*-kiss biz-an-*teen*-ah)

TYPE: perennial
HEIGHT: 10 to 45 cm (4 to 18 in.)
WIDTH: 30 cm (12 in.)
SOIL: average, moist, well drained
LIGHT: full sun to light shade
FLOWERING TIME: early summer to fall
GROWING TIPS: requires excellent drainage; deadhead to prevent self-seeding; drought tolerant once established
ALTERNATIVES: *Artemisia absinthium* 'Lambrook Silver', *A. ludoviciana* 'Valerie Finnis'; *Lavandula angustifolia* (lavender)

Hemerocallis AND *Rosa*

LESLEY REYNOLDS

Most roses are prized for their opulent blooms—attractive leaves are merely an afterthought. Not so for the redleaf rose, whose balance of delightful flowers, fine foliage, and showy rose hips makes it an elegant addition to the mixed or shrub border. The redleaf rose produces arching canes with gray-purple leaves; a prolific flush of clustered, single, mauve-pink flowers with pale pink centers and yellow stamens are followed later by bright orange-red hips. Accompany the redleaf rose with graceful daylilies, which offer a range of flowering times and enduring fountains of foliage to complement the rose throughout the growing season. Late-blooming bronze, red, or orange daylilies, such as 'Autumn Minarette', 'Golden Prize', and 'Lady Lucille', reflect the color of ripening rose hips.

DAYLILY
Hemerocallis (bottom)
(hem-er-oh-*kal*-iss)

TYPE: perennial
HEIGHT: 30 to 90 cm (12 to 36 in.)
WIDTH: 60 to 90 cm (24 to 36 in.)
SOIL: average to fertile, well drained
LIGHT: full to part sun
FLOWERING TIME: early to late summer
GROWING TIPS: plant crowns just below soil level; use organic mulch for moisture retention and winter protection; deadhead daily; remove entire flower stalk after last blossom is spent; excellent for hiding dying bulb foliage
ALTERNATIVE: *Iris sibirica* (Siberian iris)

REDLEAF ROSE
Rosa glauca (top)
(*roh*-zah *glau*-kah)

TYPE: deciduous shrub
HEIGHT: 1.8 m (6 ft.)
WIDTH: 1.5 m (5 ft.)
SOIL: fertile, moist, well drained
LIGHT: full sun
FLOWERING TIME: late spring to early summer
GROWING TIPS: use organic mulch for moisture retention and winter protection; fertilize regularly; deadhead; prune in spring to remove tip kill and old woody canes; water well in fall
ALTERNATIVE: *Rosa pimpinellifolia* var. *altaica* (Altai rose)

Heuchera AND *Hosta*

LIESBETH LEATHERBARROW

Shaded borders, once the bane of a gardener's existence, can now be as exciting as their sunny counterparts, although often in more subtle ways. With an increasing variety of foliage plants available at garden centers, it is easy to introduce interest and drama into corners where sunshine is scarce. Hostas and coral bells, two well-known shade lovers, always work wonders together. For example, 'Patriot' hosta, with its boldly variegated, lance-shaped foliage, and 'Ring of Fire' coral bells, sporting attractive silvery, lobed leaves with deep purple veining, demonstrate the contrasting leaf forms, coloration, and size found in these genera. Although their hardiness varies, 'Checkers', 'Chocolate Ruffles', and 'Velvet Night' coral bells can flourish in prairie gardens with winter protection.

'RING OF FIRE' CORAL BELLS

Heuchera americana 'Ring of Fire' (right)
(*hue*-kerr-ah ah-mare-ih-*kan*-ah)

TYPE: perennial
HEIGHT: 60 cm (24 in.)
WIDTH: 30 cm (12 in.)
SOIL: fertile, moist, well drained
LIGHT: light shade to full sun
FLOWERING TIME: early to mid summer
GROWING TIPS: avoid planting in hot, dry areas; use organic mulch for moisture retention and winter protection; deadhead
ALTERNATIVES: *Heuchera* x *brizoides* 'Brandon Pink', 'Northern Fire', 'Ruby Mist', *H. sanguinea*

'PATRIOT' HOSTA

Hosta 'Patriot' (left)
(*hoss*-tah)

TYPE: perennial
HEIGHT: 56 cm (22 in.)
WIDTH: 90 cm (36 in.)
SOIL: fertile, moist, well drained
LIGHT: part sun to full shade
FLOWERING TIME: mid-summer
GROWING TIPS: avoid planting in hot, dry areas; plant in sheltered areas; use organic mulch for moisture retention and winter protection; excellent for hiding dying bulb foliage
ALTERNATIVES: *Hosta* 'Ground Master', 'Regal Splendor'

Heuchera AND *Stachys*

LIESBETH LEATHERBARROW

Silver-leaved plants such as lambs' ears are useful garden companions, blending effortlessly with their neighbors. What's more, they enhance the blues, pinks, and magentas of plants close at hand and mediate successfully between plants with clashing colors. It is no wonder, then, that lambs' ears and 'Brandon Pink' coral bells make such a pretty twosome edging flower borders. 'Brandon Pink' produces dense mounds of green, lobed foliage with slightly scalloped edges, topped by delicate sprays of tiny, pink flowers on tall, naked stems. In contrast, lambs' ears form rosettes of incredibly soft, woolly, gray-green foliage that beg to be touched. Equally woolly, spiky bloom stalks support whorls of small, pink-purple flowers. 'Big Ears', 'Margery Fish', and 'Silver Carpet' are favorite cultivars.

'BRANDON PINK'
CORAL BELLS
Heuchera x *brizoides*
'Brandon Pink' (top)
(*hue*-kerr-ah x briz-*oi*-deez)

TYPE: perennial
HEIGHT: 60 cm (24 in.)
WIDTH: 30 cm (12 in.)
SOIL: fertile, moist, well drained
LIGHT: light shade to full sun
FLOWERING TIME: early to mid summer
GROWING TIPS: avoid planting in hot, dry areas; use organic mulch for moisture retention and winter protection; deadhead
ALTERNATIVES: *Heuchera americana*, *H. micrantha* 'Palace Purple', *H. sanguinea*

LAMBS' EARS
Stachys byzantina (bottom)
(*sta*-kiss biz-an-*teen*-ah)

TYPE: perennial
HEIGHT: 10 to 45 cm (4 to 18 in.)
WIDTH: 30 cm (12 in.)
SOIL: average, moist, well drained
LIGHT: full sun to light shade
FLOWERING TIME: early summer to fall
GROWING TIPS: requires excellent drainage; deadhead to prevent self-seeding; drought tolerant once established
ALTERNATIVES: *Artemisia absinthium* 'Lambrook Silver', *A. ludoviciana* 'Valerie Finnis'; *Lavandula angustifolia* (lavender); *Perovskia atriplicifolia* (Russian sage)

Heuchera AND *Veronica*

LIESBETH LEATHERBARROW

Individually, coral bells and woolly speedwell are versatile perennials, each complementing a host of summer-blooming plants. Together, these stellar performers, both endowed with long-lasting blooms and delightful foliage, form one of the most satisfactory partnerships in the garden. 'Brandon Pink' produces tidy mounds of attractive lobed leaves that are appealing even without blooms and are a perfect setting for its long-stemmed sprays of delicate, coral-pink bells. Woolly speedwell offers an entirely different flower form, its icy purple-blue floral spires stiff and bristling next to the gently nodding coral bells. Frosty gray foliage completes the cool contrast with 'Brandon Pink'. Some woolly speedwells are mat-forming with pink, blue, or no flowers. 'Wendy' is a tall, blue-flowered cultivar.

'BRANDON PINK'
CORAL BELLS
Heuchera x *brizoides*
'Brandon Pink' (left)
(*hue*-kerr-ah x briz-*oi*-deez)

TYPE: perennial
HEIGHT: 60 cm (24 in.)
WIDTH: 30 cm (12 in.)
SOIL: fertile, moist, well drained
LIGHT: light shade to full sun
FLOWERING TIME: early to mid summer
GROWING TIPS: avoid planting in hot, dry areas; use organic mulch for moisture retention and winter protection; deadhead
ALTERNATIVES: *Heuchera sanguinea;* x *Heucherella* 'Bridget Bloom', 'Rosalie' (foamy bells)

WOOLLY SPEEDWELL
Veronica spicata subsp. *incana* (right)
(ver-*on*-ih-kah spih-*ka*-tah subsp. in-*ka*-nah)

TYPE: perennial
HEIGHT: 30 to 60 cm (12 to 24 in.)
WIDTH: 30 cm (12 in.)
SOIL: fertile, moist, well drained
LIGHT: full to part sun
FLOWERING TIME: early to late summer
GROWING TIPS: use organic mulch for moisture retention and winter protection; deadhead
ALTERNATIVES: *Veronica austriaca* (Hungarian speedwell), *V. spicata* (spike speedwell), *V.* x 'Sunny Border Blue'

Hosta AND *Hosta*

LIESBETH LEATHERBARROW

The possibilities presented by combining hostas in the lightly shaded border are endless. Indeed, with new cultivars being introduced every year in a broad range of color, size, and leaf form, hostas are a collector's dream come true. Available in every shade of yellow, green, and blue, with or without distinct variegations, hostas are also popular for their variable leaf form. Their foliage can be small and dainty or colossal; creeping, mound-forming, or upright; heart-shaped, round, oval, or lance-shaped; and smooth, deeply veined, or even crinkled. With so many options, gardeners can mix and match hostas to their heart's content. The combination of golden yellow 'Fragrant Gold' and variegated 'Ginko Craig' is one of countless hosta partnerships that give an outstanding performance.

'FRAGRANT GOLD' HOSTA
Hosta 'Fragrant Gold' (right)
(*hoss*-tah)

TYPE: perennial
HEIGHT: 45 cm (18 in.)
WIDTH: 60 cm (24 in.)
SOIL: fertile, moist, well drained
LIGHT: part sun to light shade
FLOWERING TIME: early summer to fall
GROWING TIPS: avoid planting in hot, dry areas; plant in sheltered areas; use organic mulch for moisture retention and winter protection; excellent for hiding dying bulb foliage
ALTERNATIVES: *Hosta* 'Lemon Lime', 'Piedmont Gold', 'Sum and Substance'

'GINKO CRAIG' HOSTA
Hosta 'Ginko Craig' (left)
(*hoss*-tah)

TYPE: perennial
HEIGHT: 25 cm (10 in.)
WIDTH: 45 cm (18 in.)
SOIL: fertile, moist, well drained
LIGHT: part sun to full shade
FLOWERING TIME: early summer to fall
GROWING TIPS: avoid planting in hot, dry areas; plant in sheltered areas; use organic mulch for moisture retention and winter protection; excellent for hiding dying bulb foliage
ALTERNATIVES: *Hosta* 'Ground Master', 'Regal Splendor'

Hosta AND *Houttuynia*

LIESBETH LEATHERBARROW

Although abundant variegated foliage can overwhelm even the most accommodating gardener, there are some "busy" combinations worth trying. In this example of white-rimmed hosta paired with 'Chameleon' houttuynia, the hosta is the easygoing member of the team. Its large, bold, textured leaves complement the attractive, multicolored houttuynia leaves, which display irregular bands of green, red, pink, cream, and white. As its heart-shaped leaves unfold, houttuynia produces small flowers consisting of a mass of fuzzy, yellow stamens emerging from the center of four white, petal-like bracts. Although houttuynia grows well in a moist border, it is equally happy with its crown submerged, making it an ideal pondside or water container inhabitant.

HOSTA
Hosta (left)
(*hoss*-tah)

TYPE: perennial
HEIGHT: 25 to 60 cm (10 to 24 in.)
WIDTH: 45 cm (18 in.)
SOIL: fertile, moist, well drained
LIGHT: part sun to full shade
FLOWERING TIME: early summer to fall
GROWING TIPS: avoid planting in hot, dry areas; plant in sheltered areas; use organic mulch for moisture retention and winter protection; excellent for hiding dying bulb foliage
ALTERNATIVES: *Hosta* 'Francee', 'Ground Master', 'Patriot', 'Regal Splendor'

'CHAMELEON' HOUTTUYNIA
Houttuynia cordata 'Chameleon' (right)
(hoo-*tie*-nee-ah kore-*dah*-tah)

TYPE: annual
HEIGHT: 30 cm (12 in.)
WIDTH: 60 cm (24 in.)
SOIL: fertile, moist
LIGHT: full sun to light shade
FLOWERING TIME: late spring
GROWING TIPS: avoid planting in hot, dry areas; may be planted in-ground or in shallow water with crown just below water surface; plant in submerged containers to control spread; use organic mulch for moisture retention when planted in soil
ALTERNATIVE: none

Hydrangea AND *Lilium*

LIESBETH LEATHERBARROW

'Annabelle' is a spectacular plant that stops passersby in their tracks; most are surprised to discover that the shrub with giant, snowball blossoms is a prairie-hardy hydrangea. Its creamy white blossoms, composed of many small flowers, are borne on stiff stems above large, bright green, oval leaves with pointed tips and serrated edges. 'Annabelle' dies back to the ground during cold prairie winters, but blooms on new wood each year. Although a stunning stand-alone plant, 'Annabelle' revels in the company of glorious, orange 'Hornpipe' Asiatic lilies, whose exotic, up-facing, starry flowers offer a complete contrast in form. The white hydrangea cultivar 'Grandiflora' blooms slightly earlier than 'Annabelle'. Other orange Asiatic lilies worth trying include 'Autumn Glory' and 'Beatrix'.

'ANNABELLE' HYDRANGEA

Hydrangea arborescens 'Annabelle' (top)
(hie-*drain*-jee-ah ar-bo-*res*-kens)

TYPE: deciduous shrub
HEIGHT: 1.5 m (5 ft.)
WIDTH: 1.5 m (5 ft.)
SOIL: fertile, moist, well drained
LIGHT: part sun to light shade
FLOWERING TIME: mid-summer to fall
GROWING TIPS: avoid planting in hot, dry areas; use organic mulch for moisture retention and winter protection; blooms may require staking; cut back to 10 cm (4 in.) in late winter; water well in fall
ALTERNATIVE: *Hydrangea paniculata* 'Grandiflora' (Pee Gee hydrangea)

'HORNPIPE' ASIATIC LILY

Lilium x *hybridum* 'Hornpipe' (bottom)
(*lil*-ee-um x *hie*-bri-dum)

TYPE: hardy true bulb
HEIGHT: 90 cm (36 in.)
WIDTH: 30 cm (12 in.)
SOIL: fertile, moist, well drained
LIGHT: full to part sun
FLOWERING TIME: early to mid summer
GROWING TIPS: plant bare bulbs in fall or spring, container-grown plants in spring; use organic mulch for moisture retention and winter protection; deadhead
ALTERNATIVES: Longiflorum-Asiatic hybrids 'Donau', 'Royal Perfume', Royal Sunset', *Lilium lancifolium* (tiger lily)

Impatiens AND *Lobelia*

LESLEY REYNOLDS

In spring, shoppers in prairie garden centers are invariably greeted by flats full of multi-colored impatiens and lobelia, two of the most popular bedding plants in North America. The continual introduction of delightful new cultivars ensures that we never tire of this long-blooming, easy-to-grow pair, perfect pot-mates for a partly sunny deck or patio. Fiesta Series impatiens feature exquisite, fully double blooms that resemble tiny roses. The compact, upright plants have succulent, branching stems and medium green, slightly toothed and scalloped leaves. The popular Regatta Series is a vigorous, trailing lobelia that produces cascades of two-lipped, tubular flowers with five petals. It is available in several colors, including 'Blue Splash', 'Lilac', 'Midnight Blue', and 'Sapphire'.

FIESTA SERIES
DOUBLE IMPATIENS
Impatiens walleriana Fiesta Series (pink)
(im-*pay*-shuns wall-er-ee-*a*-na)

TYPE: annual
HEIGHT: 25 cm (10 in.)
WIDTH: 20 cm (8 in.)
SOIL: average to fertile, moist, well drained
LIGHT: part sun to full shade
FLOWERING TIME: early to late summer
GROWING TIPS: avoid planting in hot, dry areas; fertilize biweekly; pinch back growing tips
ALTERNATIVES: *Impatiens walleriana* Super Elfin Series, Accent Series; *Begonia semperflorens* (wax begonia)

REGATTA SERIES
TRAILING LOBELIA
Lobelia erinus Regatta Series (white)
(low-*bee*-lee-yah *air*-in-us)

TYPE: annual
HEIGHT: 10 to 20 cm (4 to 8 in.)
WIDTH: 10 to 15 cm (4 to 6 in.)
SOIL: average to fertile, moist, well drained
LIGHT: part sun to light shade
FLOWERING TIME: early to late summer
GROWING TIPS: avoid planting in hot, dry areas; fertilize biweekly; trim lightly after flowering
ALTERNATIVES: *Lobelia erinus* Cascade Series; *Bacopa* 'Snowstorm'

Juniperus AND *Picea*

LIESBETH LEATHERBARROW

In winter, the beauty of evergreens never fails to raise the spirits of housebound gardeners. Resplendent in their white winter cloaks, evergreen shrubs protect perennials, dormant bulbs, and small creatures from the bitter cold. Prairie gardeners can choose from many hardy evergreen shrubs, including the new and improved cultivars that enter the market every year. With sizes to suit any garden, junipers offer columnar, weeping, and creeping forms with varied foliage textures and colors. 'Paul's Gold' is a spreading, flat-topped, vase-shaped shrub with scaly, gold-tipped, flat-lying leaves. The bright foliage of 'Paul's Gold' shines against the dark green needles of the nest spruce, a small Norway spruce that produces semi-erect branches curving outward to create a depression that looks like a nest.

'PAUL'S GOLD' JUNIPER

Juniperus x *pfitzeriana*
'Paul's Gold' (bottom)
(you-*nip*-er-us fitz-ur-ee-*an*-ah)

TYPE: evergreen shrub
HEIGHT: 1.2 m (4 ft.)
WIDTH: 3 m (10 ft.)
SOIL: average, well drained
LIGHT: full sun
FLOWERING TIME: not applicable
GROWING TIPS: drought tolerant once established, but gold-leaved varieties may become dessicated in extremely hot and dry locations; prune in spring to remove dead branches; if desired, prune lightly to shape in summer; water well in fall
ALTERNATIVE: *Juniperus communis* 'Depressa Aurea' (common juniper)

NEST SPRUCE

Picea abies 'Nidiformis' (top)
(pie-*see*-ah *eh*-bees)

TYPE: evergreen shrub
HEIGHT: 90 to 120 cm (36 to 48 in.)
WIDTH: 1.2 to 1.5 m (4 to 5 ft.)
SOIL: fertile, moist, well drained
LIGHT: full to part sun
FLOWERING TIME: not applicable
GROWING TIPS: use organic mulch for moisture retention and winter protection; water well in fall before ground freezes
ALTERNATIVES: *Picea pungens* f. *glauca* 'Globosa' (Globe Colorado blue spruce), 'Procumbens'

Lactuca AND *Tropaeolum*

LIESBETH LEATHERBARROW

A vegetable plot may be out of the question in a small garden. However, you don't have to give up the idea of fresh salad greens and herbs; most will grow happily in a large container located within easy reach of the kitchen. Lettuce comes in many types and textures, including soft leaf lettuce and crispy cos (romaine), butterhead, and iceberg. Both edible and ornamental, leaf lettuce cultivars may be light to deep green, red, or bronze in color; some even have attractively crinkled leaves. Complement decorative lettuce with sprightly, edible, yellow, orange, and red Alaska Series nasturtiums, which feature cream-marbled leaves. Not only are nasturtium flowers and leaves a peppery addition to a green salad, but the young seedpods may also be pickled as a substitute for capers.

LETTUCE
Lactuca sativa (top)
(lak-*too*-kah sa-*tee*-vah)

TYPE: annual
HEIGHT: 15 to 45 cm (6 to 18 in.)
WIDTH: 15 to 30 cm (6 to 12 in.)
SOIL: fertile, moist, well drained
LIGHT: part sun to light shade
FLOWERING TIME: not applicable
GROWING TIPS: avoid planting in hot, dry areas; make successive plantings every two to three weeks; prone to slugs
ALTERNATIVES: *Eruca vesicaria* (arugula); *Beta vulgaris* var. *flavescens* 'Bright Lights' (multicolored Swiss chard)

ALASKA SERIES NASTURTIUM
Tropaeolum Alaska Series (bottom)
(tro-*pie*-oh-lum)

TYPE: annual
HEIGHT: 30 cm (12 in.)
WIDTH: 45 cm (18 in.)
SOIL: poor to average, well drained
LIGHT: full to part sun
FLOWERING TIME: early to late summer
GROWING TIPS: can be seeded directly outdoors; do not fertilize; deadhead
ALTERNATIVES: *Tropaeolum majus* (common nasturtium); *Calendula officinalis* (pot marigold); *Tagetes tenuifolia* (edible citrus-scented marigold)

Lavatera AND *Rosa*

LIESBETH LEATHERBARROW

Canadian-bred Explorer and Parkland Series roses have left an indelible mark on prairie gardens, dazzling their owners with untold beauty, fragrance, disease resistance, and long periods of continuous bloom. 'Adelaide Hoodless', released in 1973, is a very red, very vigorous Parkland Series rose. Plants produce elegant double flowers in extravagant clusters that sometimes contain as many as thirty-five blossoms each! Because this rose puts on such a lavish mid-summer display, one approach is to give it a partner with clean, simple lines. 'Pink Beauty' rose mallow, a shrubby annual with large, hibiscuslike blossoms, is the perfect match for 'Adelaide Hoodless'. Prominent, deep red veining of its pale pink, saucer-shaped flowers establishes a strong bond between 'Pink Beauty' and the rose.

'PINK BEAUTY' ROSE MALLOW
Lavatera trimestris
'Pink Beauty' (bottom)
(la-vah-*tair*-ah tri-*mess*-triss)

TYPE: annual
HEIGHT: 60 to 120 cm (24 to 48 in.)
WIDTH: 45 cm (18 in.)
SOIL: average to fertile, well drained
LIGHT: full sun
FLOWERING TIME: mid to late summer
GROWING TIPS: plant in sheltered areas; fertilize biweekly; deadhead
ALTERNATIVES: *Alcea rosea* (hollyhock); *Malope trifida* (annual mallow); *Malva moschata* (musk mallow), *M. sylvestris* (high mallow)

'ADELAIDE HOODLESS' ROSE
Rosa 'Adelaide Hoodless' (top)
(*roh*-zah)

TYPE: deciduous shrub
HEIGHT: 90 cm (36 in.)
WIDTH: 90 cm (36 in.)
SOIL: fertile, moist, well drained
LIGHT: full sun
FLOWERING TIME: early summer; some repeat blooming
GROWING TIPS: use organic mulch for moisture retention and winter protection; fertilize regularly; deadhead; prune in spring to remove tip kill and old woody canes; water well in fall
ALTERNATIVES: *Rosa* 'John Franklin', 'Morden Cardinette', 'Winnipeg Parks'

Ligularia AND *Rudbeckia*

'Othello' ligularia and 'Goldsturm' rudbeckia appear an unlikely duo at first thought—after all, 'Othello' prefers some shade, while 'Goldsturm' loves sun. However, given moist, mulched soil and a little mid-afternoon shade, 'Othello' performs well in otherwise sunny conditions. It is a striking feature plant for the back of the border with huge, toothed, heart-shaped leaves that emerge a deep mahogany red in spring, maturing to dark purple. Rising from amid its long-stemmed leaves are rounded clusters of yellow-orange, daisylike flowers composed of ray florets surrounding a dark brown disk. A sturdy daisy of a different sort, 'Goldsturm' mirrors 'Othello' with golden yellow petals encircling dark brown disks. It has rough, dark green, oval to lance-shaped leaves and branching flower stems.

'OTHELLO' LIGULARIA

Ligularia dentata 'Othello' (top)
(lig-ew-*lah*-ree-ah den-*tah*-tah)

TYPE: perennial
HEIGHT: 1.2 m (4 ft.)
WIDTH: 1.0 m (3.3 ft.)
SOIL: fertile, moist
LIGHT: light shade to part sun
FLOWERING TIME: mid to late summer
GROWING TIPS: avoid planting in hot, dry areas; use organic mulch for moisture retention and winter protection
FLOWERING TIME: mid to late summer
ALTERNATIVES: *Ligularia* 'Gregynog Gold', *L. hodgsonii*, *L. przewalskii*, *L. stenocephala* 'The Rocket' (rayflower)

'GOLDSTURM' RUDBECKIA

Rudbeckia fulgida var. *sullivantii* 'Goldsturm' (bottom)
(rude-*beck*-ee-ah *full*-gi-dah var. sull-i-*van*-te-ee)

TYPE: perennial
HEIGHT: 60 cm (24 in.)
WIDTH: 60 cm (24 in.)
SOIL: average to fertile, well drained
LIGHT: full to part sun
FLOWERING TIME: mid-summer to fall
GROWING TIPS: deadhead to prevent self-seeding and encourage reblooming
ALTERNATIVES: *Rudbeckia fulgida* (black-eyed Susan), annual *R. hirta* (gloriosa daisy); *Helenium autumnale* (sneezeweed); *Heliopsis helianthoides* (false sunflower)

Lilium AND *Verbascum*

LIESBETH LEATHERBARROW

For most gardeners there is no such thing as too many lilies, and indeed, it is a rare prairie garden that doesn't boast several of these versatile plants. Their showy trumpet-shaped blossoms herald the onset of summer, and depending on the hybrid and cultivar, provide dependable accents to mixed borders throughout the growing season. Lilies have the added advantage of combining well with just about any other plant. An equally outstanding perennial that overlaps in bloom time with mid-season Asiatic lilies is the nettle-leaved mullein. Contributing an attractive vertical accent to mixed and perennial borders, the mullein's sturdy flower spikes are smothered in tight buds that, throughout the summer, gradually transform into soft yellow, outward-facing blossoms, each with a reddish purple eye.

ASIATIC LILY
Lilium x *hybridum* (right)
(*lil*-ee-um x *hie*-bri-dum)

TYPE: hardy true bulb
HEIGHT: 45 to 150 cm (18 to 60 in.)
WIDTH: 30 to 45 cm (12 to 18 in.)
SOIL: fertile, moist, well drained
LIGHT: full sun
FLOWERING TIME: early to mid summer
GROWING TIPS: plant bare bulbs in fall or spring, container-grown plants in spring; use organic mulch for moisture retention and winter protection; deadhead
ALTERNATIVES: Aurelian-Asiatic hybrids, Longiflorum-Asiatic hybrids, *Lilium martagon, L. monadelphum*

NETTLE-LEAVED MULLEIN
Verbascum chaixii (left)
(ver-*bass*-kum *shay*-zee-ee)

TYPE: perennial
HEIGHT: 90 cm (36 in.)
WIDTH: 45 cm (18 in.)
SOIL: poor to average, well drained
LIGHT: full sun
FLOWERING TIME: mid to late summer
GROWING TIPS: soil that is too moist or fertile may shorten the plant's lifespan or necessitate staking; drought tolerant once established
ALTERNATIVES: *Verbascum* x *hybridum, V. nigrum* (black mullein), *V. phoeniceum* (purple mullein); *Digitalis purpurea* (common foxglove)

Lilium AND *Veronica*

LIESBETH LEATHERBARROW

The explosion of new lily hybrids and cultivars in the past few years has made these spectacular flowers more popular than ever. Early-blooming, dependable Asiatics are the easiest to grow, but new prairie-bred hybrids are outstanding choices for all gardeners. Whether they are brilliant shades of orange, red, or coral, or soft pastel hues of pink, yellow, or creamy white, all lilies look fabulous next to brilliant blue spike speedwell. In contrast to the visual feast of opulent bowl-, trumpet-, or star-shaped lily flowers, the intensely colored, bottle-brush spikes of speedwell blossoms are composed of many small, individual blooms, with crinkled and toothed leaves that complement the glossy smoothness of the lily foliage. 'Blue Charm' and 'Goodness Grows' are recommended cultivars.

ASIATIC LILY
Lilium x *hybridum* (left)
(*lil*-ee-um x *hie*-bri-dum)

TYPE: hardy true bulb
HEIGHT: 45 to 150 cm (18 to 60 in.)
WIDTH: 30 to 45 cm (12 to 18 in.)
SOIL: fertile, moist, well drained
LIGHT: full sun
FLOWERING TIME: early to mid summer
GROWING TIPS: plant bare bulbs in fall or spring, container-grown plants in spring; use organic mulch for moisture retention and winter protection; deadhead
ALTERNATIVES: Aurelian-Asiatic hybrids, Longiflorum-Asiatic hybrids, *Lilium martagon, L. monadelphum*

SPIKE SPEEDWELL
Veronica spicata (right)
(ver-*on*-ih-kah spih-*ka*-tah)

TYPE: perennial
HEIGHT: 30 to 60 cm (12 to 24 in.)
WIDTH: 30 cm (12 in.)
SOIL: fertile, moist, well drained
LIGHT: full to part sun
FLOWERING TIME: early to mid summer
GROWING TIPS: use organic mulch for moisture retention and winter protection; deadhead
ALTERNATIVES: *Veronica austriaca* (Hungarian speedwell), *V.* x 'Sunny Border Blue'; *Nepeta* x *faassenii*, *N. racemosa, N. sibirica* (catmint)

Lonicera AND *Parthenocissus*

LIESBETH LEATHERBARROW

Whether they are clothing fences, scrambling up trees or wall-mounted trellises, or draping a pergola or arbor, vines give gardens an old-world charm. Planted side by side, hardy 'Dropmore Scarlet' honeysuckle and Virginia creeper combine to enhance gardens with brilliant flowers and lush foliage from early summer well into fall. Enthusiastic climbers, both vines require some means of support. 'Dropmore Scarlet', developed by Dr. Frank Skinner in Manitoba, bears a profusion of bright scarlet, two-lipped, tubular flowers in terminal clusters all summer long. A handsome foliage plant, Virginia creeper has deep green leaves consisting of five oval, sharply toothed leaflets that turn a fabulous burgundy red in September. 'Engelmannii' is a slightly smaller, less hardy, self-supporting cultivar.

'DROPMORE SCARLET'
CLIMBING HONEYSUCKLE

Lonicera x *brownii*
'Dropmore Scarlet' (left)
(lon-ih-*sair*-ah x *brown*-ee-ee)

TYPE: perennial vine
HEIGHT: 5 m (16 ft.)
WIDTH: 2 m (6.5 ft.)
SOIL: fertile, moist, well drained
LIGHT: full to part sun
FLOWERING TIME: early to late summer
GROWING TIPS: use organic mulch for moisture retention and winter protection; prune after flowering
ALTERNATIVES: *Clematis orientalis*, *C. tangutica* (golden clematis)

VIRGINIA CREEPER

Parthenocissus quinquefolia (right)
(par-then-oh-*kis*-us kwin-kwe-*foh*-lee-ah)

TYPE: perennial vine
HEIGHT: 15 m (50 ft.)
WIDTH: 1 m (3.3 ft.)
SOIL: average to fertile, well drained
LIGHT: full sun to light shade
FLOWERING TIME: inconspicuous flowers in mid-summer
GROWING TIPS: drought tolerant once established; if pruning is necessary to tidy vine, it is easiest to prune while dormant
ALTERNATIVES: *Humulus lupulus* (hops); *Vitis riparia* (riverbank grape)

Lupinus AND *Rosa*

LIESBETH LEATHERBARROW

A combination of sweetly scented roses and aristocratic lupines is the essence of an English cottage garden. Unfortunately, lupine hybrids are not fond of prairie growing conditions. Our alkaline soils, drying winds, and hot temperatures often result in stressed, aphid-susceptible plants. However, if you crave the look of lupines in your garden, consider growing silvery lupine, a native prairie wildflower. With a softer, much less formal look than its hybrid cousins, its loose spires of bluish violet, pealike blossoms and deeply divided, silvery foliage show to advantage beside short, pastel pink hardy shrub roses such as 'Lambert Closse'. A very floriferous member of the Explorer Series, this rose produces deep pink buds that fade to a lovely pale pink as they open and mature.

SILVERY LUPINE
Lupinus argenteus (top)
(loo-*pee*-nuss ar-*jen*-tee-uss)

TYPE: perennial
HEIGHT: 30 to 60 cm (12 to 24 in.)
WIDTH: 30 to 60 cm (12 to 24 in.)
SOIL: poor to average, moist, well drained
LIGHT: full to part sun
FLOWERING TIME: early to mid summer
GROWING TIPS: requires excellent drainage; deadhead to prevent self-seeding; drought tolerant once established
ALTERNATIVES: *Lupinus* Gallery Hybrids, Minarette Hybrids, Russell Hybrids

'LAMBERT CLOSSE' ROSE
Rosa 'Lambert Closse' (bottom)
(*roh*-zah)

TYPE: deciduous shrub
HEIGHT: 90 cm (36 in.)
WIDTH: 90 cm (36 in.)
SOIL: fertile, moist, well drained
LIGHT: full sun
FLOWERING TIME: early summer; some repeat blooming
GROWING TIPS: use organic mulch for moisture retention and winter protection; fertilize regularly; deadhead; prune in spring to remove tip kill and old woody canes; water well in fall
ALTERNATIVES: *Rosa* 'Charles Albanel', 'Frontenac', 'Morden Blush'

Lychnis AND *Sambucus*

LESLEY REYNOLDS

The elder, with its attractive foliage, delicately scented blossoms, and colorful fruit, is one of many hardy, low-maintenance shrubs that offer great potential for interest in the mixed border. Butterflies and birds rely on the elder for food and shelter, making it a superb choice for a wildlife garden. 'Aurea' is a golden-leaved version of the American elder, a fast-growing, native North American shrub, well suited to an informal garden. Its leaves are composed of nine or more leaflets that serve as a bright backdrop to white flower clusters in spring, followed by red berries in summer. Accompany 'Aurea' with Maltese cross, an upright, old-fashioned perennial with rounded clusters of vibrant, orange-scarlet flowers that blaze like hot coals against the elder's golden leaves.

MALTESE CROSS

Lychnis chalcedonica (bottom)
(*lick*-niss kal-ky-*don*-i-ka)

TYPE: perennial
HEIGHT: 1.2 m (4 ft.)
WIDTH: 60 cm (24 in.)
SOIL: average to fertile, moist, well drained
LIGHT: full to part sun
FLOWERING TIME: early to mid summer
GROWING TIPS: avoid planting in hot, dry areas; use organic mulch for moisture retention and winter protection; may require staking; deadhead to encourage reblooming
ALTERNATIVES: *Lychnis* x *arkwrightii* 'Vesuvius', *L. haageana* (campion)

GOLDEN AMERICAN ELDER

Sambucus canadensis 'Aurea' (top)
(sam-*boo*-kus ka-na-*den*-siss)

TYPE: deciduous shrub
HEIGHT: 2 m (6.5 ft.)
WIDTH: 1.8 m (6 ft.)
SOIL: fertile, moist, well drained
LIGHT: full sun to light shade
FLOWERING TIME: late spring
GROWING TIPS: prefers full sun to maintain golden color, but burns if sun gets too hot; prune when dormant; water well in fall
ALTERNATIVES: *Sambucus nigra* 'Aurea' (black elder), *S. racemosa* 'Sutherland Golden', 'Plumosa Aurea' (European red elder)

Lysimachia AND *Paeonia*

LIESBETH LEATHERBARROW

Although at first glance yellow loosestrife (not to be confused with noxious purple loosestrife) and peonies seem to make strange bedfellows, a closer look shows why they work so well together. Simply put, they are a study in opposites, strongly linked by a common color—brilliant yellow. Nestled at the blossom centers of many peony cultivars is a showy boss of stamens/staminoids the exact same shade as the bright yellow flowers of loosestrife. However, that is where the similarity ends. Whereas loosestrife blossoms are star-shaped and hug erect stems above whorled, lance-shaped leaves, peonies produce lavish, large-petaled, single, semi-double, and double blossoms above shrubby clumps of shiny, deeply lobed, dark green foliage. Even the simple common peony works well with loosestrife.

YELLOW LOOSESTRIFE

Lysimachia punctata (top)
(li-si-*mak*-ee-ah punk-*tah*-tah)

TYPE: perennial
HEIGHT: 90 cm (36 in.)
WIDTH: 60 cm (24 in.)
SOIL: fertile, moist
LIGHT: full to part sun
FLOWERING TIME: early to late summer
GROWING TIPS: avoid planting in hot, dry areas; use organic mulch for moisture retention and winter protection; deadhead to prevent self-seeding
ALTERNATIVES: *Coreopsis lanceolata* (lance-leaved tickseed), *C. verticillata* 'Golden Shower', 'Zagreb' (thread-leaved tickseed)

COMMON PEONY

Paeonia officinalis (bottom)
(pay-*own*-ee-ah o-fi-ki-*nah*-lis)

TYPE: perennial
HEIGHT: 90 cm (36 in.)
WIDTH: 90 cm (36 in.)
SOIL: fertile, moist, well drained
LIGHT: full sun
FLOWERING TIME: late spring to early summer
GROWING TIPS: plant the crown no deeper than 5 cm (2 in.); use organic mulch for moisture retention and winter protection; requires staking; deadhead; susceptible to botrytis
ALTERNATIVES: *Paeonia* 'Auguste Dessert', 'Constance Spry', 'Dragon's Nest'

Lysimachia AND *Salix*

LIESBETH LEATHERBARROW

An identical color shared between species in a plant partnership forges a strong visual bond. Such a color link exists between 'Firecracker' fringed loosestrife and 'Nana' dwarf arctic willow, making this an excellent combination for pondside plantings or mixed borders. The purple-brown foliage of 'Firecracker' is the same color as the straight but supple, non-branching stems belonging to 'Nana'. A finely textured shrub, 'Nana' produces linear, two-tone foliage immediately after catkins emerge in mid-spring. Its attractive, bicolor leaves are blue-green on top and silver-gray on the underside. Like 'Annabelle' hydrangea, 'Nana' dies back to the snowline, but yearly rejuvenation pruning results in colorful first-year growth for continuous interest in the landscape.

'FIRECRACKER' FRINGED LOOSESTRIFE
Lysimachia ciliata 'Firecracker' (bottom)
(li-si-*mak*-ee-ah ki-lee-*ah*-tah)

TYPE: perennial
HEIGHT: 90 cm (36 in.)
WIDTH: 60 cm (24 in.)
SOIL: fertile, moist
LIGHT: full to part sun
FLOWERING TIME: mid-summer
GROWING TIPS: avoid planting in hot, dry areas; use organic mulch for moisture retention and winter protection
ALTERNATIVES: *Lysimachia punctata* (yellow loosestrife), *L. clethroides* (gooseneck loosestrife)

DWARF ARCTIC WILLOW
Salix purpurea 'Nana' (top)
(*say*-licks purr-*purr*-ee-ah)

TYPE: deciduous shrub
HEIGHT: 1.2 m (4 ft.)
WIDTH: 1.2 m (4 ft.)
SOIL: average, moist
LIGHT: full sun to light shade
FLOWERING TIME: mid-spring
GROWING TIPS: use organic mulch for moisture retention and winter protection; drought tolerant once established; cut back to 10 cm (4 in.) in late winter; water well in fall
ALTERNATIVES: *Salix brachycarpa* 'Blue Fox', *S. exigua* (coyote willow), *S.* 'Flame'

Lysimachia AND *Salvia*

LIESBETH LEATHERBARROW

Spiky plants, whether they are short or tall, make wonderful vertical accents in flower beds. Their shape provides a welcome visual break for observers as their eyes rove from one end of a flower border to the other. One approach with spiky plants is to cluster two or more species with an upright aspect; another is to group different colors of the same species. The combination of 'Alexander' yellow loosestrife, and 'Snowhill' (white) and 'May Night' (indigo blue) sage incorporates both these ideas. 'Alexander' is a tidy yellow loosestrife cultivar, identified by its green leaves edged in cream and its bright yellow, out-facing flowers. The neighboring sages form tidy clumps; their aromatic, triangular leaves and small, tubular flowers also hug narrow, erect spikes.

'ALEXANDER' YELLOW LOOSESTRIFE

Lysimachia punctata 'Alexander' (right)
(li-si-*mak*-ee-ah punk-*tah*-tah)

TYPE: perennial
HEIGHT: 90 cm (36 in.)
WIDTH: 60 cm (24 in.)
SOIL: fertile, moist
LIGHT: full to part sun
FLOWERING TIME: early to late summer
GROWING TIPS: avoid planting in hot, dry areas; use organic mulch for moisture retention and winter protection
ALTERNATIVES: *Lysimachia punctata* (yellow loosestrife), *L. clethroides* (gooseneck loosestrife)

SAGE

Salvia x *sylvestris* (left)
(*sal*-vee-ah x sill-*vess*-tris)

TYPE: perennial
HEIGHT: 70 cm (28 in.)
WIDTH: 45 cm (18 in.)
SOIL: average, well drained
LIGHT: full to part sun
FLOWERING TIME: mid-summer to fall
GROWING TIPS: requires excellent drainage; too much water and fertilizer cause legginess; drought tolerant once established
ALTERNATIVES: annual *Salvia farinacea* (mealycup sage), *S. verticillata*, *S. viridis* (clary sage)

Matteuccia AND *Polygonatum*

LESLEY REYNOLDS

Many graceful ferns are available to prairie gardeners, but none is so hardy and easy to grow as the ostrich fern. This elegant, vase-shaped, North American native spreads by rhizomes, making it an excellent groundcover for planting beneath deciduous trees or for naturalization beside a pond. The ostrich fern has large, erect fronds composed of many pale green leaflets; smaller, dark brown, fertile fronds appear in the summer. Transform a patch of ostrich ferns into a woodland garden with the addition of variegated Solomon's seal. This exceptional perennial has arching stems clothed with alternating, elliptical leaves edged in creamy white. Adding to its charm are sweetly fragrant, white, bell-shaped flowers that dangle from the leaf axils and mature into blue-black berries in the fall.

OSTRICH FERN

Matteuccia struthiopteris (top)
(ma-*too*-key-ah stroo-thee-*op*-ter-iss)

TYPE: perennial
HEIGHT: 90 to 120 cm (36 to 48 in.)
WIDTH: 60 to 90 cm (24 to 36 in.)
SOIL: average to fertile, moist
LIGHT: full shade to part sun
FLOWERING TIME: not applicable
GROWING TIPS: avoid planting in hot, dry areas; plant with crowns just below soil level; use organic mulch for moisture retention; plant in sheltered areas
ALTERNATIVES: *Osmunda regalis* (Royal fern), *O. cinnamomea* (cinnamon fern), *O. claytoniana* (interrupted fern)

VARIEGATED SOLOMON'S SEAL

Polygonatum odoratum 'Variegatum' (bottom)
(po-lih-go-*na*-tum oh-dor-*a*-tum)

TYPE: perennial
HEIGHT: 60 cm (24 in.)
WIDTH: 30 cm (12 in.)
SOIL: fertile, moist, well drained
LIGHT: full shade to part sun
FLOWERING TIME: late spring
GROWING TIPS: avoid planting in hot, dry areas; use organic mulch for moisture retention and winter protection
ALTERNATIVES: *Polygonatum biflorum* (small Solomon's seal), *P. multiflorum* (Eurasian Solomon's seal)

Monarda AND *Veronicastrum*

LIESBETH LEATHERBARROW

Just as the familiar spires of spike speedwell begin to fade in mid-summer, the less familiar Culver's root is initiating a similarly lovely spiky display. Once actually classified as speedwell, Culver's root now occupies a genus of its own, producing candelabra-style spires of tubular, white, pale pink, or purplish white flowers. Long, protruding stamens add a delicate, lacy aspect to the flower spikes. This elegant plant adds a pleasing vertical accent to late-summer mixed borders and is perfect paired with the likes of shaggy monarda by virtue of its contrasting flower form. Attractive to bees and butterflies, monarda has aromatic foliage and tubular flowers arranged in rounded tufts, supported by colored bracts. Medium pink 'Marshall's Delight' is especially resistant to powdery mildew.

'MARSHALL'S DELIGHT'
MONARDA

Monarda didyma
'Marshall's Delight' (top)
(moh-*nar*-dah dih-*dih*-mah)

TYPE: perennial
HEIGHT: 90 cm (36 in.)
WIDTH: 60 cm (24 in.)
SOIL: average to fertile, moist, well drained
LIGHT: full sun to light shade
FLOWERING TIME: mid-summer to fall
GROWING TIPS: avoid planting in hot, dry areas; use organic mulch for moisture retention and winter protection; deadhead
ALTERNATIVE: *Monarda fistulosa* (wild bee balm)

CULVER'S ROOT

Veronicastrum virginicum (bottom)
(ve-ro-ni-*kas*-trum vir-*jin*-i-kum)

TYPE: perennial
HEIGHT: 60 cm (24 in.)
WIDTH: 45 cm (18 in.)
SOIL: fertile, moist, well drained
LIGHT: full sun to light shade
FLOWERING TIME: mid-summer to fall
GROWING TIPS: use organic mulch for moisture retention and winter protection; deadhead; drought tolerant once established
ALTERNATIVES: *Lysimachia clethroides* (gooseneck loosestrife); *Veronica spicata* 'Snow White' (spike speedwell), *V. longifolia* 'Icicles' (longleaf speedwell)

Nemesia AND *Osteospermum*

LIESBETH LEATHERBARROW

Osteospermum, the African daisy, is one genus among a bouquet of sun-loving, daisylike annuals hailing from Africa that are winning favor in prairie container gardens. *Dimorphotheca*, a close relative, is also commonly known as African daisy. Delightful annuals for sunny, hot locations, *Osteospermum* cultivars expand the daisy palette from shades of yellow to include cool blues and violets, hot magentas and pinks, and blue- and purple-tinted whites, many with centers and petal backs of beautifully contrasting colors. Accompany long-blooming *Osteospermum* with annuals of a daintier aspect in harmonizing colors, such as *Nemesia caerulea*, a taller version of the commonly grown *Nemesia strumosa*. This versatile annual features racemes of two-lipped, blue, pink, or white flowers with yellow throats.

NEMESIA

Nemesia caerulea (bottom)
(nem-*ee*-sha kye-*ru*-lee-ah)

TYPE: annual
HEIGHT: 30 to 60 cm (12 to 24 in.)
WIDTH: 30 cm (12 in.)
SOIL: fertile, moist, well drained
LIGHT: full to part sun
FLOWERING TIME: late spring to late summer
GROWING TIPS: fertilize biweekly; in areas with hot, dry summers, provide shade from afternoon sun; deadhead; pinch back growing tips
ALTERNATIVES: *Nemesia strumosa*; *Schizanthus pinnatus, S.* x *wisetonensis* (butterfly flower)

AFRICAN DAISY

Osteospermum (top)
(oss-tee-oh-*spur*-mum)

TYPE: annual
HEIGHT: 15 to 30 cm (6 to 12 in.)
WIDTH: 15 to 30 cm (6 to 12 in.)
SOIL: average to fertile, well drained
LIGHT: full sun
FLOWERING TIME: early to late summer
GROWING TIPS: fertilize biweekly; deadhead; pinch back growing tips
ALTERNATIVES: *Osteospermum caulescens, O. ecklonis, O. jucundum*; *Argyranthemum* cultivars (Cobbity daisy); *Dimorphotheca* cultivars (African daisy, cape marigold); *Gazania* cultivars

Nemesia AND *Pelargonium*

LESLEY REYNOLDS

Despite their common name, zonal geraniums are not members of the *Geranium* (cranesbill) genus, belonging instead to the *Pelargonium* (stork's bill) genus. Whatever you call them, these dashing kings of the container garden are long blooming and easy to grow. Geranium colors range from hot and fluorescent to cool and pale, but it is the red geranium that is the horticultural equivalent of the little black dress—it never goes out of style. The geranium's dense, globe-shaped clusters of orange- to scarlet-red flowers benefit from daintier companions, such as a striking red and white nemesia cultivar. Nemesia flowers are small, trumpet-shaped, and two-lipped, and their lance-shaped, toothed leaves are a pleasing change of shape and texture from the large, scalloped geranium leaves.

NEMESIA

Nemesia strumosa (top)
(nem-*ee*-sha stroo-*mo*-sa)

TYPE: annual
HEIGHT: 15 to 30 cm (6 to 12 in.)
WIDTH: 10 to 15 cm (4 to 6 in.)
SOIL: fertile, moist, well drained
LIGHT: full to part sun
FLOWERING TIME: late spring to late summer
GROWING TIPS: fertilize biweekly; in areas with hot, dry summers, provide shade from afternoon sun; deadhead; pinch back growing tips
ALTERNATIVES: *Lobelia erinus* cultivars

ZONAL GERANIUM

Pelargonium x *hortorum* (bottom)
(pell-are-*go*-nee-um x hor-*tor*-um)

TYPE: annual
HEIGHT: 30 to 90 cm (12 to 36 in.)
WIDTH: 30 to 45 cm (12 to 18 in.)
SOIL: fertile, moist, well drained
LIGHT: full to part sun
FLOWERING TIME: early summer to fall
GROWING TIPS: fertilize biweekly; deadhead; pinch back growing tips
ALTERNATIVES: *Pelargonium* x *domesticum* (Martha Washington geranium), *P. peltatum* (ivy-leaved geranium)

Nepeta AND *Penstemon*

LIESBETH LEATHERBARROW

Plant combinations based on bold contrast are usually easy to spot and can often be appreciated from afar. Duos based on more subtle differences are less obvious but equally delightful once they are discovered. Both 'Six Hills Giant' catmint and 'Husker Red' beardtongue have tubular, two-lipped blossoms that look similar until you get up close. Then you discover that catmint "lips" are irregularly shaped and beardtongue "lips" are beautifully lobed. Furthermore, whereas 'Husker Red' produces up to fifty creamy white blooms on each upright, red flower stalk—a stunning contrast to its wine red foliage—'Six Hills Giant' bears tall spikes of striking lavender-blue blossoms above gray-green, textured leaves. Although delicate in appearance, this plant combination is definitely a winner!

CATMINT
Nepeta x *faassenii*
'Six Hills Giant' (purple)
(*ne*-peh-tah x fah-*sen*-ee-ee)

TYPE: perennial
HEIGHT: 90 cm (36 in.)
WIDTH: 60 cm (24 in.)
SOIL: average, moist, well drained
LIGHT: full sun to light shade
FLOWERING TIME: early summer to fall
GROWING TIPS: use organic mulch for moisture retention and winter protection; shear after flowering to keep plant compact; drought tolerant once established
ALTERNATIVES: *Nepeta racemosa*, *N. sibirica*

'HUSKER RED' WHITE BEARDTONGUE
Penstemon digitalis 'Husker Red' (white)
(*pen*-ste-mon di-ji-*ta*-liss)

TYPE: perennial
HEIGHT: 76 cm (30 in.)
WIDTH: 30 cm (12 in.)
SOIL: average to fertile, well drained
LIGHT: full sun to light shade
FLOWERING TIME: early to mid summer
GROWING TIPS: requires excellent drainage; use organic mulch for moisture retention and winter protection; deadhead
ALTERNATIVES: *Penstemon barbatus* (common beardtongue), *P. strictus* (stiff beardtongue); *Physostegia virginiana* (obedient plant)

Nepeta AND *Potentilla*

Two robust plants that put on an outstanding, long-lived display of color in prairie gardens are catmint and potentilla. Each is a brilliant performer in its own right and a very compatible partner for dozens of garden inhabitants in sunny borders, but together they strike the perfect balance between vibrant color and complementary form. Catmint's misty clouds of lavender-blue, two-lipped blossoms crown compact mounds of soft, textured, gray-green leaves. In contrast, attractive potentilla blossoms are buttercuplike—broadly bowl-shaped with five smooth, rounded petals. Originally available only in bright yellow, potentillas now boast a range of blossom colors, from white ('Abbotswood') to yellow ('Goldfinger'), and orange ('Mango Tango') to pink ('Pink Beauty') to red ('Red Robin').

CATMINT

Nepeta x *faassenii* (left)
(*ne*-peh-tah x fah-*sen*-ee-ee)

TYPE: perennial
HEIGHT: 45 cm (18 in.)
WIDTH: 45 cm (18 in.)
SOIL: average, moist, well drained
LIGHT: full sun to light shade
FLOWERING TIME: early summer to fall
GROWING TIPS: use organic mulch for moisture retention and winter protection; shear after flowering to keep plant compact; drought tolerant once established
ALTERNATIVES: *Nepeta racemosa*, *N. sibirica*

POTENTILLA

Potentilla fruticosa (right)
(po-ten-*till*-ah froo-ti-*ko*-sah)

TYPE: deciduous shrub
HEIGHT: 90 cm (36 in.)
WIDTH: 90 cm (36 in.)
SOIL: average, well drained
LIGHT: full to part sun
FLOWERING TIME: late spring to fall
GROWING TIPS: use organic mulch for moisture retention; prune in early spring, removing dead or weak growth at ground level; thin out older branches to prevent crowding; water well in fall
ALTERNATIVES: *Caragana frutex* 'Globosa' (globe caragana), *C. pygmaea* (pygmy caragana)

Opuntia AND *Sedum*

LIESBETH LEATHERBARROW

The duo of plains prickly pear cactus and two-row stonecrop is a perfect, carefree constituent of xeriscape gardens, eschewing the need for supplementary water once established. Evoking images of the desert, plains prickly pear cactus is a native species that consists of flattened, club-shaped, segmented pads covered in clusters of five to nine mixed, short and long spines that can cause intense skin irritation and are often difficult to remove, so beware! Its bright yellow to pinkish orange flowers are numerous and usually bloom over an extended period, from mid-June to July. Two-row stonecrop is a vigorous, extremely adaptable, succulent groundcover. In late summer, it produces a profusion of rosy magenta-red, star-shaped flowers above a mat of fleshy, toothed leaves.

PLAINS PRICKLY PEAR CACTUS
Opuntia polyacantha (top)
(oh-*pun*-tee-ah po-lee-ah-*kanth*-a)

TYPE: perennial
HEIGHT: 15 to 30 cm (6 to 12 in.)
WIDTH: 90 cm (36 in.)
SOIL: poor to average, gritty, well drained
LIGHT: full sun
FLOWERING TIME: late spring to early summer
GROWING TIPS: plant in sheltered areas; requires excellent drainage; mulch with layer of grit to prevent rotting at soil level
ALTERNATIVES: *Opuntia compressa* (compressed prickly pear cactus), *O. fragilis* (brittle prickly pear cactus)

TWO-ROW STONECROP
Sedum spurium (bottom)
(*see*-dum *spur*-ee-em)

TYPE: groundcover
HEIGHT: 10 cm (4 in.)
WIDTH: 60 cm (24 in.)
SOIL: poor to average, well drained
LIGHT: full sun to light shade
FLOWERING TIME: early to late summer
GROWING TIPS: requires excellent drainage; trim lightly after flowering to maintain shape; drought tolerant once established
ALTERNATIVES: *Sedum elwesii*, *S. kamtschaticum* 'Rosy Glow', *S.* 'Vera Jameson'

Osmunda AND *Saxifraga*

LIESBETH LEATHERBARROW

An unexpected pairing at first glance, the duo of interrupted fern and golden London pride saxifrage performs sensationally in shady borders and woodland gardens. A lovely foliage plant and also one of the easiest to grow, the interrupted fern has slightly arching fronds divided into many segments. Some inner fronds also have brownish, spore-bearing leaflets that wither and drop once the spores have been dispersed, leaving an empty space, or interruption, in the middle of the frond. Golden London pride is a leafy saxifrage that forms a carpet of deep green rosettes splashed with bright yellow, irregular patches. In early summer, abundant upright stems boast masses of loosely clustered, tiny, star-shaped white flowers that are flushed with pale pink and held high above the foliage.

INTERRUPTED FERN

Osmunda claytoniana (top)
(oz-*mun*-dah clay-ton-ee-*ah*-nah)

TYPE: perennial
HEIGHT: 60 cm (24 in.)
WIDTH: 60 cm (24 in.)
SOIL: fertile, moist
LIGHT: full shade to part sun
FLOWERING TIME: not applicable
GROWING TIPS: plant in sheltered areas; avoid planting in hot, dry areas; plant with crowns just below soil level; use organic mulch for moisture retention and winter protection
ALTERNATIVES: *Osmunda cinnamomea* (cinnamon fern), *O. regalis* (royal fern); *Matteuccia struthiopteris* (ostrich fern)

GOLDEN LONDON PRIDE

Saxifraga x *urbium*
'Aureopunctata' (bottom)
(sacks-*iff*-ra-gah x *er*-bee-um)

TYPE: perennial
HEIGHT: 30 cm (12 in.)
WIDTH: 30 cm (12 in.)
SOIL: fertile, moist, well drained
LIGHT: light shade to part sun
FLOWERING TIME: early summer
GROWING TIPS: use organic mulch for moisture retention and winter protection; to prevent winter drying of evergreen foliage, cover with mulch or evergreen boughs; deadhead
ALTERNATIVE: *Saxifraga* x *geum* (kidneyleaf saxifrage)

Oxalis AND *Sedum*

LIESBETH LEATHERBARROW

When scoping out garden centers for unique plant combinations, keep in mind the possibilities of exotic houseplants. Treated as tender annuals, many houseplants are the perfect choice for rounding out a container planting or for tucking in between more traditional garden plants. The red velvet shamrock, one such "indoor-outdoor" plant, has exquisite triangular, two-tone leaves in shades of deepest burgundy-purple and dark magenta that resemble mysterious butterflies pausing in flight. Linked by a common color, 'Dragon's Blood' two-row stonecrop makes a dramatic mid-summer companion for the shamrock when it is smothered with dark magenta-red, star-shaped blossoms that echo the angular lines of the shamrock foliage. Other two-row stonecrops include 'Splendens' and 'Tricolor'.

RED VELVET SHAMROCK
Oxalis regnellii 'Triangularis' (right)
(ox-*al*-iss reg-*nell*-ee-ee)

TYPE: annual
HEIGHT: 20 cm (8 in.)
WIDTH: 30 cm (12 in.)
SOIL: average to fertile, moist, well drained
LIGHT: part sun to light shade
FLOWERING TIME: early summer to fall
GROWING TIPS: plant outdoors when all risk of frost has passed; fertilize biweekly; lift in the fall before first frost and grow indoors as a houseplant for the winter
ALTERNATIVE: *Heuchera micrantha* 'Palace Purple' (coral bells)

'DRAGON'S BLOOD' TWO-ROW STONECROP
Sedum spurium 'Dragon's Blood' (left)
(*see*-dum *spur*-ee-em)

TYPE: perennial
HEIGHT: 10 cm (4 in.)
WIDTH: 60 cm (24 in.)
SOIL: poor to average, well drained
LIGHT: full sun
FLOWERING TIME: early to late summer
GROWING TIPS: requires excellent drainage; tolerates light shade; trim after flowering to maintain shape; drought tolerant once established
ALTERNATIVES: *Sedum elwesii*, *S. kamtschaticum* 'Rosy Glow', *S.* 'Vera Jameson'

Paeonia AND *Philadelphus*

Sweetly scented mock orange and opulent peonies are the ultimate pairing for imparting an air of decadence to mixed borders. Every prairie garden should have at least one mock orange in its repertoire. In early summer it is smothered with fragrant, bowl-shaped blossoms of purest white. Extravagant peonies are the perfect companion for mock orange, adding immeasurably to create a feast for the senses. In late spring and early summer, their lavish blossoms unfold to reveal layer upon layer of intricate petals that shine in all imaginable shades of red, pink, and white. Most valued in the ornamental garden are the named cultivars of *Paeonia lactiflora*, such as 'Felix Crousse', 'Festiva Maxima', 'M. Jules Elie', and 'Sarah Bernhardt', all cherished for their exotic scent and appearance.

PEONY

Paeonia lactiflora (bottom)
(pay-*own*-ee-ah lak-tih-*flor*-ah)

TYPE: perennial
HEIGHT: 90 cm (36 in.)
WIDTH: 90 cm (36 in.)
SOIL: fertile, moist, well drained
LIGHT: full sun
FLOWERING TIME: late spring to early summer
GROWING TIPS: plant the crown no deeper than 5 cm (2 in.); use organic mulch for moisture retention and winter protection; requires staking; deadhead; susceptible to botrytis
ALTERNATIVE: *Paeonia officinalis* (common peony)

'WATERTON' MOCK ORANGE

Philadelphus lewisii 'Waterton' (top)
(fill-a-*dell*-fuss loo-*wiss*-ee-ee)

TYPE: deciduous shrub
HEIGHT: 2.1 m (7 ft.)
WIDTH: 1.5 m (5 ft.)
SOIL: fertile, moist, well drained
LIGHT: full sun
FLOWERING TIME: late spring to early summer
GROWING TIPS: prune after flowering; don't prune first-year branches as flowers form on second-year wood; drought tolerant once established; water well in fall
ALTERNATIVES: *Philadelphus coronarius* 'Aureus', *P.* x 'Galahad', *P.* x *virginalis* 'Minnesota Snowflake'

Petunia AND *Schizanthus*

LIESBETH LEATHERBARROW

Gone are the days of spindly, boring petunias lined up in rows in narrow flower beds; a wealth of new hybrids offers diverse flower forms and colors, improved weather tolerance, and versatile growth habits, including vigorous trailing or groundcover types. Long-blooming petunias are ideal to combine in a container with annuals that may not equal their longevity, continuing to flower after their spent companions are removed. The exotic butterfly flower is such a short-lived annual, nonetheless irresistible for the sheer beauty of its showy clusters of tubular, flared blooms. Also known as poor man's orchids, butterfly flowers usually have yellow throats streaked with violet or marked with other contrasting colors. 'Royal Pierrot Mix' is one of the longest-blooming cultivars.

PETUNIA

Petunia (bottom)
(pe-*tewn*-ee-ah)

TYPE: annual
HEIGHT: 15 to 35 cm (6 to 14 in.)
WIDTH: 30 to 90 cm (12 to 36 in.)
SOIL: average to fertile, well drained
LIGHT: full to part sun
FLOWERING TIME: early summer to fall
GROWING TIPS: fertilize biweekly; pinch back growing tips; if plants become leggy, cut back by half to encourage bushy growth and more flowers
ALTERNATIVE: *Calibrachoa* (million bells)

BUTTERFLY FLOWER

Schizanthus pinnatus (top)
(shiz-*an*-thus pin-*a*-tus)

TYPE: annual
HEIGHT: 20 to 50 cm (8 to 20 in.)
WIDTH: 23 to 30 cm (9 to 12 in.)
SOIL: average to fertile, moist, well drained
LIGHT: full to part sun
FLOWERING TIME: early to late summer
GROWING TIPS: avoid planting in hot, dry areas; fertilize biweekly; pinch back growing tips; individual plants will not bloom all summer so succession planting is recommended
ALTERNATIVE: *Schizanthus* x *wisetonensis*

Portulaca AND *Tropaeolum*

LIESBETH LEATHERBARROW

Portulaca and nasturtium comprise a moderately drought-tolerant duo of annuals that is perfect for planting in hot, sunny borders or containers. Both plants are "spreaders" and come in a similar suite of colors, namely, hot and pastel shades of red, pink, orange, and yellow, plus purple for portulaca, but that's where the similarity ends. All aspects of nasturtium are rounded and bold—its leaves are almost perfectly round with slightly scalloped edges, and its tubular flowers flare into five rounded petals with prominent spurs. The opposite is true for portulaca, which has red stems clothed in abundant small, bright green, cylindrical, succulent leaves and showy single or double, roselike blossoms. Calypso Mixed, Sundance Hybrids, and Sundial Series portulacas are good choices.

SUNDIAL SERIES PORTULACA

Portulaca grandiflora
Sundial Series (bottom)
(por-tew-*lah*-kah grand-i-*flo*-rah)

TYPE: annual
HEIGHT: 10 to 20 cm (4 to 8 in.)
WIDTH: 30 to 45 cm (12 to 18 in.)
SOIL: poor to average, well drained
LIGHT: full sun
FLOWERING TIME: early summer to fall
GROWING TIPS: requires excellent drainage; cut back by half in mid-summer to encourage reblooming; drought tolerant once established
ALTERNATIVES: *Calendula officinalis* (pot marigold); *Tagetes* cultivars (marigold)

NASTURTIUM

Tropaeolum (top)
(tro-*pie*-oh-lum)

TYPE: annual
HEIGHT: 30 to 60 cm (12 to 24 in.)
WIDTH: 45 to 60 cm (18 to 24 in.)
SOIL: average, well drained
LIGHT: full to part sun
FLOWERING TIME: early summer to fall
GROWING TIPS: requires excellent drainage; do not fertilize; rich soil promotes leaf growth at the expense of flowers; dead-head; drought tolerant once established
ALTERNATIVE: *Eschscholzia californica* (California poppy)

Rosa AND *Rosa*

LIESBETH LEATHERBARROW

With their luxuriant flush of semi-double flowers in June, 'Hazeldean' and 'Prairie Dawn' are among the first shrub roses to bloom. Sturdy, upright, and extremely hardy, bearing masses of large, semi-double, deep yellow flowers, 'Hazeldean' is a hybrid of 'Persian Yellow' and the Altai rose, developed by Saskatchewan's Percy Wright. It retains the desirable deep yellow color of 'Persian Yellow' without its nasty predisposition to blackspot. 'Prairie Dawn', which dates from 1959, is one of the many outstanding hardy roses developed in Morden, Manitoba. More lax and spreading than its partner, 'Prairie Dawn' has lightly scented, pink, semi-double flowers that open when mature to reveal yellow-tinted centers and stamens that emphasize the rich yellow petals of 'Hazeldean'.

'HAZELDEAN' ROSE

Rosa 'Hazeldean' (bottom)
(*roh*-zah)

TYPE: deciduous shrub
HEIGHT: 1.8 m (6 ft.)
WIDTH: 1.5 m (5 ft.)
SOIL: fertile, moist, well drained
LIGHT: full sun
FLOWERING TIME: early summer
GROWING TIPS: use organic mulch for moisture retention and winter protection; fertilize regularly; deadhead; prune in spring to remove tip kill and old woody canes; water well in fall
ALTERNATIVES: *Rosa* 'Frühlingsgold', *R.* x *harisonii* 'Harison's Yellow'

'PRAIRIE DAWN' ROSE

Rosa 'Prairie Dawn' (top)
(*roh*-zah)

TYPE: deciduous shrub
HEIGHT: 1.5 m (5 ft.)
WIDTH: 1.5 m (5 ft.)
SOIL: fertile, moist, well drained
LIGHT: full sun
FLOWERING TIME: early summer; some repeat blooming from mid to late summer
GROWING TIPS: use organic mulch for moisture retention and winter protection; fertilize regularly; deadhead; prune in spring to remove tip kill and old woody canes; water well in fall
ALTERNATIVES: *Rosa* 'Jens Munk', 'John Davis', 'Prairie Youth'

Rudbeckia AND *Solidago*

LIESBETH LEATHERBARROW

From mid-summer onward, the arching yellow sprays of goldenrod impart a warm glow to mixed borders and wild-flower gardens. Although the species can be invasive, several named cultivars (e.g., 'Crown of Rays', 'Golden Baby', 'Golden Wings') are well behaved. Any one of these partnered with 'Indian Summer' gloriosa daisies results in an eye-catching yellow tone-on-tone combination that makes a big impact in the late summer. Gloriosa daisies are short-lived perennials, commonly grown as annuals on the prairies. The species has orange-yellow ray petals surrounding a dark center, but cultivars, which may be single or double, often come in shades of yellow or gold with streaks of mahogany or bronze. 'Becky', 'Goldilocks', and 'Toto' are other good gloriosa daisy choices.

'INDIAN SUMMER'
GLORIOSA DAISY
Rudbeckia hirta
'Indian Summer' (bottom)
(rude-*beck*-ee-ah *her*-tah)

TYPE: annual
HEIGHT: 60 to 90 cm (24 to 36 in.)
WIDTH: 60 cm (24 in.)
SOIL: average to fertile, well drained
LIGHT: full to part sun
FLOWERING TIME: early summer to fall
GROWING TIPS: deadhead to maintain a tidy appearance; drought tolerant once established; very low maintenance
ALTERNATIVES: *Rudbeckia fulgida* var. *sullivantii* 'Goldsturm'; *Helianthus annuus* (sunflower)

GOLDENROD
Solidago (top)
(so-li-*dah*-go)

TYPE: perennial
HEIGHT: 60 cm (24 in.)
WIDTH: 45 cm (18 in.)
SOIL: average, moist, well drained
LIGHT: full to part sun
FLOWERING TIME: mid-summer to fall
GROWING TIPS: deadhead to prevent self-seeding; may require staking if soil is too rich; drought tolerant once established
ALTERNATIVES: *Helenium autumnale* (sneezeweed); *Heliopsis helianthoides* (false sunflower); *Verbascum chaixii* (nettle-leaved mullein)

Salix AND *Spiraea*

LIESBETH LEATHERBARROW

Even gardeners on a budget can afford to adorn their gardens with silver and gold if they choose 'Polar Bear' willow and 'Goldflame' spirea. Like other silver-leaved plants, 'Polar Bear' is a cool and neutral companion, offering an elegant background to 'Goldflame' spirea's golden foliage. 'Polar Bear' is a fast-growing, non-spreading, multi-stemmed shrub with hairy, slender branches and soft, linear foliage the color of moonlight. In spring this lovely willow is covered with fuzzy catkins. Unlike the tall 'Polar Bear', 'Goldflame' is small and rounded, fitting perfectly in front of the willow in a mixed or shrub border. It is attractive for the entire growing season, its golden leaves changing to red when fall frosts nip the garden. In summer, 'Goldflame' produces clusters of light pink flowers.

'POLAR BEAR' WILLOW

Salix silicola 'Polar Bear' (top)
(*say*-licks sill-ee-*ko*-lah)

TYPE: deciduous shrub
HEIGHT: 3 m (10 ft.)
WIDTH: 1.5 m (5 ft.)
SOIL: fertile, moist, well drained
LIGHT: full sun to light shade
FLOWERING TIME: not applicable
GROWING TIPS: use organic mulch for moisture retention and winter protection; to rejuvenate, prune back every three or four years; water well in fall
ALTERNATIVE: *Salix exigua* (coyote willow)

'GOLDFLAME' DWARF PINK SPIREA

Spiraea x *bumalda* 'Goldflame' (bottom)
(spy-*ree*-ah x bu-*mall*-dah)

TYPE: deciduous shrub
HEIGHT: 90 cm (36 in.)
WIDTH: 90 cm (36 in.)
SOIL: fertile, moist, well drained
LIGHT: full sun to light shade
FLOWERING TIME: mid-summer
GROWING TIPS: prune in early spring as buds begin to swell; deadhead; water well in fall
ALTERNATIVES: *Spiraea japonica* 'Golden Princess'; *Sambucus racemosa* 'Goldenlocks' (European red elder)

Salvia AND *Scabiosa*

LESLEY REYNOLDS

Growing annuals need not entail a large investment in bedding plants or time spent coaxing plants to grow from seed indoors. Left to their own devices, several frost-tolerant, long-blooming annuals self-seed in the garden year after year, making them useful companions for perennials in the mixed border. Clary sage, one member of this accommodating group, is remarkable not for its flowers—they are insignificant and hidden in the leaf axils—but for its showy spikes of white, pink, or purple bracts with dark veins. Clary sage harmonizes beautifully in color and form with the pincushion flower, an equally long-blooming plant with soft violet-blue or white, saucer-shaped flowers composed of large, overlapping petals surrounding a central mound of disk florets studded with spiky stamens.

CLARY SAGE
Salvia viridis (left)
(*sal*-vee-ah vir-*ih*-dis)

TYPE: annual
HEIGHT: 30 to 50 cm (12 to 20 in.)
WIDTH: 23 cm (9 in.)
SOIL: average to fertile, moist, well drained
LIGHT: full to part sun
FLOWERING TIME: early summer to fall
GROWING TIPS: fertilize biweekly; deadhead to prevent self-seeding
ALTERNATIVES: *Salvia coccinea* (Texas sage), *S. farinacea* (mealycup sage); *Consolida ajacis* 'Dwarf Hyacinth Flowered' (larkspur)

PINCUSHION FLOWER
Scabiosa caucasica (right)
(skab-ee-*oh*-sah kaw-*ka*-si-kah)

TYPE: perennial
HEIGHT: 45 to 90 cm (18 to 36 in.)
WIDTH: 60 cm (24 in.)
SOIL: average to fertile, moist, well drained
LIGHT: full sun to light shade
FLOWERING TIME: early summer to fall
GROWING TIPS: requires excellent drainage; use organic mulch for moisture retention and winter protection; deadhead to encourage continuous bloom and prevent self-seeding
ALTERNATIVES: annual *Scabiosa atropurpurea* (sweet scabious), *S. columbaria* (small scabious)

Sedum AND *Solidaster*

LIESBETH LEATHERBARROW

Prairie gardeners can thank enterprising plant breeders for the exciting duo of 'Matrona' stonecrop and solidaster, which burst into bloom just when the garden most needs a lift. 'Matrona', a hybrid of 'Autumn Joy' and 'Atropurpureum', combines the best attributes of its illustrious parents. In late summer, the rounded, developing flower clusters add a pale green hue to the border before opening into tiny, pink, star-shaped blooms that later turn to bronze. 'Matrona' has striking burgundy stems and succulent, gray-green foliage with rosy edges. Combine dramatic 'Matrona' with lighthearted solidaster, an intergeneric hybrid of *Solidago* and *Aster*. Solidaster is an upright, branching perennial that bears masses of daisylike flowers with creamy yellow petals and darker yellow centers.

'MATRONA' STONECROP

Sedum 'Matrona' (bottom)
(*see*-dum)

TYPE: perennial
HEIGHT: 60 cm (24 in.)
WIDTH: 30 to 60 cm (12 to 24 in.)
SOIL: average to fertile, well drained
LIGHT: full sun
FLOWERING TIME: fall
GROWING TIPS: requires excellent drainage; do not fertilize; drought tolerant once established
ALTERNATIVES: *Sedum* 'Atropurpureum', 'Autumn Joy', *S. spectabile*

SOLIDASTER

x *Solidaster luteus* (top)
(x so-lid-*as*-ter loo-*tay*-us)

TYPE: perennial
HEIGHT: 90 cm (36 in.)
WIDTH: 30 to 80 cm (12 to 32 in.)
SOIL: average to fertile, well drained
LIGHT: full sun
FLOWERING TIME: fall
GROWING TIPS: use organic mulch for moisture retention and winter protection; may require staking
ALTERNATIVES: *Solidago* hybrids (goldenrod)

The rich, warm colors of this fall-blooming hardy mum are perfectly complemented by golden variegated sage. LIESBETH LEATHERBARROW

CHAPTER FOUR

Fall

On the prairies, fall is defined by glorious contrasts, a season of blue skies and golden fields, mellow afternoons and crisp nights. Warm days and spectacular fall foliage invite us outdoors to enjoy our gardens before bitter winter winds and drifting snow are upon us, and we perform the pleasant tasks of bulb-planting and leaf-raking with satisfaction and gratitude for the privilege of gardening in this beautiful part of the world. Around us bloom the last perennials of the season, as asters and mums unfurl their petals in a rainbow of shades from white, pink, and purple, to yellow, orange, and bronze.

Fall is harvest season on the prairies, and our gardens are filled with fruits, berries, and seeds, both edible and ornamental. Plant partnerships can be formed based on the beauty of these elements, and long after the leaves have fallen, they remain to enhance the garden and provide food for the birds during the frigid winter months. Ornamental crabapples, mountain ash, and highbush cranberry have conspicuous red fruit, backed up by splendid fall foliage color. Many perennials, including alliums, ornamental grasses, stonecrop, coneflower, globe thistle, astilbe, and poppies, bear attractive seed capsules or spikes, and although it usually results in extra weeding of unwanted seedlings

Perennials, herbs, and grasses bring diverse colors and textures to this warm and harmonious fall border. LIESBETH LEATHERBARROW

Combining bright red berries, attractive foliage, and shiny, coppery bark, mountain ash and Amur cherry are winners in the fall prairie landscape. LIESBETH LEATHERBARROW

in the spring, gardeners may wish to suppress the urge to cut them down. Everlastings, those flowers prized for dried flower arrangements, give a similar effect; try 'Annabelle' hydrangea, strawflowers, and statice.

In fall, trees and shrubs that have been mere backdrops during summer's floral extravaganza become the center of attention as their leaves transform from green to fiery shades of yellow, orange, and red. When it comes to planning gardens for fall foliage, some gardeners like the bonfire approach, choosing tree and shrub partners that change color in a simultaneous blaze of glory. Others prefer to maintain fabulous fall foliage in the garden for as long as possible by selecting various species of trees and shrubs that turn color at different times. Gardeners with small properties don't have the luxury of combining several birch, oak, ash, or mountain ash trees for a parklike effect, but they can achieve comparable results on a smaller scale with tree and shrub, or shrub and shrub, partnerships. Several shrubs with impressive fall color, including burning bush, cotoneaster, viburnum, and ninebark, are ideal for small gardens. Keep in mind that bold foliage color is not restricted to trees and shrubs; Virginia creeper, bergenia, and many cranesbills display splendid red autumn leaves.

While the emphasis in the fall garden is usually on deciduous trees, evergreens are particularly useful now as cool and neutral foils for the brilliant foliage of deciduous trees and shrubs. Whether they are magnificent fifty-foot specimens or dwarf or weeping varieties in a foundation planting or shrub border, spruce, pines, and junipers cannot be overlooked as perfect partners for any season. Evergreen needles come in many textures and sizes, from blue-tinted, spiky, and stubby to emerald green, long, and flexible. Some junipers have shaggy, flaking, red-brown bark that is particularly striking in the winter garden.

As the last leaves drift to the ground and snowflakes begin to fall, tuck a few "perfect partners" in a favorite container and place it on your doorstep. Select small boughs of evergreens, such as spruce, mugo pine, or different varieties of junipers, as the foundation of your winter container. Add twiggy branches of pleasing color and texture from weeping birch, dogwood, willow, or burning bush, and finish with branches of mountain ash, viburnum, or cotoneaster berries and interesting perennial seed heads harvested from the garden.

While the garden sleeps, there's plenty of time to recall the successes of the past gardening season and plan the inevitable changes that need to be made. We gardeners enjoy, and indeed require, this time of reflection; we can put the winter to good use in gaining inspiration from catalogues, books, magazines, and most of all, fellow gardeners. Next spring there will be new flower beds to dig and new plant partnerships to form. We wait in pleasant anticipation of all the wondrous possibilities next year presents.

Clad in its fall finery, a majestic bur oak rises above the changing foliage of a collection of prairie-hardy shrubs. LIESBETH LEATHERBARROW

Acer AND *Picea*

LIESBETH LEATHERBARROW

Although prairie gardeners cannot aspire to groves of sugar maples, several other maples are both hardy and ornamental. Chief among them is the Amur maple, one of the best trees for brilliant orange or red fall color. Grown as a large, multi-stemmed shrub or as a single-trunked, small tree, the Amur maple has attractive gray bark and glossy, three-lobed leaves with red leaf veins and leaf stalks. In spring, scented, greenish white flowers appear that by fall have transformed into bright red, winged seedpods called samaras. With its solid presence, superb color, and fine texture, the Colorado blue spruce is an excellent supporting player for the Amur maple, gaining center stage in the late fall and winter garden once the maple's flaming leaves have drifted to the ground.

AMUR MAPLE
Acer tataricum var. *ginnala* (front)
(*ay*-ser tah-*tahr*-ih-cum var. jin-*a*-lah)

TYPE: deciduous tree
HEIGHT: 6 m (20 ft.)
WIDTH: 4.5 m (15 ft.)
SOIL: average, well drained
LIGHT: full to part sun
FLOWERING TIME: late spring
GROWING TIPS: drought tolerant once established; susceptible to lime-induced chlorosis; to prevent bleeding, prune only after the tree is in full leaf; water well in fall
ALTERNATIVE: *Acer tataricum* (tatarian maple)

COLORADO BLUE SPRUCE
Picea pungens f. *glauca* (back)
(pie-*see*-ah *pun*-jenz f. *glau*-kah)

TYPE: evergreen tree
HEIGHT: up to 12 m (40 ft.)
WIDTH: up to 4.5 m (15 ft.)
SOIL: fertile, moist, well drained
LIGHT: full to part sun
FLOWERING TIME: not applicable
GROWING TIPS: use organic mulch for moisture retention and winter protection; water well in fall
ALTERNATIVES: *Picea abies* (Norway spruce), *P. glauca* (white spruce)

Aconitum AND *Picea*

LIESBETH LEATHERBARROW

Monkshood is familiar in the late-summer garden, producing slender spires of unique hooded blossoms in a range of shades from azure to indigo. Less familiar is its twining cousin, climbing monkshood, which is also proving hardy on the prairies. Decked in dangling clusters of blossoms with three rounded lower petals and an upper hood-like structure, this vine adds a striking touch of the loveliest lavender blue to fall woodland gardens. Although it can be supported on a homemade trellis, climbing monkshood looks much better clambering over dwarf coniferous shrubs. The short, spiky, blue-green needles of weeping blue spruce, for example, are an excellent foil for this plant, enhancing the soft blues of its blossoms and providing a welcome contrast to its shiny, deeply incised foliage.

CLIMBING MONKSHOOD

Aconitum volubile (front)
(ahk-oh-*nye*-tum vol-*ewe*-bill-ee)

TYPE: deciduous vine
HEIGHT: 2 m (6.5 ft.)
WIDTH: 1 m (3.3 ft.)
SOIL: fertile, moist, well drained
LIGHT: part sun to light shade
FLOWERING TIME: fall
GROWING TIPS: avoid planting in hot, dry areas; use organic mulch for moisture retention and winter protection
ALTERNATIVE: *Aconitum episcopale* (climbing monkshood)

WEEPING COLORADO BLUE SPRUCE

Picea pungens f. *glauca* 'Pendula' (back)
(pie-*see*-ah *pun*-jenz f. *glau*-kah)

TYPE: evergreen tree
HEIGHT: up to 4 m (13 ft.)
WIDTH: up to 4.5 m (15 ft.)
SOIL: fertile, moist, well drained
LIGHT: full to part sun
FLOWERING TIME: not applicable
GROWING TIPS: use organic mulch for moisture retention and winter protection; water well in fall
ALTERNATIVES: *Picea abies* (Norway spruce), *P. glauca* (white spruce)

Aesculus AND *Fraxinus*

By "pushing the limits," dedicated gardeners have gradually introduced hardy, exotic-looking trees into the prairie landscape. An example is Ohio buckeye, one of the first trees to leaf out in spring. It produces decidedly tropical, palm-shaped leaves and pale, vertical flower clusters that soon turn into smooth, brown nuts encased in prickly, green husks. Just as it is one of the first trees to leaf out, the buckeye is also one of the first to lose its foliage. By the time it sheds in late summer, its leaves are aflame in brilliant red-orange. For a continuous burst of color in the mixed border, plant Ohio buckeye next to a Manchurian ash. The ash, with its almost perfectly shaped canopy, begins to cast its spell of gold just as the last red buckeye leaves tumble to the ground.

OHIO BUCKEYE
Aesculus glabra (front)
(*eye*-skew-lus *glah*-brah)

TYPE: deciduous tree
HEIGHT: 12 m (40 ft.)
WIDTH: 12 m (40 ft.)
SOIL: fertile, moist, well drained
LIGHT: full to part sun
FLOWERING TIME: late spring to early summer
GROWING TIPS: keep well watered; use organic mulch at base for moisture retention; prune when dormant, removing dead, damaged, or crossing branches; water well in fall
ALTERNATIVES: *Juglans cinerea* (butternut), *J. nigra* (black walnut)

MANCHURIAN ASH
Fraxinus mandshurica (back)
(*fracks*-in-us man-*choo*-rih-kah)

TYPE: deciduous tree
HEIGHT: 12 m (40 ft.)
WIDTH: 6 m (20 ft.)
SOIL: average to fertile
LIGHT: full sun
FLOWERING TIME: late spring
GROWING TIPS: performs well in wet or dry sites; prune when dormant, removing dead, damaged, or crossing branches; water well in fall
ALTERNATIVES: *Fraxinus americana* 'Fall Blaze', *F. nigra* 'Fallgold' (black ash), *F.* x 'Northern Gem', 'Northern Treasure', *F. pennsylvanica* var. *subintegerrima* (green ash)

Aster AND *Helictotrichon*

LIESBETH LEATHERBARROW

Popular among prairie gardeners, blue oat grass puts on a fine display throughout the year. In fact, the combined effect of cool blue, spiky grass blades and wispy, tan flowers held high on arching stems is quite striking. What's more, this bristling, round dome of foliage does not falter when many other perennials begin to fade in autumn, making it an excellent partner for late-bloomers, such as asters. A popular aster is the Michaelmas daisy, whose attractive starry blossoms warn that cold weather is approaching. On the prairies, killer frosts sometimes arrive too soon for aster blossoms to reach their full glory, but cultivars such as 'Alert', 'Audrey', 'Pink Beauty', and 'Professor Kippenberg' are worth a try, since they perform well through the first light frosts and beyond.

MICHAELMAS DAISY
Aster novi-belgii (front)
(*ass*-ter no-vee-*bell*-jee-ee)

TYPE: perennial
HEIGHT: 35 cm (14 in.)
WIDTH: 45 cm (18 in.)
SOIL: average to fertile, moist, well drained
LIGHT: full to part sun
FLOWERING TIME: late summer to fall
GROWING TIPS: use organic mulch for moisture retention and winter protection; provide good air circulation to prevent powdery mildew; may not bloom if hard frost is exceptionally early
ALTERNATIVES: *Aster ericoides* (heath aster), *A. lateriflorus*, *A. novae-angliae* (New England aster)

BLUE OAT GRASS
Helictotrichon sempervirens (back)
(hell-ick-toe-*try*-kon sem-per-*veer*-ens)

TYPE: perennial
HEIGHT: 90 cm (36 in.)
WIDTH: 60 cm (24 in.)
SOIL: poor to average, well drained
LIGHT: full sun
FLOWERING TIME: early to mid summer
GROWING TIPS: use organic mulch for moisture retention; cut leaves back to form tight bun in spring to encourage neat, new growth; drought tolerant once established
ALTERNATIVE: *Festuca glauca* (blue fescue)

Aster AND *Rosa*

As the first light frosts touch prairie gardens, the asters begin to bloom, their masses of purple, pink, red, and white blossoms like brilliant bouquets in waning perennial borders. Splendid flowers for the cutting garden, New England asters are branching, clump-forming perennials with medium green, lance-shaped leaves and showy clusters of daisylike flowers that close at night. Part of the New England aster Fall Fashion Series, 'Sylvia' is a vivacious companion to the redleaf rose. It bears rich, reddish purple flowers with orangey red centers that perfectly match the outstanding orange-red rose hips. After producing single, mauve-pink flowers earlier in the growing season, the redleaf rose also earns its keep in late summer and fall with elegant gray-purple foliage and arching canes.

'SYLVIA' NEW ENGLAND ASTER
Aster novae-angliae 'Sylvia' (bottom)
(*ass*-ter no-vye-*an*-glee-eye)

TYPE: perennial
HEIGHT: 90 cm (36 in.)
WIDTH: 45 cm (18 in.)
SOIL: average to fertile, moist, well drained
LIGHT: full to part sun
FLOWERING TIME: late summer to fall
GROWING TIPS: use organic mulch for moisture retention and winter protection; provide good air circulation to prevent powdery mildew; may not bloom if hard frost is exceptionally early
ALTERNATIVES: *Aster ericoides* (heath aster), *A. lateriflorus*, *A. novi-belgii* (Michaelmas daisy)

REDLEAF ROSE
Rosa glauca (top)
(*roh*-zah *glau*-kah)

TYPE: deciduous shrub
HEIGHT: 1.8 m (6 ft.)
WIDTH: 1.5 m (5 ft.)
SOIL: fertile, moist, well drained
LIGHT: full sun
FLOWERING TIME: late spring to early summer
GROWING TIPS: use organic mulch for moisture retention and winter protection; fertilize with compost or well-rotted manure; deadhead; prune in spring to remove tip kill and old woody canes
ALTERNATIVE: *Rosa pimpinellifolia* var. *altaica* (Altai rose)

Betula AND *Cotoneaster*

LIESBETH LEATHERBARROW

Every community on the prairies boasts at least a few cotoneaster hedges. It's easy to take this hardy and useful shrub for granted throughout much of the year, but when autumn arrives, its amazing display of orange-red foliage is impossible to ignore. Cotoneaster bears small, cup-shaped, pinkish white flowers that turn into black, berrylike fruit in late summer. An easily maintained hedge shrub, cotoneaster may be allowed to grow in its natural shape or sheared for a denser, more formal look. In their fall finery, cotoneaster hedges look spectacular next to the bright yellow autumn leaves of the European white birch. This white-trunked beauty has dainty, diamond-shaped, toothed leaves on slightly weeping branches that droop increasingly with age.

EUROPEAN WHITE BIRCH
Betula pendula (top)
(*bet*-ewe-lah *pen*-dew-lah)

TYPE: deciduous tree
HEIGHT: 15 m (50 ft.)
WIDTH: 9 m (30 ft.)
SOIL: fertile, moist, well drained
LIGHT: full sun
FLOWERING TIME: not applicable
GROWING TIPS: susceptible to bronze birch borer and birch leaf miners; to prevent bleeding, prune only after tree is in full leaf; drought results in significant tip kill; water regularly, especially in fall
ALTERNATIVES: *Betula papyrifera* (paper birch), *B. nana* (Arctic birch); *Populus tremuloides* (trembling aspen)

HEDGE COTONEASTER
Cotoneaster lucidus (bottom)
(ko-toe-nee-*ass*-ter *loo*-si-duss)

TYPE: deciduous shrub
HEIGHT: 2 m (6.5 ft.)
WIDTH: 2 m (6.5 ft.)
SOIL: average to fertile, well drained
LIGHT: full sun to light shade
FLOWERING TIME: mid to late spring
GROWING TIPS: drought tolerant once established; prune when dormant; trim hedge plants to desired shape during the growing season; water well in fall
ALTERNATIVE: *Cotoneaster acutifolius* (Peking cotoneaster)

Betula AND *Pinus*

LIESBETH LEATHERBARROW

Pines, identified by their long needles grouped in clusters of two, three, or five, lend character to mixed borders or small groves of woody ornamentals. Open and asymmetrical in form, and sometimes even twisted in shape, these trees lend a softness to the landscape that the stiff, more formal profiles of popular spruce trees lack. The comforting sound of the wind whispering through emerald green pine needles is also part of this tree's magic. Because pine trees retain their needles year round, they are handsome in the winter landscape, especially under a dusting of snow. They also make excellent companions to birch trees of all types, greatly enhancing the brilliant yellows of their fall foliage and the pure white of their mature bark.

EUROPEAN WHITE BIRCH

Betula pendula (left)
(*bet*-ewe-lah *pen*-dew-lah)

TYPE: deciduous tree
HEIGHT: 15 m (50 ft.)
WIDTH: 9 m (30 ft.)
SOIL: fertile, moist, well drained
LIGHT: full sun
FLOWERING TIME: not applicable
GROWING TIPS: susceptible to bronze birch borer and birch leaf miners; to prevent bleeding, prune only after tree is in full leaf; drought results in significant tip kill; water regularly, especially in fall
ALTERNATIVES: *Betula papyrifera* (paper birch), *B. nana* (Arctic birch)

LODGEPOLE PINE

Pinus contorta var. *latifolia* (right)
(*pee*-nus or *py*-nus kon-*tor*-tah var. lah-ti-*foe*-lee-ah)

TYPE: evergreen tree
HEIGHT: 15 m (50 ft.)
WIDTH: 6 m (20 ft.)
SOIL: average to fertile, well drained
LIGHT: full sun
FLOWERING TIME: not applicable
GROWING TIPS: requires excellent drainage; no pruning necessary; water well in fall
ALTERNATIVES: *Pinus aristata* (bristlecone pine), *P. cembra* (Swiss stone pine), *P. flexilis* (limber pine), *P. sylvestris* (Scots pine)

Calamagrostis AND *Echinops*

LIESBETH LEATHERBARROW

'Karl Foerster' is highly acclaimed and one of the most versatile and attractive ornamental grasses available to prairie gardeners. It makes a glorious vertical statement in mixed borders, performing with panache year round. Loose, feathery flowers emerge tinted pink, gradually turning a golden tan color that persists through fall and beyond. The flower stems tower above the underlying tuft of shiny green grass in a narrow, tight configuration. A perfect fall partner for 'Karl Foerster' is the globe thistle, which always adds zip and intrigue to flower beds. A study in textural diversity, globe thistle has coarse, jagged, incised leaves and metallic blue, spherical clusters of short, spiky flower buds. Both plants are also standouts in the winter garden.

'KARL FOERSTER' FEATHER REED GRASS

Calamagrostis x *acutiflora* 'Karl Foerster' (left)
(ka-la-mah-*gross*-tiss x a-kute-ih-*flor*-ah)

TYPE: perennial
HEIGHT: 1.8 m (6 ft.)
WIDTH: 60 cm (24 in.)
SOIL: fertile, moist, well drained
LIGHT: full to part sun
FLOWERING TIME: mid to late summer
GROWING TIPS: tolerates wide range of soil types; cut leaves back to form tight bun in spring to encourage neat, new growth
ALTERNATIVES: *Molinea caerulea* subsp. *arundinacea* 'Karl Foerster', 'Skyracer' (purple moor grass)

GLOBE THISTLE

Echinops ritro (right)
(*eck*-ih-nops *rih*-tro)

TYPE: perennial
HEIGHT: 1.2 m (4 ft.)
WIDTH: 60 cm (24 in.)
SOIL: average, well drained
LIGHT: full to part sun
FLOWERING TIME: mid-summer to fall
GROWING TIPS: plant crown at or slightly below soil level; may require staking if soil is too rich; drought tolerant once established
ALTERNATIVES: *Echinops bannaticus, E. giganteus, E. sphaerocephalus; Eryngium* cultivars (sea holly)

Caragana AND *Hydrangea*

LIESBETH LEATHERBARROW

For a look of understated elegance in the late-fall garden, plant 'Annabelle' hydrangea and weeping caragana side by side. Neither is blessed with flaming color as it gracefully exits from the warm days of summer, but both transform into warm shades of golden brown when the days shorten. 'Annabelle's spectacular flower heads, much sought after for dried bouquets, are equally showy when left to dry outdoors. Even as other shrubs and perennials waste away, 'Annabelle' maintains a dramatic look throughout fall and winter, especially when rimmed in frost or brushed with snow. The caragana's strength lies in the curvature of its branches. With its weeping form becoming more prominent as it sheds its leaves, this shrub's silhouette is splendid no matter what the time of year.

WEEPING CARAGANA

Caragana arborescens 'Pendula' (top)
(ka-ra-*gah*-nah ar-bo-*res*-kens)

TYPE: deciduous shrub
HEIGHT: 90 cm (36 in.)
WIDTH: 90 cm (36 in.)
SOIL: poor to fertile
LIGHT: full sun
FLOWERING TIME: late spring
GROWING TIPS: drought tolerant once established; rarely needs pruning; keep an eye out for suckers at the base, trim them to the ground if they appear; water well in fall
ALTERNATIVE: *Larix decidua* 'Pendula' (weeping European larch)

'ANNABELLE' HYDRANGEA

Hydrangea arborescens
'**Annabelle**' (bottom)
(hie-*drain*-jee-ah ar-bo-*res*-kens)

TYPE: deciduous shrub
HEIGHT: 1.5 m (5 ft.)
WIDTH: 1.5 m (5 ft.)
SOIL: fertile, moist, well drained
LIGHT: part sun to light shade
FLOWERING TIME: mid-summer to fall
GROWING TIPS: avoid planting in hot, dry areas; use organic mulch for moisture retention and winter protection; blooms may require staking; cut back to 10 cm (4 in.) in late winter; water well in fall
ALTERNATIVE: *Hydrangea paniculata* 'Grandiflora' (Pee Gee hydrangea)

Chrysanthemum AND *Rudbeckia*

LIESBETH LEATHERBARROW

Chrysanthemums are often considered the quintessential autumn flower. When paired with 'Goldsturm' rudbeckia, they speak volumes, reminding us that winter will soon be upon us. Thanks to the wizardry of Canadian plant breeders in Morden, Manitoba, a series of early-flowering mums is available. However, another early-blooming species with a more delicate aspect than Morden mums is 'Clara Curtis', which produces single, rose-pink, yellow-centered, daisylike flowers on tall, stiff stems. In contrast, 'Goldsturm' has a much bolder look. Its brilliant, slightly down-curved petals are substantial and radiate outward from a dark brown, central "eye." A single plant is lavished with so many long-lived blossoms, it creates a veritable golden storm (or 'Goldsturm') for weeks on end.

'CLARA CURTIS' HARDY MUM

Chrysanthemum x *rubellum*
'Clara Curtis' (bottom)
(kriss-*an*-the-mum x roo-*bell*-um)

TYPE: perennial
HEIGHT: 60 cm (24 in.)
WIDTH: 60 cm (24 in.)
SOIL: average to fertile, moist, well drained
LIGHT: full sun
FLOWERING TIME: mid-summer to fall
GROWING TIPS: requires excellent drainage; may require staking; pinch back growing tips once in June to encourage bushy growth
ALTERNATIVES: *Chrysanthemum* x *morifolium, C. weyrichii*

'GOLDSTURM' RUDBECKIA

Rudbeckia fulgida var. *sullivantii*
'Goldsturm' (top)
(rude-*beck*-ee-ah *full*-gi-dah var. sull-i-*van*-te-ee)

TYPE: perennial
HEIGHT: 60 cm (24 in.)
WIDTH: 60 cm (24 in.)
SOIL: average to fertile, well drained
LIGHT: full to part sun
FLOWERING TIME: mid-summer to fall
GROWING TIPS: deadhead to prevent self-seeding and encourage reblooming
ALTERNATIVES: *Rudbeckia fulgida* (black-eyed Susan); annual *R. hirta* (gloriosa daisy); *Helenium autumnale* (sneezeweed); *Heliopsis helianthoides* (false sunflower)

Cornus AND *Rosa*

Recent years have brought increased emphasis on the use of native plants to create gardens that enhance rather than remove wildlife habitat. Two of the finest shrubs to introduce into a native prairie garden, or indeed any mixed or shrub border, are red osier dogwood and common wild rose. Although most renowned for its cherry-red stems, a boon to the winter garden, red osier dogwood is also valued in autumn for its purple-red foliage. This species can spread widely, so choose a small cultivar, such as 'Isanti', for small gardens. The common wild rose bears fragrant, clustered, pink flowers that develop into round, red hips that mimic the dogwood's glowing fall foliage. As frost nips the prairies, the rose assumes a golden mantle of leaves, in bright contrast to its companion.

RED OSIER DOGWOOD
Cornus sericea (left)
(*kor*-nuss say-ri-*kee*-ah)

TYPE: deciduous shrub
HEIGHT: 3 m (10 ft.)
WIDTH: 3 m (10 ft.)
SOIL: fertile, moist
LIGHT: full sun to light shade
FLOWERING TIME: late spring to early summer
GROWING TIPS: avoid planting in hot, dry areas; needs periodic rejuvenation pruning to maintain vivid stem coloration; suckers and spreads slowly by stolons, so requires plenty of space; water well in fall
ALTERNATIVES: clump-forming *Cornus alba* 'Aurea', 'Elegantissima', 'Ivory Halo', 'Sibirica'

COMMON WILD ROSE
Rosa woodsii (right)
(*roh*-zah *wood*-see-ee)

TYPE: deciduous shrub
HEIGHT: 1.5 m (5 ft.)
WIDTH: 1.0 m (3.3 ft.)
SOIL: fertile, moist, well drained
LIGHT: full sun
FLOWERING TIME: early summer
GROWING TIPS: use organic mulch for moisture retention and winter protection; fertilize regularly; deadhead; prune in spring to remove tip kill and old woody canes; water well in fall
ALTERNATIVES: *Rosa acicularis* (prickly wild rose), *R. arkansana* (prairie rose)

Cornus AND *Sorbus*

LIESBETH LEATHERBARROW

For gardeners with a hankering for some "big red" to punctuate the golden autumn glow of prairie poplars and ashes, the combination of red osier dogwood and showy mountain ash is about as red as it gets. What's more, both of these plants earn their keep year round in the mixed border. Red osier dogwood is a hardy species that bears white flowers in spring, produces clusters of white fruit in summer, has excellent purple-red fall color, and best of all, enlivens the winter garden with its bright, cherry-red stems. Fireblight-resistant 'Grootendorst' has equal value in the landscape. It also produces white spring blossoms, attractive foliage with fiery fall color, and brightly colored fruit that remains on the tree until hordes of hungry bohemian waxwings descend to pick it clean.

RED OSIER DOGWOOD
Cornus sericea (bottom)
(*kor*-nuss say-ri-*kee*-ah)

TYPE: deciduous shrub
HEIGHT: 3 m (10 ft.)
WIDTH: 3 m (10 ft.)
SOIL: fertile, moist
LIGHT: full sun to light shade
FLOWERING TIME: late spring to early summer
GROWING TIPS: avoid planting in hot, dry areas; needs periodic rejuvenation pruning to maintain vivid stem coloration; suckers and spreads slowly by stolons, so requires plenty of space; water well in fall
ALTERNATIVES: clump-forming *Cornus alba* 'Aurea', 'Elegantissima', 'Ivory Halo', 'Sibirica'

'GROOTENDORST' SHOWY MOUNTAIN ASH
Sorbus decora 'Grootendorst' (top)
(*sore*-bus day-*kore*-ah)

TYPE: deciduous tree
HEIGHT: 8 m (26 ft.)
WIDTH: 5 m (16 ft.)
SOIL: average to fertile, well drained
LIGHT: full to part sun
FLOWERING TIME: late spring
GROWING TIPS: avoid wet or low-lying locations; use organic mulch for moisture retention; prune after flowering, once leaves have fully emerged; may suffer sunscald in winter in extremely sunny locations; water well in fall
ALTERNATIVE: *Sorbus americana* (American mountain ash)

Cotoneaster AND *Sorbus*

LIESBETH LEATHERBARROW

Against the blue of the autumn prairie sky, the fiery foliage of cotoneaster and mountain ash brings the growing season to a festive finale. Cotoneaster, a hardy and versatile hedging shrub, is attractive throughout the growing season, with rounded, shiny, dark green leaves that are slightly hairy underneath. In fall, the leaves gradually turn from green to radiant shades of orange and red. The autumn colors of mountain ash are equally spectacular, ranging from shades of yellow and orange to bright red. However, in contrast with the simple foliage form of cotoneaster, mountain ash has elegant compound leaves composed of up to fifteen toothed, lance-shaped leaflets. Clusters of large, red berries provide a bold accent to the highly ornamental foliage.

HEDGE COTONEASTER

Cotoneaster lucidus (bottom)
(ko-toe-nee-*ass*-ter *loo*-si-duss)

TYPE: deciduous shrub
HEIGHT: 2 m (6.5 ft.)
WIDTH: 2 m (6.5 ft.)
SOIL: average to fertile, well drained
LIGHT: full sun to light shade
FLOWERING TIME: mid to late spring
GROWING TIPS: drought tolerant once established; prune when dormant; trim hedge plants to desired shape during the growing season; water well in fall
ALTERNATIVE: *Cotoneaster acutifolius* (Peking cotoneaster)

MOUNTAIN ASH

Sorbus (top)
(*sore*-bus)

TYPE: deciduous tree
HEIGHT: 8 m (26 ft.)
WIDTH: 5 m (16 ft.)
SOIL: average to fertile, well drained
LIGHT: full to part sun
FLOWERING TIME: late spring
GROWING TIPS: avoid wet or low-lying locations; use organic mulch for moisture retention; prune after flowering, once leaves have fully emerged; may suffer sunscald in winter in extremely sunny locations; water well in fall
ALTERNATIVES: *Sorbus americana* (American mountain ash), *S. decora* (showy mountain ash)

Euonymus AND *Fraxinus*

LIESBETH LEATHERBARROW

With its dense, naturally rounded form, Manchurian ash is one of the most beautifully shaped hardy trees for prairie gardens. Its foliage is also superb, consisting of large, compound, pinnate leaves that transform this lovely tree into a bright yellow globe every autumn. Like all ash trees, Manchurian ash leafs out later than most other deciduous trees, so it does not cast shade on spring-flowering bulbs, perennials, or shrubs as early in the growing season. Accompany Manchurian ash with the unusual Turkestan burning bush, an upright shrub that bears red-brown flowers, followed by exotic looking four-lobed, red-pink fruit with orange seeds. The narrow, toothed, dark green leaves change to red-pink in the fall, just in time to enhance the ash's golden splendor.

TURKESTAN BURNING BUSH

Euonymus nanus 'Turkestanicus' (left)
(you-*on*-ih-mus *na*-nus)

TYPE: deciduous shrub
HEIGHT: 1 to 1.5 m (3.3 to 5 ft.)
WIDTH: 1 to 1.5 m (3.3 to 5 ft.)
SOIL: fertile, moist, well drained
LIGHT: full to part sun
FLOWERING TIME: mid-summer
GROWING TIPS: use organic mulch for moisture retention and winter protection; prune when dormant; water well in fall
ALTERNATIVE: *Euonymus alatus* (winged burning bush)

MANCHURIAN ASH

Fraxinus mandshurica (right)
(*fracks*-in-us man-*choo*-rih-kah)

TYPE: deciduous tree
HEIGHT: 12 m (40 ft.)
WIDTH: 6 m (20 ft.)
SOIL: average to fertile
LIGHT: full sun
FLOWERING TIME: late spring
GROWING TIPS: performs well in wet or dry sites; prune when dormant, removing dead, damaged, or crossing branches; water well in fall
ALTERNATIVES: *Fraxinus americana* 'Fall Blaze', *F. nigra* 'Fallgold' (black ash), *F.* x 'Northern Gem', *F.* x 'Northern Treasure', *F. pennsylvanica* var. *subintegerrima* (green ash)

Euonymus AND *Picea*

LESLEY REYNOLDS

Some of the best autumn pairs rely on the contrast of evergreens with the colorful fall foliage of deciduous trees or shrubs. This is illustrated in spectacular fashion by the pairing of 'Compactus' burning bush and Colorado blue spruce. A crimson beacon in the fall landscape, 'Compactus' is also an asset to the summer garden for its compact, dense form and lobed, red-purple fruit that splits to reveal orange seeds. Although 'Compactus' is a suitable companion for any evergreen, the glaucous needles of Colorado blue spruce intensify the burning bush's vivid hue. Colorado blue spruce come in all shapes—weeping, globular, columnar, and prostrate—and all sizes. Two popular choices are 'Hoopsii', a large, pyramidal spruce with silvery blue needles, and 'Globosa', an outstanding dwarf cultivar.

COMPACT BURNING BUSH

Euonymus alatus 'Compactus' (bottom)
(you-*on*-ih-mus ah-*lah*-tus)

TYPE: deciduous shrub
HEIGHT: 1 to 1.5 m (3.3 to 5 ft.)
WIDTH: 1.5 to 2 m (5 to 6.5 ft.)
SOIL: fertile, moist, well drained
LIGHT: full to part sun
FLOWERING TIME: mid-summer
GROWING TIPS: use organic mulch for moisture retention and winter protection; prune when dormant; water well in fall
ALTERNATIVE: *Euonymus nanus* 'Turkestanicus'

COLORADO BLUE SPRUCE

Picea pungens f. *glauca* (top)
(pie-*see*-ah *pun*-jenz f. *glau*-kah)

TYPE: evergreen tree
HEIGHT: up to 12 m (40 ft.)
WIDTH: up to 4.5 m (15 ft.)
SOIL: fertile, moist, well drained
LIGHT: full to part sun
FLOWERING TIME: not applicable
GROWING TIPS: use organic mulch for moisture retention and winter protection; water well in fall
ALTERNATIVES: *Picea abies* (Norway spruce), *P. glauca* (white spruce)

Juniperus AND *Parthenocissus*

LIESBETH LEATHERBARROW

There is no rule that says vines must be supported by trellises. Left to their own devices, many vines make admirable ground-covers, mingling with the plants they meet along the way and adding a touch of color and texture to otherwise bare ground. Virginia creeper is one such multi-purpose vine that adds beauty to the landscape, especially intertwined with evergreen shrubs such as Savin junipers. In summer, the two form a tone-on-tone combination in green, displaying a marked contrast in texture between the shiny, broad-leaved Virginia creeper foliage and the dull, sharp, needlelike leaves of the juniper. However, it's not until fall that the duo reaches its peak performance with the brilliant red Virginia creeper foliage illuminating the juniper like so many Christmas lights.

SAVIN JUNIPER

Juniperus sabina (green)
(you-*nip*-er-us sa-*been*-ah)

TYPE: evergreen shrub
HEIGHT: 1.2 to 1.8 m (4 to 6 ft.)
WIDTH: 3 m (10 ft.)
SOIL: average, well drained
LIGHT: full sun
FLOWERING TIME: not applicable
GROWING TIPS: drought tolerant once established; prune in spring to remove any dead branches; if desired, prune lightly to shape in summer; water well in fall
ALTERNATIVES: *Juniperus communis* (common juniper), *J. horizontalis* (spreading juniper), *J. x pfitzeriana*, *J. scopulorum* (Rocky Mountain juniper); *Pinus mugo* (mugo pine)

VIRGINIA CREEPER

Parthenocissus quinquefolia (red)
(par-then-oh-*kis*-us kwin-kwe-*foh*-lee-ah)

TYPE: perennial vine
HEIGHT: 15 m (50 ft.)
WIDTH: 1 m (3.3 ft.)
SOIL: average to fertile, well drained
LIGHT: full sun to light shade
FLOWERING TIME: inconspicuous flowers in mid-summer
GROWING TIPS: drought tolerant once established; if pruning is necessary to tidy vine, it is easiest to prune while dormant
ALTERNATIVES: *Humulus lupulus* (hops); *Vitis riparia* (riverbank grape)

Larix AND *Picea*

When larches shine like golden spires in the landscape, it is a sure sign that fall has arrived. These needled trees look like evergreens in spring and summer, but in fall they blaze in shades of fiery yellow and orange, then drop their needles in deciduous fashion. More airy and graceful than familiar evergreens, larches have shapely branches and persistent cones that create winter interest, even in the absence of foliage. Their spectacular golden fall color is best displayed against a background of evergreens. Because larches are trees of large proportion, best suited to large properties or acreages, you can pair them with the equally large and ever-lovely Colorado blue spruce. Dwarf spruce cultivars include 'Bakeri', 'Fastigiata', 'Montgomery', and 'Pendula'.

SIBERIAN LARCH
Larix sibirica (left)
(*lair*-ix sy-*bee*-ri-kah)

TYPE: deciduous tree
HEIGHT: 18 m (60 ft.)
WIDTH: 5 m (16 ft.)
SOIL: average to fertile, well drained
LIGHT: full sun
FLOWERING TIME: not applicable
GROWING TIPS: avoid planting in hot, dry areas; use organic mulch at the base for moisture retention; no pruning required on specimen trees; water well in fall
ALTERNATIVES: *Larix decidua* (European larch), *L. laricina* (tamarack)

COLORADO BLUE SPRUCE
Picea pungens f. *glauca* (right)
(pie-*see*-ah *pun*-jenz f. *glau*-kah)

TYPE: evergreen tree`
HEIGHT: up to 12 m (40 ft.)
WIDTH: up to 4.5 m (15 ft.)
SOIL: fertile, moist, well drained
LIGHT: full sun
FLOWERING TIME: not applicable
GROWING TIPS: use organic mulch for moisture retention and winter protection; water well in fall
ALTERNATIVES: *Picea abies* (Norway spruce), *P. glauca* 'Densata' (Black Hills spruce)

Malus AND *Viburnum*

LIESBETH LEATHERBARROW

Whether they are grown separately or in combination, both 'Dolgo' ornamental crabapple and American highbush cranberry are very decorative, with complementary features that commend them as mates in mixed borders year round. In late spring, their spreading branches bear charming clusters of fragrant, white flowers that eventually transform into quite large, wine-red crabapples on the 'Dolgo' and contrasting small, scarlet red fruit on the cranberry. If you don't pick them for jelly or jam, both apples and cranberries persist through fall and winter, attracting abundant wildlife to the garden, especially hordes of bohemian waxwings. Their fall foliage, too, is a sight to behold, varying from bright yellow on the 'Dolgo', to gold, crimson, deep wine red, and even purple on the cranberry.

'DOLGO' CRABAPPLE

Malus x 'Dolgo' (right)
(*ma*-luss)

TYPE: deciduous tree
HEIGHT: 8 m (26 ft.)
WIDTH: 8 m (26 ft.)
SOIL: average, well drained
LIGHT: full to part sun
FLOWERING TIME: late spring
GROWING TIPS: drought tolerant once established; prune after flowering and once leaves have fully emerged; water well in fall
ALTERNATIVES: *Malus* x 'Kerr', 'Rescue', *M.* x *adstringens* 'Kelsey', 'Selkirk', 'Thunderchild'

AMERICAN HIGHBUSH CRANBERRY

Viburnum trilobum (left)
(vie-*burr*-num try-*loh*-bum)

TYPE: deciduous shrub
HEIGHT: 4 m (13 ft.)
WIDTH: 3 m (10 ft.)
SOIL: fertile, moist, well drained
LIGHT: full sun to light shade
FLOWERING TIME: late spring to early summer
GROWING TIPS: susceptible to aphids, flush regularly with a strong spray of water; prune after flowering, once leaves have fully emerged; water well in fall
ALTERNATIVES: *Viburnum dentatum* (arrowwood), *V. lantana* (wayfaring tree), *V. lentago* (nannyberry)

Physocarpus AND *Ribes*

LIESBETH LEATHERBARROW

In autumn, common ninebark and golden flowering currant prove their worth in prairie gardens with an eye-catching display of fall color. These North American native shrubs are ideal choices for a shrub border; however, both spread by suckers and are best suited to large gardens. Ninebark has arching branches, intriguing cinnamon-colored, shredding bark, and three-lobed, toothed leaves that turn bright yellow in the fall. Although ninebark's small, pinkish white flowers are inconspicuous, its clusters of red seedpods are showy. Golden flowering currant is notable for its scarlet fall foliage, but it also shines in the spring, when it bears an abundance of fragrant, yellow, tubular flowers. In late summer, its blue-black fruit provides a feast for the birds.

COMMON NINEBARK
Physocarpus opulifolius (right)
(fie-zo-*kar*-pus op-ew-li-*fo*-lee-us)

TYPE: deciduous shrub
HEIGHT: 1.5 to 2.5 m (5 to 8 ft.)
WIDTH: 2 m (6.5 ft.)
SOIL: fertile, moist, well drained
LIGHT: full sun to light shade
FLOWERING TIME: early summer
GROWING TIPS: use organic mulch for moisture retention; after flowering, prune 20 percent of old shoots to base to promote replacement growth; may suffer winter die-back; water well in fall
ALTERNATIVE: *Spiraea* x *bumalda* (dwarf pink spirea)

GOLDEN FLOWERING CURRANT
Ribes odoratum (left)
(*rih*-bees oh-dor-*a*-tum)

TYPE: deciduous shrub
HEIGHT: 1 to 2 m (3.3 to 6.5 ft.)
WIDTH: 1 to 2 m (3.3 to 6.5 ft.)
SOIL: average to fertile, well drained
LIGHT: full sun
FLOWERING TIME: late spring
GROWING TIPS: drought tolerant once established; prone to powdery mildew; prune after flowering, removing older stems; water well in fall
ALTERNATIVE: *Cotoneaster lucidus* (hedge cotoneaster)

References

Bennett, Jennifer, and Forsyth, Turid. *The Annual Garden.* Willowdale, ON: Firefly Books Ltd., 1998.

The Best of Fine Gardening: Perennials. Newtown, CT: Taunton Press, 1993.

The Best of Fine Gardening: Shrubs and Trees. Newtown, CT: Taunton Press, 1993.

Bird, Richard. *Hardy Perennials.* London, Eng.: Ward Lock, 1998.

Brickell, C., Cole, T., and Zuk, J., eds. *Reader's Digest A-Z Encyclopedia of Garden Plants.* Westmount, QC: The Reader's Digest Association, Inc., 1997.

Calgary Horticultural Society. *The Calgary Gardener.* Calgary, AB: Fifth House Publishers, 1996.

Cavendish Books. *Cavendish Plant Guides: Bulbs.* Vancouver, BC: Cavendish Books Inc., 1997.

Cavendish Books. *Cavendish Plant Guides: Perennials.* Vancouver, BC: Cavendish Books Inc., 1996.

Cavendish Books. *Cavendish Plant Guides: Shrubs and Climbers.* Vancouver, BC: Cavendish Books Inc., 1996.

Coombes, Allen J. *Dictionary of Plant Names.* Portland, OR: Timber Press, 1985.

Coombes, Allen, and Tripp, Kim. *The Complete Book of Shrubs.* Pleasantville, NY: The Reader's Digest Association, Inc., 1998.

Cutler, Karan D., ed. *Vines.* Charlotte, VT: Camden House Publishing, Inc., 1992.

Ellis, Barbara W. *Taylor's Guide to Growing North America's Favorite Plants.* New York, NY: Houghton Mifflin Company, 1998.

Harris, Marjorie. *The Canadian Gardener's Guide to Foliage and Garden Design.* Toronto, ON: Random House, 1993.

Heger, Mike, and Whitman, John. *Growing Perennials in Cold Climates.* Chicago, IL: Contemporary Books, 1998.

Hessayon, D. G. *The Bulb Expert.* London, Eng.: Transworld Publishers, 1996.

Hessayon, D. G. *The New Bedding Plant Expert.* London, Eng.: Expert Books, 1997.

Hogue, Marjorie M. *Amazing Annuals.* Willowdale, ON: Firefly Books Ltd., 1999.

Hole, Lois. *Bedding Plant Favorites.* Edmonton, AB: Lone Pine Publishing, 1994.

Hole, Lois. *Favorite Trees and Shrubs.* Edmonton, AB: Lone Pine Publishing, 1997.

Hole, Lois. *Perennial Favorites.* Edmonton, AB: Lone Pine Publishing, 1995.

Hole, Lois. *Rose Favorites.* Edmonton, AB: Lone Pine Publishing, 1997.

Jacobson, Arthur L. *North American Landscape Trees.* Berkeley, CA: Ten Speed Press, 1996.

Kelly, John, ed. *The Hillier Gardener's Guide to Trees and Shrubs.* Pleasantville, NY: The Reader's Digest Association, Inc., 1997.

Knowles, Hugh. *Woody Ornamentals for the Prairies.* Rev. ed. Edmonton, AB: University of Alberta, Faculty of Extension, 1995.

Lane, Clive. *Cottage Garden Annuals.* London, Eng.: David and Charles, 1997.

Leatherbarrow, Liesbeth, and Reynolds, Lesley. *Best Bulbs for the Prairies.* Calgary, AB: Fifth House Publishers, 2001.

Leatherbarrow, Liesbeth, and Reynolds, Lesley. *The Calgary Gardener, Volume Two: Beyond the Basics.* Calgary, AB: Fifth House Publishers, 1998.

Leatherbarrow, Liesbeth, and Reynolds, Lesley. *101 Best Plants for the Prairies.* Calgary, AB: Fifth House Publishers, 1999.

Lima, Patrick. *The Art of Perennial Gardening.* Willowdale, ON: Firefly Books Ltd., 1998.

Mathew, Brian, and Swindells, Phillip. *The Complete Book of Bulbs, Corms, Tubers, and Rhizomes.* Pleasantville, NY: The Reader's Digest Association, 1994.

The 1998 Prairie Garden. Winnipeg, MB: Winnipeg Horticultural Society, 1998.

The 1999 Prairie Garden. Winnipeg, MB: Winnipeg Horticultural Society, 1999.

Osborne, Robert. *Hardy Trees and Shrubs.* Toronto, ON: Key Porter Books Ltd., 1996.

Phillips, Roger, and Rix, Martyn. *The Random House Book of Perennials, Volume 1: Early Perennials.* New York, NY: Random House, 1991.

Phillips, Roger, and Rix, Martyn. *The Random House Book of Perennials, Volume 2: Late Perennials.* New York, NY: Random House, 1991.

Proctor, Rob. *Annuals and Bulbs.* Emmaus, PA: Rodale Press, 1995.

Proctor, Rob. *Perennials: Enduring Classics for the Contemporary Garden.* New York, NY: Running Heads Incorporated, 1990.

Rice, Graham. *The Complete Book of Perennials.* Pleasantville, NY: The Reader's Digest Association, Inc., 1996.

Stearn, William. *Stearn's Dictionary of Plant Names for Gardeners.* London, Eng.: Cassell Publishers, 1992.

Toop, Edgar. *Annuals for the Prairies.* Edmonton, AB: Lone Pine Publishing, 1993.

Toop, Edgar, and Williams, Sara. *Perennials for the Prairies.* Edmonton, AB: University of Alberta, Faculty of Extension, 1991.

Van der Horst, Arend Jan, and Benvie, Sam. *Tulips.* Toronto, ON: Key Porter Books, 1997.

Williams, Sara. *Creating the Prairie Xeriscape.* Saskatoon, SK: University Extension Press, University of Saskatchewan, 1997.

Winterrowd, Wayne. *Annuals for Connoisseurs.* New York, NY: Prentice Hall, 1992.

Woods, Christopher. *Encyclopedia of Perennials: A Gardener's Guide.* New York, NY: Facts on File, Inc., 1992.

Zucker, Isabel. *Flowering Shrubs and Small Trees.* New York, NY: Michael Friedman Publishing Group, 1990.

Index

In this index, numbers appearing in Roman bold type (e.g., **52**) identify main entries in the book; each main entry is accompanied by a photograph. Numbers appearing in italic bold type (e.g., *137*) identify photographs that are not associated with a main entry.

JUN 2 5 2003